Thomas Guthrie

The Gospel in Ezekiel

Illustrated in a series of discourses

Thomas Guthrie

The Gospel in Ezekiel
Illustrated in a series of discourses

ISBN/EAN: 9783337285289

Printed in Europe, USA, Canada, Australia, Japan

Cover: Foto ©Lupo / pixelio.de

More available books at **www.hansebooks.com**

THE

GOSPEL IN EZEKIEL

ILLUSTRATED IN

A SERIES OF DISCOURSES.

BY THE

REV. THOMAS GUTHRIE, D.D.,

EDINBURGH.

AUTHOR OF "THE INHERITANCE OF THE SAINTS," "WAY TO LIFE,"
"SPEAKING TO THE HEART," ETC.

NEW YORK:

ROBERT CARTER & BROTHERS,
No. 530 BROADWAY.

1870.

REV. WILLIAM HANNA, LL. D.

To you, my dear Sir, I dedicate these Discourses, the substance of which was preached to our Congregation, not so much as an expression of my high admiration of the genius and talents which you have consecrated to the cause of our common Lord, as a mark of the warm affection which I cherish for you, and of the kind, cordial, and most happy intercourse which we have enjoyed since our union as colleagues and pastors of the same flock.

THOMAS GUTHRIE.

CONTENTS.

———◆———

THE GOSPEL IN EZEKIEL.

The Messenger.

Moreover, the word of the Lord came unto me, saying, Son of man.—.
Ezekiel xxxvi. 16, 17.

HAVING scattered over an open field the bones of
the human body, bring an anatomist to the scene.
Conduct him to the valley where Ezekiel stood, with
his eye on the skulls and dismembered skeletons of an
unburied host. Observe the man of science how he
fits bone to bone and part to part, till from those scat-
tered members he constructs a framework, which,
apart from our horror at the eyeless sockets and flesh
less form, appears perfectly, divinely beautiful. In
hands which have the patience to collect, and the skill
to arrange these materials, how perfectly they fit!
bone to bone, and joint to joint, till the whole figure
rises to the polished dome, and the dumb skeleton
seems to say, "I am fearfully and wonderfully made."
Now as with these parts of the human frame, so is it
with the doctrines of the Gospel, in so far as they are
intelligible to our understandings. Scattered over the
pages of sacred Scripture, let them also be collected
and arranged in systematic order, and how beautifully
they fit! doctrine to doctrine, duty to duty; till, all
connected with each other, all "members one of an-

other," they rise up into a form of perfect symmetry, and present that very system which, with minor differences but substantial unity, is embodied in the confessions, creeds, and catechisms of Evangelical Christendom. I have said, so far as they are intelligible to us; for it is ever to be borne in mind, that while the Gospel has shallows through which a child may wade and walk on his way to heaven, it has deep, dark, unfathomed pools, which no eye can penetrate, and where the first step takes a giant beyond his depth.

There is a difference, which even childhood may discern, between the manner in which the doctrines and duties of the Gospel are set forth in the Word of God, and their more formal arrangement in our catechisms and confessions. They are scattered here and there over the face of Scripture, much as the plants of nature are upon the surface of the globe. There, for example, we meet with nothing corresponding to the formal order, systematic classification, and rectangular beds of a botanical garden; on the contrary, the creations of the vegetable kingdom lie mingled in what, although beautiful, seems to be wild confusion. Within the limits of the same moor or meadow the naturalist gathers grasses of many forms, he finds it enamelled with flowers of every hue; and in those forests which have been planted by the hand of God, and beneath whose deep shades man still walks in rude and savage freedom, trees of every form and foliage stand side by side like brothers. With the Sabbath hills around us, far from the dust and din, the splendor and squalor of the city, we have sat on a rocky bank, to wonder at the varied and rich profusion with which God had clothed the scene. Nature, like Joseph, was dressed in a coat of many colors—

lichens, gray, black and yellow, clad the rock; the glossy ivy, like a child of ambition, had planted its foot on the crag, and, hanging on by a hundred arms, had climbed to its stormy summit; mosses, of hues surpassing all the colors of the loom, spread an elastic carpet round the gushing fountain; the wild thyme lent a bed to the weary, and its perfume to the air; heaths opened their blushing bosoms to the bee; the primrose, like modesty shrinking from observation, looked out from its leafy shade; at the foot of the weathered stone the fern raised its plumes, and on its summit the foxglove rang his beautiful bells; while the birch bent to kiss the stream, as it ran away laughing to hide itself in the lake below, or stretched out her arms to embrace the mountain ash and evergreen pine. By a very slight exercise of fancy, in such a scene one could see Nature engaged in her adorations, and hear her singing, "The earth is full of the glory of God." "How manifold are thy works, Lord God Almighty! in wisdom thou hast made them all."

Now, although over the whole surface of our globe, as in that spot, plants of all forms and families seem confusedly scattered, amid this apparent disorder the eye of science discovers a perfect system in the floral kingdom; and just as—although God has certainly scattered these forms over the face of nature without apparent arrangement—there is a botanical system, so there is as certainly a theological system, although its doctrines and duties are not classified in the Bible according to dogmatic rules. Does it not appear from this circumstance, that God intended his Word to be a subject of study as well as faith, and that man should find in its saving pages a field for the exercise of his highest faculties? We are commanded to compare "spiritual things with spiritual;" we are to "search the Scriptures," to dig for their treasures, to dive for the pearls. Hence the prayer of David, "Give me understanding, that I may learn thy commandments."

While the trees and flowers that clothe the fields of nature are scattered without much apparent order over the wide surface of the earth, still there are mountain regions lying within the tropics, where, in the course of a single day, the traveler may find laid out in regular arrangement, every vegetable form peculiar to every line of latitude between the equator and the poles. Leaving the palms which cover the mountain's feet, he ascends into the regions of the olive; from these, to a more temperate climate, where the vine festoons the trees, or trails its limbs along the naked rock; still ascending, he next reaches a belt of oaks and chestnuts; from that he passes to heights shaggy with the hardy pine; by and by, he enters a region where trees are dwarfed into bushes; rising above that, his foot presses a carpet of lowly mosses; till, climbing the rocks where only the lichen lives, he leaves all life beneath him; and now, shivering in the cold, panting in the thin air for breath, he stands on those dreary elevations, where eternal winter sits on a throne of snow, and, waving her icy scepter, says to vegetation, "Hither shalt thou come, and no further." Like some such lofty mountain of the tropics, there are portions of the Divine Word, where, in a space also of limited extent—within the short compass of a chapter, or even part of it—the more prominent doctrines of Salvation are brought into juxtaposition, and set side by side, almost in systematic order.

This chapter offers to our attention one of the most

remarkable of these; and in illustration of that, I remark—

I. That this portion of Scripture. extending onwards from the 16th verse, presents an epitome or outline of the Gospel.

Its details, with their varied beauties, are here, so to speak, in shade; but the grand truths of redemption stand boldly up, much as we have seen from sea the lofty headlands of a dim and distant coast. We are aware that the Mosaic economy, and many of God's dealings with his ancient people, were but the shadows of good things to come; and that, when the things are come, as come they certainly are, you may meet us on the very threshold with this question, Why look at the shadow when you possess the substance? However valued in his absence the portrait of a son may be, what mother, when he is folded in her arms, and she has his living face to look on, turns to the picture? What artist studies a subject in twilight, when he may see it in the blaze of day? True —true at least in general. Yet such study has its advantages. It not seldom happens that a portrait brings to view some shade of expression which we had not previously observed in the face of the veritable man; and when some magnificent form of architecture, or the serried ridges and rocky needles of a mountain, have stood up between us and the last lights of day, we have found, that although the details, the minor beauties, of fluted columns or frowning crags were lost in the shades of evening, yet, drawn in sharp and simple outline against a twilight sky, the effect of the whole was more impressive then when eyed in the glare of day.

Thus it may be well, occasionally at least, to examine the Gospel in the broad shadows and strongly defined outlines of an old economy; and through God's government of his ancient people, to study the motives, the nature, and the ends of his dealings with ourselves. In this way the passage before us has peculiar claims upon our attention. Applicable, in the first instance, to the condition of the Jews, it presents a remarkable summary of Gospel doctrines, and that in a form approaching at least to systematic order.

In the 17th verse, we have man sinning—"Son of man, when the house of Israel dwelt in their own land, they defiled it by their own way, and by their doings."

In the 18th verse, we have man suffering—"Wherefore I poured my fury upon them."

In the 21st verse, man appears an object of mercy—"but I had pity."

In the 22d verse, man is an object of free mercy—mercy without merit—"I do not this for your sakes, O, house of Israel."

In the 24th verse, man's salvation is resolved on—"I will bring you into your own land."

In the 25th verse, man is justified—"Then will I sprinkle clean water upon you, and ye shall be clean."

In the 26th and 27th verses, man is renewed and sanctified—"A new heart also will I give you, and a new spirit will I put within you; and I will take away the stony heart out of your flesh, and I will give you an heart of flesh. And I will put my spirit within you, and cause you to walk in my statutes, and ye shall keep my judgments, and do them."

In the 28th verse, man is restored to the place and privileges which he forfeited by his sins—"Ye shall be my people, and I will be your God." "This land that was desolate, is become like the garden of the Lord." We have our security for these blessings in the assurance of the 36th verse—"I the Lord have spoken it, and I will do it;" and the means of obtaining them in the declaration of the 37th verse—"I will yet for this be enquired of by the house of Israel, to do it for them."

Such is the wide and interesting field that lies before us. But before entering upon it, let us consider—

II. The party who is commissioned to deliver God's message.

Who, what is this ambassador of Heaven? An angel? No; but a man. "Son of man," says the Lord. In the first verse of this chapter he says—"Son of man, prophesy unto the mountains." In the 3d verse of the following one he asks— "Son of man, can these bones live?" Again, in the 9th verse of the same chapter, he says—"Son of man, prophesy unto the wind." And, still addressing him by the same title, in the 11th verse, he tells the prophet—"Son of man, these bones are the whole house of Israel." By this title Ezekiel is so often addressed, "Son of man," "Son of man," is so constantly sounded both in his ears and ours, that it forces on our attention this remarkable fact, that God deals with man through the instrumentality of man, and by men communicates his will to men. The rain which descends from heaven falls upon the surface of our earth, sinks through the porous soil, and, flowing along rocky fissures or veins of sand, is conveyed below ground to the fountain whence it springs. Now, although out of the earth, that water is not "of the earth, earthy." The world's

deepest well owes its treasures to the skies. So it was
with the revealed will of God. It flowed along hu-
man channels, yet its origin was more than celestial—
it was divine. Those waters, at whose springs Faith
drinks and lives, while conveyed to man through the
instrumentality of man, had their source far away in
the throne of God; their fountain-head is the Godhead.
No doubt, God could have used other instrumentality.
He might have commissioned angels on his errands of
mercy, and spoke at all times, as he did sometimes, by
their lips. With rare exceptions, however, his am-
bassadors were men. The patriarchs, prophets, and
apostles, by whom in days of old he revealed his will—
those missionaries of heaven—were all sons of man.
Now in this arrangement observe, in the first place—

The kindness of God to man. Who has read the
story of Moses without feeling that it was a great kind
ness, both to him and his mother, that he had a mo-
ther's bosom to lie on—that God in his providence so
arranged matters that the mother was hired to be the
nurse of her son? who else would have treated the
outcast so lovingly and kindly? And I hold it a
singular kindness to man that he is selected to be the
instrument of saving his fellow-men. The God of sal-
vation, the author and finisher of our faith, might have
arranged it otherwise. "Who shall limit the Holy
One of Israel?" The field is the world; and as the
husbandman ploughs his fields and sows his seed in
spring by the very hands that bind the sheaves of
autumn, God might have sent those angels to sow the
Gospel, who shall descend at judgment to reap the
harvest. But although these blessed and benevolent
spirits take a lively interest in the work, and are
sent forth to minister to them that are heirs of salva

tion—although watching from on high the progress of the Redeemer's cause, they rejoice in each new jewel that is added to his crown, and in every new province that is won for his kingdom; and although there be more joy even in heaven than on earth when man is saved—a higher joy among these angels "over one sinner that repenteth than over ninety and nine just persons"—yet theirs is little more than the pleasure of spectators. Theirs is the joy of those who, occupying the shore, or crowded on its heights, with eager eyes and beating heart follow the bold swimmer's movements, and watching his head as it rises and sinks among the waves, see him near the drowning child, and pluck its half-drowned prey from the billow; and, still trembling lest strength should fail him, look on with anxious hearts, till, buffeting his way back, he reaches the strand, and amid their shouts and sympathies restores her boy to the arms of a fainting mother.

To man, however, in salvation, it is given to share, not a spectator's but a Saviour's joy; and with his lips at least to taste the cup for which Jesus endured the cross and despised the shame. If that parent is happy who snatches a child from the flood or fire, and the child, thus saved, and twice given him, becomes doubly dear, what happiness in purity or permanence to be compared with his, who is a laborer with God in saving souls? Let me invite you to share in these pleasures, the sweetest, I assure you, out of heaven. This is a privilege and a pleasure free to all. It is one which kings cannot purchase, and yet beggars may enjoy; and one also (and what more could be said of it?) which enhances the joy of heaven. While every saint shall have one heaven, some shall have more; those who have helped to fill its mansions shall possess many heavens in one. In proportion to the number they have brought to Christ, they shall multiply their joys—the joys which eye hath not seen, nor ear heard, and which entereth not into the heart of man to conceive. In this arrangement I observe again—

The honor conferred on man. Did Moses occupy a noble position when he stood aloft on a rock amid the dying Israelites, and there, the central figure of the camp, on whom all eyes were turned, raised that serpent, to look on which was life? Nobler still his attitude and office, who, with his foot on this dying world, lifts up the cross—"Jesus Christ and him crucified"—that, whosoever looketh and believeth on him, might not perish, but have everlasting life. Give me the bleeding Saviour, make me the instrument of converting a single soul, and I grudge not Moses his "piece of brass;" nor envy him the honor of saving a thousand lives, that are now all quenched in death. Great honor to the memory of the mighty men who swept like a hurricane through the camp of the Philistines, and, cleaving their way through opposing foes, drew the water of Bethlehem for their king; yet, rather than be one of David's mighty men, it would content me to be one of Christ's humblest, and hold the cup of life to a pauper's lips. All honor to the prophet who went up to heaven in a chariot of fire; but nobler still his departure, who, as he ascends to glory, leaves spiritual sons behind him to weep by the cast-off mantle of his flesh, and cry, "My father, my father, the chariots of Israel and the horsemen thereof!" What honors does this world offer? what stars, what jeweled honours flash on her swelling breast, to be

for one moment compared with those which they win
on earth, and wear in heaven, who have turned souls
from darkness to light—from the cursed power of Satan
to the living God? Each soul a gem in their crown,
they that have turned many to righteousness shall
shine with the brightness of the firmament, as the stars,
for ever and ever. How has the hope of this touched,
as with fire, the preacher's lips, sustained his heart,
held up prayer's weary hands, and proved an ample
recompense for those scanty rewards which God's ser-
vants too often received at the hands of men, for the
penury which has embittered, and the hardships which
have pressed on their lot! Their master was rejected
and despised of men—a man of sorrows and acquaint-
ed with grief, and the disciple being no better than
his Lord, they have shared in his sufferings. But, if
fellow-sufferers, they are fellow-laborers with Christ—
his associates in the noblest work beneath the sun.
Despised as the teacher of the Gospel may be, the
apostle raises him to an eminence from which he may
contemplate this world, with all its grandeur and glory,
rolling away into dark oblivion. Viewed in the light
of eternity, the church stands on a loftier elevation
than the palace, and the pulpit offers man a grander
position than the throne of empires. To ministers
of the Gospel belongs the high pre-eminence of being
able to say, " we are fellow-laborers with God;" and,
with such an associate—in such lofty company, devot-
ing his life to such a cause—no wonder that Paul con-
fronted a skeptic, sneering, scoffing world, and bravely
said, " I am not ashamed of the Gospel of Christ."

I am anxious that you should understand that the
honors that I have spoken of are not reserved for
pulpits. The youth who, finding Sabbath rest in Chris-

tian labors, holds his Sabbath-class; the mother, with her children grouped around her, sweet solemnity sitting in her face, and the Bible resting on her knee; the friend who deals faithfully with another's soul; any man who kindly takes a poor sinner by the hand, and seeking to conduct him to the Saviour, says, "Come with us, and we will do you good;" "Arise, for we have seen the land, and behold it is very good;" these, not less than ministers of the Gospel, are fellow-laborers with God. Think not that this noblest work is our exclusive privilege, nor stand back as if you had neither right nor call to set to your hand. What although in the church you hold no rank? No more does the private who wears neither stripes on his arm nor epaulettes on his shoulder; but although a private, may he not die for the colors which it is not his privilege to carry? If it is not his business to train recruits, it is his business, and shall be his reward to enlist them. Now to this office, to recruit the ranks of the cross, the Gospel calls you—calls all—calls the meanest soldier in the army of the faith. "The Spirit and the bride say come." But more than they should call. Where sinners are perishing, where opportunity offers, where a door is open, where the rule, "Let all things be done decently and in order," is not outraged and violated—call it preaching if you choose, but in God's name let hearers preach. Has God gifted any with power to speak of Christ? Then, with such high interests at stake, from forms which churches, not their Head—man, not God, has established, we say, "loose him and let him go." "Let him that *heareth say come,* and let him that is athirst come; and whosoever will, let him take of the water of life freely."

Thou art a "son of man:" you bear the prophet's title.

whatsoever otherwise you may be. Let me call you
to the prophet's office. The Master hath need—much
need of you. Thousands, tens of thousands, are dying
in their sins. Although every minister were as a
flaming fire in the service of his God, every bishop were
a Latimer, every reformer were a Knox, every preach-
er were a Whitefield, every missionary were a Martyn,
the work is greater than ministers can accomplish;
and if men will not submit that the interests of nations
and the success of armies shall be sacrificed to routine
and forms of office, much less should these be tolerated
where the cause of souls is at stake. I say, therefore,
to every Christian, "the Master hath need" of you.
Take a living, loving interest in souls. Don't leave
them to perish. It may be the duty of others per-
manently and formally to instruct, but it is yours
to enlist. "This honor have all his saints." And in
attempting to engage you in the work at least of en-
listing others, and of recruiting, out of your family,
and friends, and neighborhood, the armies of the
faith, I call you to a work in which every man may
bear his share, and one which offers honor as exalted
as its pleasures are pure. It was no honor to Elijah
to gird up his loins, and with the storm at his back to
run abreast of the smoking horses of Ahab's chariot.
Considering who the parties were, it had been as meet,
I think, that the king should have run and the pro-
phet ridden. But to run by the chariot where Jesus sits,
his crown on his head, his bow in his hand, and his
sword by his thigh; to employ our feet in offices
that have employed angels' wings; to bear the news
of mercy to a dying sinner; and to gather crowds
around the Saviour, that they may strew his path
with palms, and swell the song of Hosanna to the Son

of David—for such a work a king might cast off robes and crown.

Yes—I think that he would not demean, but rather dignify his office, who should descend from a throne where subjects kneel, to bend his knee before God by a peasant's bed, or leave his palace for a cell, to watch, and weep, and pray with one whom crime had consigned to death. And, as surely as yon planet worlds that roll and shine above us draw radiance from the sun around which they move, so surely shall they shine who spend and are spent in Jesus' service; they shall share his honors, and shine in his luster. The man, however lowly his condition, who, some way between his cradle and the tomb, has converted even one soul to God, has not lived in vain, nor labored for nought; but has achieved a great work. He may be well content to go down into the grave by men unpraised, by the world unknown. His works, if they have not preceded, shall follow him; and needing no tablet raised among mouldering bones and tombstones, he has a monument to his memory, where there are neither griefs nor graves, more costly than brass or marble. Others may have filled the world with the breath of their name; he has helped to fill heaven. Others may have won an earthly renown; but he who, one himself, has sought to make others Christians—who, reaching the rock himself, draws another, a perishing child, brother, friend, neighbor, up—plucked from the flood himself, pulls another out —who has leaped into the depths that he might rise with a pearl, and set it lustrous in Jesus' crown—he is the man who shall wear heaven's brightest honors, and to whom, before all else, the Lord will say, "Well done, good and faithful servant, enter thou into the joy of thy Lord." Weak in yourselves, but strong in God, go forth on this enterprise, your prayer the wish of Brainerd, "Oh that I were a flaming fire in the service of my God!" In this arrangement we see, lastly,

The wisdom of God. However highly gifted he may otherwise be, it is a valid objection to a preacher, that he does not feel what he says; that spoils more than his oratory. An obscure man rose up to address the French Convention. At the close of his oration, Mirabeau, the giant genius of the Revolution, turned round to his neighbor, and eagerly asked, Who is that? The other, who had been in no way interested by the address, wondered at Mirabeau's curiosity. Whereupon the latter said, That man will yet act a great part; and, asked to explain himself, added, he speaks as one who believes every word he says. Much of pulpit power under God depends on that— admits of that explanation, or one allied to it. They make others feel who feel themselves. How can he plead for souls who does not know the value of his own? How can he recommend a Saviour to others who himself personally despises and rejects him? Unhappy indeed, and doubly blind those whose leader is as blind as they are; and unhappiest of all the blind preacher; for while leader and led shall fall into the ditch, he falls undermost—his the heaviest condemnation, the deepest and most damned perdition. In possession of such a man—of one who has adopted the church as other men the law, or army, or navy, as a mere profession, and goes through the routine of its duties with the coldness of an official—the pulpit seems filled with the ghastly form of a skeleton, that in its cold and bony fingers holds a burning lamp.

It is true that a man may impart light to others who does not himself see the light. It is true that, like a concave speculum cut from a block of ice, which, concentrating the rays of the sun, kindles touchwood or gunpowder, a preacher may kindle fire in others, when his own heart is cold as frost. It is also true that he may stand like a finger-post on a road, where he neither leads nor follows; and God may thus in his sovereign mercy bless others by one who is himself unblessed. Yet commonly it happens, that it is what comes from the heart of preachers that reaches the heart of hearers. Like a ball red hot from the cannon's mouth, he must burn himself who would set others on fire. Still, although the ministry of men who are themselves strangers to piety—although a Judas or Simon Magus in office—is an evil to which the church, in every age and under every form of government, stands more or less exposed, it were a poor refuge to seek exemption from such an evil, even in the ministry of angels; because, while man may not feel what he preaches, angels could not. How could they? They never felt the stings of conscience; they never hung over hell's fiery gulf, and saw the narrow ledge they stood on crumbling away beneath their feet, and sent up to heaven the piercing cry, " Lord, save me, I perish;" they never felt the power and peace of Jesus' blood; pursued by a storm of wrath, they never flew to the Rock of Ages, and folded their wings in the sweet and safe serenity of its welcome clefts; they never thirsted for salvation; in an agony for pardon, they never felt ready to give a thousand worlds for one Christ; they never, as we have done, trod the valley of humiliation, and walked with bleeding feet and weeping eyes its flinty path; they never knew what it is, between them and their home in heaven, to see death's gloomy passage, and, more appalling still, a sight which makes the saint grasp his sword with a firmer hand, and lift up his shield on high—Satan, the enemy, posted there, and striding across the passage to dispute the way—never knowing what it is to have been in bondage, having neither country nor kindred here, how could they preach like Paul? how could their bosoms burn with this apostolic fire—"I could wish that I myself were accursed from Christ for my brethren, my kinsmen according to the flesh?"

We have somewhere read of a traveler who stood one day beside the cages of some birds, that, exposed for sale, ruffled their sunny plumage on the wires, and struggled to be free. A way-worn and sun-browned man, like one returned from foreign lands, he looked wistfully and sadly on these captives, till tears started in his eye, and turning round on their owner, he asked the price of one, paid it in strange gold, and opening the cage set the prisoner free; and thus and thus he did with captive after captive, till every bird was away, soaring to the skies and singing on the wings of liberty. The crowd stared and stood amazed; they thought him mad, till to the question of their curiosity he replied—"I was once myself a captive; I know the sweets of liberty." And so they who have experience of guilt, have felt the serpent's bite, the burning poison in their veins, who on the one hand have felt the sting of conscience, and on the other the peace of faith, the joys of hope, the love, the light, the liberty, the life, that are found in Jesus—they, not excepting heaven's highest angels, are the fittest to preach a Saviour, to plead with man for God, or plead with God

for man. Each Sabbath morning the gates of heaven
might have opened, and, sent by God on a mission
worthy of seraphic fire, an angel might have lighted
down upon this sanctuary, and, flying into the pulpit,
when he had folded his wings and used them to vail
his glory, he might have taken up the wondrous theme
of salvation and the cross. No angel would leave
heaven to be a king and fill a throne; but, I believe,
were it God's will, there is no angel there but would
hold himself honored to be a preacher and fill a pul-
pit. Another and very different messenger appears—
a frail, dying, sinful man—one who is bone of your
bone, and flesh of your flesh; and if his humanity
made Jesus the better Saviour, it makes his servants the
better ambassadors, that they also are touched with
their people's infirmities, and are made in all points
like as they are, and especially in this point, that we
cannot add, "yet without sin."

It is true that in us the instrument which God
employs is in itself a humble one—in itself worthy
neither of honor nor respect: the treasure is commit-
ted to earthen vessels, sometimes of the rudest form
and the coarsest clay. What of that? If the letter
from a foreign land brings good tidings of his son,
does the father quarrel with the meanness of the pa-
per? While tears of joy and gratitude drop on the
page, does he so much as notice it? If the dish offers
safe or savory meat, a starving man enjoys it none the
less that it is not served up on gold or porcelain. An
ointment worthy of the Master's head, and exhaling
odors that fill the house, is as welcome from a sinner's
as an angel's hand—from a vessel of the poorest earth
as of the purest alabaster. Even so will saving truth
be to you, if God's people. Without turning him into

an idol, and giving the honor to the servant which is due to the Master, I am sure you will respect the servant for his Master's sake. Are some of you yet sinners in the gall of bitterness and bond of iniquity? Because we are ourselves sinners, and know what it is to have been captives, we are the fitter to address you. We know that you are not happy, nor can be happy in sin; its pleasures perish in the using, and pain in the recollection; and it is madness, the height of madness—for a man to stake eternity on the chances of a to-morrow, and purchase sin's short-lived joys at the expense of eternal happiness. We know that out of Christ, as you have no safety, you can find no true peace. "There is no peace, saith my God, to the wicked;" "they are like the troubled sea which cannot rest;" in storms a raging ocean, and in summer's serenest day ebbing or flowing, and breaking its billows, like the world's joys and happiness, on a beach of wrecks and withered weeds. Seek Christ, seek your peace through him and in him; and, saved yourself—yourself plucked from the wreck—oh, remember the perishing, and let the first breath and effort of your new life be spent for others. I give you an example; and in the words spoken for a fellow-sufferer's life, see what you should do for a fellow-sinner's soul.

During a heavy storm off the coast of Spain, a dismasted merchantman was observed by a British frigate drifting before the gale. Every eye and glass were on her, and a canvas shelter on a deck almost level with the sea suggested the idea that there yet might be life on board. With all his faults, no man is more alive to humanity than the rough and hardy mariner; and so the order instantly sounds to put the ship about, and presently a boat puts off with instructions to bear

down upon the wreck.   Away after that drifting hulk
go these gallant men through the swell of a roaring
sea ; they reach it; they shout; and now a strange
object rolls out of that canvas screen against the lee
shroud of a broken mast.   Hauled into the boat, it
proves to be the trunk of a man, bent head and knees
together, so dried and shrivelled as to be hardly felt
within the ample clothes, and so light that a mere boy
lifted it on board.   It is laid on the deck; in horror
and pity the crew gather round it; it shows signs of
life ; they draw nearer; it moves, and then mutters—
mutters in a deep, sepulchral voice—" *There is another
man.*"   Saved himself, the first use the saved one made
of speech was to seek to save another.   Oh! learn
that blessed lesson. ·Be daily practising it.   And so
long as in our homes, among our friends, in this wreck
of a world which is drifting down to ruin, there lives
an unconverted one, there is " *another man,*" let us go
to that man, and plead for Christ; go to Christ and
plead for that man ; the cry, " Lord save me, I perish,"
changed into one as welcome to a Saviour's ear, " Lord
save them, they perish."

The Defiler.

Son of man, when the house of Israel dwelt in their own land, they defiled it by their own way, and by their doings.—EZEK. xxxvi. 17.

"THY holy cities are a wilderness; Zion is a wilderness; Jerusalem is a desolation." So low as this had the fortunes of Israel ebbed, when the words of my text were penned. Judah was in chains; the people were captives in the hands of heathen—exiles in the land of Babylon. Jerusalem lay in ruins; the grass grew long and rank in her deserted streets; an awful silence filled the temple; the fox looked out of the window, and the foul satyr had her den in the Holy of Holies. No plough turned a furrow in the field; the vines grew wild and tangled on the crumbling terraces; nor cock crew, nor dog bayed, nor flock bleated, nor maid sang, nor shepherd piped, nor smoke curled up from homestead among the lonely hills. The land was desolate, almost utterly desolate. She now enjoyed what the love of pleasure and the greed of gain had denied her; she rested, and had a long Sabbath; while over an expatriated people, far away beyond the desert, and beside the river, the seventy years' captivity rolled wearily on. A few pious men, who had in vain tried to stem the flood-tide of sin which swept the nation on to ruin, were mourning over the guilt of which captivity was the punishment. Wearying to be home again they cried, "How long, O Lord, how long? Wilt thou be angry for ever?

Shall thy jealousy burn like fire?" "Be not wroth very sore, O Lord, neither remember iniquity for ever. Behold, see, we beseech thee, we are all thy people; thy holy cities are a wilderness; Zion is a wilderness; Jerusalem a desolation." "Turn us again, Lord God of Hosts, and cause thy face to shine on us, and so we shall be saved."

So they felt and prayed who were as salt in the putrid mass. The larger portion, however, as has too often been the case in the visible church, lived only to dishonor their faith, their creed, their country and their race. Like many still who go abroad, and in leaving their native land leave behind them all appearance of piety, they profaned God's holy name, and gave the scoffer abundant occasion for this bitter and biting sneer—"These are the people of the Lord!" In its application to the contemporaries of Ezekiel, the prophet briefly describes these sad and sinful days, and also refers to that preceding period of deep and wide degeneracy, when the corruption of kings, princes, priests and people, had grown so great, that, to use the words of Scripture, "Their trespass was grown up to the heavens." The patience of God at length exhausted, as he "drove" the man and woman from the garden, he drove Israel from a land which their sins had defiled.

However much we may abhor their crimes, it is impossible not to pity the sufferers—in a sense to sympathise with them. Are we men who, in the case of an invasion, would take a bold position on the shore, and fight every inch of ground, and when driven back would take our last stand in our own doorway, nor allow the foot of foe to pass there but over our dead body? If our bosom burns with any patriotic

fire, if we have the common affections of men for
family and friends, it is impossible to look with insen-
sibility at that bleeding fragment of a nation gathered
for the march to Babylon, amid the blackened and
blood-stained ruins of their capital. What a mournful
company! The sick, the bedrid, the blind, old men
tottering forth on the staff of age, and plucking their
gray beards with grief; the skeleton infant hanging
on a breast that famine and sorrow have dried; mothers
with terror-stricken children clinging to their sides,
or, worse still, with gentle daughters imploring their
protection from these rude and ruffian soldiers; a few
gallant men, the survivors of the fight, wasted by
famine, bleeding from unbandaged wounds, their arms
bound, and burning tears streaming down their cheeks,
as they looked on wives and daughters shrieking and
helpless in the arms of brutal passion; how they
strain at their bonds! and bitterly envy their more
fortunate companions who lay in the bloody breach,
nor had survived to see the horrors of that day! The
piety that abhors the sins of this people is not incom-
patible with the pity that sympathises with their
sorrows; and could sit down and weep with Jeremiah,
as, seated on a broken pillar of the temple, desolation
around him, and no sound in his ear but the long, wild
wail of the captive band, he wrung his hands, raised
them to heaven, and cried, "Oh that my head were
waters, and mine eyes a fountain of tears, that I might
weep day and night for the slain of the daughter of
my people."

There was a home-leaving, however, in which we
feel a nearer interest. I do not refer to that eventful
morning when some of us left a father's house; and
the gates of that happy sanctuary opened, amid tears

and fears and many a kind farewell—and when watch
ed by a father's eye, and followed by a mother's pray-
ers, we pushed out our bark on the swell of life's
treacherous sea.   The turning time of many a young
man's history,—the crisis of his destiny,—that day
may have exerted an influence as permanent on our
fate as its impression remains indelible on our mem-
ory.   I refer to a home-leaving of far older date; to
one, not of personal, nor of national, but of universal
interest.   My eye is turned back on the day when our
first parents, who had fallen into sin and forfeited their
inheritance, were expelled from man's first home.   And,
recollecting the reluctance with which I have seen a
heart broken mother make up her mind to disown the
prodigal, and drive him from her door,—knowing,
when with slow and trembling hand she had barred
him out, how it seemed to her as if in that horrid
sound she had heard the door of heaven bolted against
him,—and feeling how much provocation we ourselves
could suffer, ere a bleeding heart would consent to
turn a child out upon the open streets, and believing
also that our Father in heaven is kinder than the
kindest, and better than the best of us, and that the
fondest, fullest heart is to his, but as the rocky pool,
—the lodge of some tiny creature—to the great ocean
which has filled it with a wave, no demonstration of
God's abhorrence of sin (always excepting the cross of
Calvary) comes so impressively to our hearts as his
expulsion of our unhappy parents from his own bliss-
ful presence and their sweet home in Eden.   When
with slow and lingering steps Adam and Eve came
weeping forth from Paradise, and the gate was locked
behind them, that was the bitterst home-leaving the
world ever saw.   Adam, the federal head of his family

—they came not alone, but are followed by a longer and sadder procession than went weeping on the way to Babylon: they are followed by a world in tears. Cast out in them—in them condemned and expatriated —we all defiled the land wherein we dwelt. In this sense the world sinned in Adam, and defiled the happy bowers of Eden; and the universality of sin stands firm on the universality of the sentence, "Death has passed upon all men, for that all have sinned."

I. Let us look at man sinning. "Ye have defiled the land."

Sin is presented here in the aspect of a defilement. But before fixing your attention on this feature, I may remark, that it offers but one of many aspects in which sin appears; all alarming, all hateful, all detestable.

As opposed to sin and its consequences, heaven and holiness are pictured forth in the Bible in colors that glow upon the canvas, through the emblems of every thing we hold most dear and desirable. Raise your eyes, for example, to the New Jerusalem. Gold paves its streets, and around them rise walls of jasper. Earth holds no such city, nor the depths of ocean such pearls as form its gates; no storms sweep its sea; no winter strips its trees; no thunder shakes its serene and cloudless sky; the day there never darkens into night; harps and palms are in the hands, while crowns of glory flash and blaze upon the heads of its sinless inhabitants. From this distant and stormy orb, as the dove eyed the ark, faith eyes this glorious vision, and, weary of the strife, longing to be gone, cries, "Oh that I had the wings of a dove, that I might fly away and be at rest!"

And how difficult would it be to name a noble

2

figure, a sweet simile, a tender or attractive relation-
ship, in which Jesus is not set forth to woo a reluctant
sinner and cheer a desponding saint! Am I wound-
ed? He is balm. Am I sick? He is medicine. Am
I naked? He is clothing. Am I poor? He is
wealth. Am I hungry? He is bread. Am I thirsty?
He is water. Am I in debt? He is a surety. Am
I in darkness! He is a sun. Have I a house to
build? He is a rock. Must I face that black and
gathering storm? He is a anchor sure and stead-
fast. Am I to be tried? He is an advocate. Is sen-
tence passed, and am I condemned? He is pardon.
To deck him out, and set him forth, Nature culls her
finest flowers, brings her choicest ornaments, and lays
these treasures at his feet. The skies contribute their
stars. The sea gives up its pearls. From fields, and
mines, and mountains, Earth brings the tribute of her
gold, and gems, and myrrh, and frankincense; the
lily of the valley, the clustered vine, and the fragrant
rose of Sharon. He is " the chiefest among ten thou-
sand, and altogether lovely;" "in Him dwelleth all
the fullness of the Godhead bodily." I offer him to
you—make a free offer of him, and doing so will chal-
lenge you to name a want for which I shall not find a
supply in Christ, something that fits your want as
accurately, as the works of a key the wards of its
lock.

> " A Way he is to lost ones that have strayed;
>   A Robe he is to such as naked be;
> Is any hungry, to all such he is Bread;
>   Is any weak, in Him how strong is he!
> To him that's dead he's Life; to sick men, Health,
> Eyes to the blind, and to the poor man Wealth."

Look now at sin; pluck off that painted mask, and

turn upon her face the **lamp** of the Bible. We start;
it reveals a death's head. I stay not to quote texts
descriptive of sin; it is a debt, a burden, a thief, a
sickness, a leprosy, a plague, a poison, a serpent, a
sting—every thing that man hates it is; a load of
evils beneath whose most crushing, intolerable pres-
sure, "the whole creation groaneth." Name me the
evil that springs not from this root—the crime that
lies not at this door. Who is the hoary sexton that
digs man a grave? Who is the painted temptress
that steals his virtue? Who is the murderess that
destroys his life? Who is the sorceress that first de-
ceives and then damns his soul!—Sin. Who, with
icy breath, blights the sweet blosssoms of youth?
Who breaks the hearts of parents? Who brings gray
hairs with sorrow to the grave? Who, by a more
hideous metamorphosis than Ovid ever fancied, changes
sweet children into vipers, tender mothers into mon-
sters, and their fathers into worse than Herods, the
murderers of their own innocents?—Sin. Who casts
the apple of discord on home hearths? Who lights
the torch of war, and carries it over happy lands?
Who, by divisions in the Church, rends Christ's seam-
less robe?—Sin. Who is this Delilah that sings the
Nazarite asleep, and delivers the strength of God into
the hands of the uncircumcised? Who, with smiles
on her face, and honied flattery on her tongue, stands
in the door to offer the sacred rites of hospitality, and
when suspicion sleeps, pierces our temples with a
nail? What Siren is this, who, seated on a rock by
the deadly pool, smiles to deceive, sings to lure, kisses
to betray, and flings her arms around our neck, to
leap with us into perdition?—Sin. Who petrifies the
soft and gentle heart, hurls reason from her throne,

and impels sinners, mad as Gadarene swine, down the precipice, into the lake of fire?—Sin. Who, having brought the criminal to the gallows, persuades him to refuse a pardon, and with his own hand to bar the door against the messenger of mercy? What witch of hell is it, that thus bewitches us?—Sin. Who nailed the Son of God to that bloody tree? and who, as if it were not a dove descending with the olive, but a vulture swooping down to devour the dying, vexes, grieves, thwarts, repels, drives off the Spirit of God? Who is it that makes man in his heart and habits baser than a beast; and him, who was once but little lower than an angel, but little better than a devil? —Sin. Sin! Thou art a hateful and horrible thing; that " abominable thing which God hates." And what wonder? Thou hast insulted his Holy Majesty? thou hast bereaved him of beloved children; thou nast crucified the Son of his infinite love; thou hast vexed his gracious Spirit; thou hast defied his power; thou hast despised his grace; and, in the body and blood of Jesus, as if that were a common thing, thou hast trodden under foot his matchless mercy. Surely, brethren, the wonder of wonders is, that sin is not that abominable thing which *we* also hate.

But let us leave what is general, to fix our attention on the view of sin which the text presents. It is set before us here as a defilement; and I may remark, that it is the only thing that in the eye of God does deform and defile us. Yet how strange it is, that some deformity of body shall prove the subject of more parental regrets and personal mortification than this foul deformity of soul. It is miserable to think how hearts have grieved, and even eyes, which got their tears surely for better uses, have wept over the stain of some costly dress, which never grieved and never wept for a sin-stained soul. What pains are taken, what costs and cares incurred, to bedeck the body for the house of God, as if that flimsy finery could conceal or compensate for a foul heart within! Your manners may have acquired a courtly polish; your dress may rival the winter's snow; unaccustomed to menial offices, and sparkling with Indian gems, your hands may bear no stain on them, yet they are not clean; nay, beneath this graceful exterior may lie concealed more foul pollution than is covered by a beggar's rags. This son of toil, from whose very touch your delicacy shrinks, and who, till Sabbath stops the wheels of business, and with her kind hand wipes the sweat of labor from his brow, never knows the full comfort of a cleanly habit, may have a heart within, which, compared with yours, is purity itself. Beneath this soiled raiment, all unseen by the world's eye, he wears the "clean linen" of a Redeemer's righteousness. His speech may be rude, his accent vulgar; but let him open his heart, unbosom its secrets, and from these there come forth such gracious thoughts, such holy desires, such heavenly aspirations, such hallowed joys, that it seems as if we had opened some rude sea-chest, brought by a foreign ship from southern lands, which, full to the lid with pearls, and gold, and diamonds, loads the air with floating odors of cassia, and myrrh, and frankincense.

Hypocrite, and dead professor! let us open thy bosom: full of all corruption, how it smells like a charnel-house! We are driven back by the noisome stench—we hasten to close the door; it is a painted but putrid sepulcher, whose fair exterior but aggra-vates the foulness within. It is not what lies without,

but within, that defiles a man. And it is well all
should remember, when you wash on a Sabbath
morning, that your soul needs washing in another
laver; and, when your person is decked for church,
that you need other robes—robes fairer than worm
spins or shuttles weave, or the wealth of banks can
buy. See that by faith ye put on that righteousness,
even that righteousness of Jesus Christ, in which God
sees neither spot, nor stain, nor any such thing.

II. The nature of this defilement.

It is internal. Like snow drift when it has leveled
the churchyard mounds, and, glistening in the winter
sun, lies so pure, and fair, and beautiful above the
dead, who fester and rot below, a very plausible
profession, wearing the semblance of innocence, may
conceal from human eyes the foulest heart-corruption.
The grass grows green upon a mountain that holds a
volcano in its bowels. Behind the rosy cheek and
soft lustrous eye of beauty, how often does there lurk
a deadly disease, the deadliest of all! Internal, but
all the more dangerous that they are internal, such
diseases are the last to be suspected or believed in by
their victims, and the hardest to cure. To other than
a skillful eye, or a mother's anxious look, this fair and
graceful form never wears bloom of higher health, nor
moves in more fascinating charms, nor wins more
admiring eyes, than when fell consumption, like a
miner working on in darkness, has penetrated the
vital organs, and is quietly sapping the foundations
of life.

Like these maladies, sin has its seat within. It is a
disease of the heart, and the worst of all heart-com-
plaints. There may be no very alarming appearance

on the surface; in the conduct that lies exposed to
the eyes of man there may be little offensive to holi-
ness; yet this fair exterior affords no criterion, no
sure or certain test by which to judge of matters
within. Thanks indeed be to God, and praise to his
sovereign grace, if sin does not find unchallenged
entrance, and meet a cordial welcome in our inner
man; yet how constant and arduous is the fight which
even gracious men have to maintain against the ten-
dency to secret errors! The old man has been nailed
to the tree, but how difficult to keep him there!
How difficult to keep pollution down, and maintain a
current of pure and hallowed desires flowing through
the channels of the heart! In judging ourselves that
we be not judged, beware how you trust to outward
appearances. What if it should be with us as with
this calm pool, which seems so clean, nay, with
heaven mirrored in its face, so beautiful? Let some
temptation stir up our passions, (and how little does
it need to stir them!) and those pure, pellucid waters
now grow foul and noisome; and, sending forth the
most offensive odors, prove what vile pollution may
lie beneath the fairest surface. Think not that the
evil is accidental—that it lies, as some say, in educa-
tion, in temptation, in external causes: it is traceable
to the heart itself. What more harmless than temp-
tations—this fiery dart launched by Satan's hand—
that flaming arrow from his bow—if they fell like
sparks in water? But alas! they fall like a torch
into a magazine of combustibles. Knowing this, and
jealous of themselves, let God's people watch and pray
that they enter not into temptation. To life's last
step, with life's latest breath, be this your prayer,
"Lead us not into temptation, but deliver us from

evil." It is another prayer, indeed, that the sinner has to offer. He has not to seek that his heart may be kept clean, but made clean; it is not health preserved, but restored, you want; you need not food, but medicine; a new nature, heart, life: this the prayer that suits your lips and case: "Create in me a clean heart, O God, and renew a right spirit within me."

This defilement is universal. Our world is inhabited by various races of men—different specimens, not different species. The Malay, the Negro, the race early cradled among Caucasian mountains, and the Red Indians of the New World; these all differ from each other in the color of the skin, in the contour of the skull, in the cast and character of their features. Whence came these different races? The Bible says that "God made of one blood all the families of the earth." According to its authority they are all sprung of one pair, who were located in a garden somewhere in the distant east. There, in that central and elevated region of the old world, man was both made and redeemed; there the cradle of our race was rocked, and the cross of salvation raised; and, breaking forth in an eastern region, the lights of knowledge and religion, learning human and divine, letters, science, and arts have, as by a law of nature, followed the track of the sun. The origin of these different races is a question of no small importance, and has formed a battle-ground between the enemies and defenders of our faith; one long and obstinately contested.

If, in order to account for these different races on the principles of unchallengeable physiology, it could be proved, that Europe, Africa, and America must, as well as Asia, have had their parent pairs; if it could be proved that there must of necessity have been as many Adams as there are races of men, then it is plain that we must yield up the divine authority of the Bible, and read the story of Moses as an old-world fable—some fragment of Egyptian wisdom which he had embalmed in the page of Genesis. Infidelity, quick to see what would serve her purpose, has attempted to prove this, and challenged religion to meet her on the field of science. Her challenge has been accepted. Men-at-arms in the ranks of the faith have taken up the gauntlet; the battle has been fought, and fought out; and now, to the confusion and complete discomfiture of the infidel, it stands demonstrated, that in this question as in others, science is in perfect harmony with revelation. Dismissing all Adams but one, she demands no more than the Bible grants, will receive no more than it offers, believe no more than it reveals; concluding that all these varieties of the human family are, in the providence of God, and in the hands of an Omnipotence which delights in variety, the offspring of a single pair.

There is one argument which these unhired, impartial, and independent defenders of our faith—these high-priests of science—did not, perhaps, feel warranted to employ, but which presents to us the most convincing evidence of a common origin. It lies where the tests of chemistry cannot detect it, nor the knife of the anatomist reach it, nor the eye of the physiognomist discover it, nor the instruments of the phrenologist measure it. Its place is in the inner man; it lies in the depths of the soul; and comes out in this remarkable fact, that, although the hues of the skin differ, and the form of the skull and the features of the face are cast in different moulds, the features, co-

lor, and character of the heart are the same in all men.
Be he pale-faced or red, tawny or black, Jew, Greek,
Scythian, bond or free ; whether he be the civilized in
habitant of Europe, or roam a painted savage in Ame-
rican woods, pant beneath the burning line, or, wrapt
in furs, shiver amid the Arctic snows; as in all classes
of society, so in all races of men, to quote the words
of the prophet, "the heart is deceitful above all things,
and desperately wicked ;" or, in the no less emphatic
language of the Apostle, "the carnal mind is enmity
against God." The pendulum vibrates slower at the
equator than the pole ; the further north we push our
way over thick-ribbed ice, the clock goes the faster;
but parallels of latitude have no modifying influence
on the motions of the heart. It beats the same in all
men ; nor, till repaired by grace, does it in any beat
true to God. In Adam all have died—have sinned,
and therefore died. Sin, like our atmosphere, em-
braces the world. Like death, it is universal; its em-
pire is coeval and co-extensive with that of the king
of terrors. And how can it be otherwise ? If man is
the child of unholy parents, how can a clean thing
come out of an unclean ? When water of its own
accord shall rise above its fountain, then may Adam's
children possess a nature loftier than his own. The
tree is diseased, not at the top, but at the root; and,
therefore, no branch of the human family can by pos-
sibility escape being affected by sin. Is any thing
more plain and palpable than this, that if the fountain
was polluted, to whatever quarter of the world the
stream of population flowed, it must have borne pol-
lution in its bosom ? Is suffering the sure index of
sin ? Then, if there be no country beneath the sun
where signs of suffering are not seen, and its sounds

are not heard, sin is every where—is in every man.
Be they dug in Arctic snows, or in the desert sands,
there is no land without its graves; nor, wherever it
stands, a city without its cemetery. Be they mon-
archies or republics, unaffected by the revolutions that
cast down other dynasties, death reigns in them all—
a king of kings. Death sits on the world's oldest
throne. Suffering the stings of conscience, sin and
serpent-bitten, man is condemned by a voice within
him; there sits a divinity enthroned in every man's
soul, whose voice is the clear, articulate, and solemn
echo of this judgment, "All have sinned, and come
short of the glory of God."

This evil is incurable.

Hear the Word of the Lord: "Though thou wash
thee with nitre, and take thee much soap, yet thine
iniquity is marked before me, saith the Lord." Again,
"Can the Ethiopian change his skin, or the leopard
his spots? Then may ye that have been accustomed
to do evil learn to do well." Again, "Why should
ye be stricken any more, ye will revolt more and
more?" Of these solemn and humbling truths I know
no more remarkable illustration than that before us.
What effect had God's judgments on his ancient peo-
ple? Some children owe their ruin to excessive in-
dulgence; others are the victims of an extreme sever-
ity, which drives them first to falsehood, and then
from that on to other crimes. Thus mismanagement
may be laid at our door; but who will impute error
to God, or challenge the wisdom of his ways? Now,
when the scourge was in the hands of a God all wise,
what effect had it on his people? Were they cured
by their afflictions, trials, and years of suffering? Did

these arrest the malady? Had they even the effect
of preventing their sinking deeper into sin? By no
means. As always happens in incurable diseases, the
patient grew worse instead of better. "Seducers wax
worse and worse." As always happens when life is
gone, the dead grew more and more offensive. The
more it shines, and the more it rains, the thicker the
dews of night, and the hotter the sun of day, the fast-
er the dead tree rots; for those agents in nature which
promote the vegetation and develop the beauty of
life, the sounding shower, the silent dews, the sum-
mer heat, have no other effect on death than to
hasten its putridity and decay. And even so, furnish-
ing us with an impressive lesson of the impotency of
all means that are unaccompanied by the divine bless-
ing—was it with God's ancient people. He sent them
servants, and he sent them sufferings; but, until the
Spirit of life descended from on high, their habits only
grew more depraved, their condition more desperate,
their profanity more profane; they but laid them-
selves more and more open to the charge—"The last
state of that man is worse than the first." Wherever
on weary feet they wandered, they dishonored reli-
gion, disgraced the faith; and, instead of extorting
the respect of their oppressors, they exposed both
themselves and their God to contempt.

The heathen sneered and said, "These are the peo-
ple of the Lord!" and, what is less common, these
down-trodden exiles, these debased and degraded sin
ners, seem themselves to have felt the desperate char-
acter of their case; they said, "Our bones are dried,
and our hope is lost."

Now, as we may learn from the case of the Jews,
the case of every sinner, apart from divine assistance.

is a desperate one. This internal and universal de-
filement is one which neither sorrows nor sufferings
can remove. God, in a passage which we have already
quoted, says, "Though thou wash thee with nitre,
and take thee much soap, yet thine iniquity is marked
before me;" sorrows have no more virtue than soap,
tears than nitre here. Trust not, therefore, in any
merely unsanctified afflictions, as if these could per-
manently and really change the true character of the
heart. I have seen the characters of the writing re-
main on paper that the flames had turned into a film
of buoyant coal; I have seen the thread that had
been passed through the fire, retain, in its cold gray
ashes, the twist which it had got in spinning; I have
found every shivered splinter of the flint as hard as
the unbroken stone: and, let trials come, in provi-
dence, sharp as the fire and ponderous as the crushing
hammer, unless God send with these something else
than these, bruised, broken, bleeding as the heart may
be, it remains the same. You may weep for your
sins; and, since all of us have need to seek a more ten-
der conscience, and that this too cold and callous heart
were warmed and softened, sorry should I be to stop
your weeping. Should a mote of dust get into the
natural eye, the irritation induced will weep out the
evil; and so, in a way, with sin in a tender and holy
conscience. But tears—an ocean of tears—wash not
out the guilt of sin. All tears are lost that fall not at
the feet of Jesus. But even the tears which bathe a
Saviour's feet wash not away our sins. When falling
—flowing fastest, we are to remember that it is not the
tears we shed, but the blood he shed, which is the
price of pardon; and that guilty souls are nowhere to
be cleansed but in that bath of blood where the foul·

est are free to wash and certain to be cleansed.   From
its crimson margin a Magdalene and a Manasseh have
gone up to glory ; and since their times, succeeding
ages have been daily and more fully proving, that
grace is still free, salvation still full, and that still the
blood of Christ cleanseth from all sin.

> "There is a fountain filled with blood,
>   Drawn from Emmanuel's veins,
> And sinners plunged beneath that flood,
> Lose all their guilty stains."

Man Sinning.

When the house of Israel dwelt in their own land, they defiled it by their own way, and by their doings.—EZEKIEL xxxvi. 17.

"I HAVE dreamed a dream," said Joseph, "and behold the sun, moon, and eleven stars made obeisance to me." Our earth was once supposed to occupy a place of no less honor in creation. Turning daily on its axis, and performing also an annual revolution round the sun, our globe is in incessant motion; but it was once believed that its state was one of perfect rest, and that, like the small pivot on which some great wheel revolves, it formed a center, around which went rolling the whole machinery of heaven, those suns and planets, both fixed and wandering stars. This dream of science met a happier fate than Joseph's; believed in the credulous ages of the world's childhood, it was obstinately clung to as an article of faith down to no very distant period. It is not so very long ago since the telescope of Galileo demonstrated that our earth, whatever the Pope might say, is a satellite of the sun, and but one of many orbs that roll around him; and he but one of many suns, which, taking millions of years to complete their circle, revolve about some greater center. At some period preceding the philosopher's discovery, the throne of Spain is said to have been occupied by a man who was acute enough to perceive, that if all these vast systems, suns, planets, and comets, were daily turning

round this earth, then, in making the greater subser
vient to the less, the Creator of the universe had con-
structed a very clumsy and cumbersome piece of
mechanism. History has preserved the profane lan-
guage of his dissent from the science of his own day.
It was something to the effect, that if God had con-
sulted him when he made the worlds, they would
have been better designed. Far be it from us, under
any perplexity felt in contemplating the mysteries
either of creation or providence, to question the wis-
dom of God, to cherish a thought so daring, or utter
an expression so profane. In his dealings with us, his
way may be in the sea, and his path in the mighty
waters, and his footsteps not known; "by terrible
things in righteousness," he may answer us; let him
dash the cup from our hand, or fill it brimful of
"wine of astonishment," we shall never deem it right
to think that God has done wrong. Whatever ap-
pearance of error his ways or works may present, be
assured that the defect is not in the object, but in the
spectator, in the eye that sees, not in the thing that is
seen; not in the plans of infinite wisdom, but in the
finite and fallible mind, which has the folly to con-
demn what it has not the understanding to compre-
hend. "Manifold are thy works, Lord God Almighty;
in wisdom hast thou made them all."

Such is the judgment of the Psalmist; and from
this no work of God's so strongly tempts us to dissent
as the condition and character of man himself; and I
know no way of so well meeting this temptation as by
receiving into our creed the doctrine of the Fall. If
with some we reject this doctrine.—if we hold that the
children are not in any sense implicated in their pa-
rents' sin—then, in the providence of God, and in the

goverLment of the world, there appears to be nothing
—I shall not say so deficient in wisdom, but so ob-
scure, inscrutable, painfully and fearfully mysterious,
as the position, condition, and character of man; for,
on the supposition that man has never fallen,—that
the vessel is as pure and perfect as when it passed
from the potter's hand—these questions are ever
rising, and, dismiss them as we may, are ever return-
ing,—how could a good God make such a wicked
creature? How could a kind God make such an un-
happy creature? How could a wise God make such
a foolish creature? How could a holy God make
such a sinful creature? If it is impossible for a pure
stream to be born of a polluted fountain, is it not as
impossible to believe that a crystal fountain can be
the parent of a polluted stream? If a clean thing
cannot come out of an unclean, is not the conclusion
as fair, as logical, as inevitable, that an unclean thing
cannot come out of a clean?

Now let us shut the Bible—exclude every ray of
inspired and celestial light; we stand in darkness;
and yet it seems to me like the dead substance, the
decaying wood, the putrid animal matter which grows
luminous through its decay, and emits in death a
phosphorescent light: by the help of man's very cor-
ruption we have light enough to see his fallen, dead,
degraded state. Indeed, I would a thousand times
sooner believe, that man made himself what he is, than
that God made him so; for in the one case I should
think ill of man only; in the other I am tempted to
blame his Maker. Just think, I pray you, to what
conclusion our reason would conduct us in any anal-
ogous case. You see, for example, a beautiful capital
still bearing some of the flowers and foliage which the

chisel of a master had carved upon the marble. It
lies prostrate on the ground, half-buried among weeds
and nettles; while beside it the rerises from its ped-
estal the headless shaft of a noble pillar. Would you
not conclude at once that its present position, so base,
mean, and prostrate, was not its original position?
You would say the lightning must have struck it
down; or an earthquake have shaken it, or some ig-
norant barbarian had climbed the shaft, and with rude
hand had hurled it to the ground. Well, we look at
man, and come to a similar conclusion. There is
something, there is much that is wrong, both in his
state and condition. His mind is carnal, and at en-
mity with God; the "imaginations of his heart are
only evil continually," so says the Bible. His body
is the seat of disease; his eyes are often swimming in
tears; care, anticipating age, has drawn deep furrows
on his brow; he possesses noble faculties, but, like
people of high descent, who have sunk into a low
estate and become menials, they drudge in the service
of the meanest passions. He has an immortal soul,
but it is clogged by the infirmities, and imprisoned
within the walls of a "body of death." His life is
vanity; he is ever seeking happiness, but like the
child who pursues the horizon, chases the rainbow, or
climbs the hills to catch the silvery moon, he never
finds the object of his search. In some respects,—
manifestly made for a sphere higher than he fills,—
he appears to us like a creature of the air which some
cruel hand has stripped of its silken wings. How like
he looks to this hapless object which has just fallen
on the pages of a book that we read by the candle on
an autumn evening! it retains the wish, but has lost
the power to fly; allured by the taper's glare, it has

brushed the flame, burned its wings, and, dropping
with a heavy fall, it now crawls wingless across the
page, and seeks the finger of mercy to end its misery.
Compare man with any of the other creatures of God,
and how directly we come to the conclusion that he
is not the creature he came from his Maker's hands!

Who has not had this borne in upon his mind
when his feet carried him forth into the fields of na-
ture? I pass out among our sylvan scenes; and here,
on the spray of the tasseled broom, there sits and
sings a little bird; it fills the glen with melody; from
his throat and throbbing breast he rings out the
sweetest music, as with keen bright eye he now looks
up to God and now down on the bush where his mate
sits with wings extended over their unfeathered nest-
lings; with songs he cheers her maternal cares, and is
then away on busy wing to cater for mother and her
young. Next, I turn my steps to the open moor; and so
soon as the intruder appears on her lonely domain, the
lapwing comes down upon the wind; brave and ven-
turesome she sweeps us with her wing, and shrieks out
her distress as she wheels round and round our head;
her brood are cowering on that naked waste; nor does
she rest until our foot is off the ground, and even then,
when the coast is clear, we hear her long, wild screams,
like the beating of a mother's heart when her child is
saved; like the mournful dash of waves upon the
shore long after the wind is down. Next I climb the
mountain, when snow-drifts thick from murky hea-
vens, and, like Satan, taking advantage of a believer's
trials, the wily fox is out upon the hunt; every mo-
ther of the flock lies there with her tender lamb be-
hind her; with her body she screens it from the rude-
ness of the storm · and with her head to the wind,

and expanded nostrils snuffing the distant danger, she
lies ready, the moment her eye catches the stealthy
foe, to receive him on her feet, and die, like a true
mother, in her lamb's defence. Such are God's crea-
tures. The work is unmarred; the workmanship
what it came from the Maker's hand; and away
among these old hoary hills, remote from man, his
cities, his sins, his works, his sorrows, we are out of
hearing of the groans of creation; and, but for the
corruption we carry with and within us, we could al-
most forget the Fall. Stretched on a flowery bank,
with the hum of bees, the song of birds, and the chirp
of the merry grasshopper in our ear, heaven serene
above us, and beneath us the placid lake, where every
flower and bush and birch-tree of the rock looks down
into the mirror of its own beauty, the murmur of the
waterfall sounds to us, like an echo from the crags of
the Creator's voice, " All is very good."

But let us retrace our steps along the dusty road
from the broom where the little bird sings, and the
moor where the lapwing screams her maternal fears,
and the hill where the timid sheep faces the fox to
die for her offspring; or the forest, where the bear
with her cubs behind her, offers her shaggy bosom to
the spear. Enter this town. Look at this mother, as
we saw her when Sabbath bells rung worshipers to
prayer, and God was calling sinners to the throne of
mercy. Her back is against the church's wall; she
has sunk on the cold pavement; her senses are steeped
in drink, and on her lap,—pitiful sight! lies an ema-
ciated, half-naked infant, with the chill, cold rain
soaking its scanty rags, and lashing its pallid face.
Is this God's handiwork? Is this the clay as it came
from the potter's wheel? Was this the shape in

which woman came from her Maker's hand? When Adam woke, was our mother Eve such as this her daughter? If so, better he had never woke; it had been good for him to be alone. Nature, to say nothing of religion, revolts from the thought.

Now, it is common enough to call such spectacles brutal; language which is a libel on creation, and a blasphemy against the Creator. Such scenes are not brutal. My very argument lies in this, that the brute beasts never present themselves in such a repulsive and revolting aspect. Under the impulse of instincts necessary for their well-being, for the due balance or races, and the general welfare of the world, they may, and indeed must prey upon each other; but did any man ever find them committing self-destruction? Do they ever pursue such suicidal conduct? Range the wide fields of nature, travel from the equator to the poles, rise from the worm that crawls on earth to the eagle that cleaves the clouds, and where shall you find any thing corresponding to our scenes of dissipation, or the bloody fields of war? Suppose, that on his return from Africa, some Park, or Bruce, or Campbell, were to tell how he had seen the lions of the desert leave their prey, and, meeting face to face in marshaled bands, amid roars that drowned the thunder, engage in deadly battle, he would find none so credulous as to believe him; the world would laugh the traveler and his tale to scorn. But should a thing so strange and monstrous occur—should we see the cattle, while the air shook with their bellowings, and the ground trembled beneath their hoofs, rush from their distant pastures, to form two vast, black, solid columns; and should these herds, with heads leveled to the charge, dash forward to bury

their horns in each other's bodies, we would proclaim
a prodigy, and ask what madness had seized creation.
Well, is not sin the parent of more awful prodigies?
Look here—turn to the horrors of this battle-field.
This is no fancy, but a fact—a bloody, sickening
fact. The ground lies thick with the mangled brave;
the air is shaken with the most horrible sounds,
every countenance expresses the passions of a fiend.
Humanity flies shrinking from the scene, and leaves
it to rage, revenge, and agony. Fiercer than the
cannon's flash shoot flames of wrath from brother's
eyes; they sheathe their swords in each other's bowels;
every stroke makes a widow, and every ringing volley
scatters a hundred orphans on a homeless world. I
would sooner believe that there was no God at all,
than that man appears in this scene as he came from
the hand of a benignant Divinity. Man must have
fallen; nature, society, the state of the world, are so
many echoes of the voice of Revelation; they pro-
claim that man is fallen—that the gold has become
dim—that the much fine gold has perished; and, in
words to which we again turn your attention, that we
have defiled the land in which we dwell, by our ways
and by our doings. Now, leaving the subject of
Original, to speak of Actual Sin, we remark—

I. Apart from derived sinfulness, we have personal
sins to answer for.

Dispose of the doctrine of original sin as you please;
suppose that you could disprove it; when that count
of the indictment is canceled, what have you gained?
Enough, more than enough, remains to convict us of
guilt, and condemn all within these walls. You may
deny Original, but can any man deny Actual Sin?

You might as well deny your existence; it sticks to you like your shadow. "If we should say that we have no sin, we make God a liar, and the truth is not in us." I say with God, "Come, let us reason together." Do you mean to affirm, on the one hand, that you have never been guilty of doing what you should not have done? or, on the other, never guilty of not doing what you should have done? Lives there a man so happy as to look back on the past and feel no remorse, or forward to the future and feel no fear? What! is there no page of your history that you would obliterate—no leaf that, with God's permission you would tear from the book? Is there no action, nor word, nor wish of days gone by, that you would not, if you could, recall? To David's prayer, "Lord, remember not the sins of my youth, nor my transgressions," have you no solemn and hearty Amen? If you could be carried back to the starting-pest, and leant again against the cradle, and stood again at your mother's knee, and sat again at the old school desk, with companions that are now changed, or scattered, or dead and gone—were you to begin life anew—would you run the self-same course; would you live over the self-same life? What! is there no speech that you would unsay? is there no act that you would undo? no Sabbath that you would spend better? none yet alive, none mouldering in the grave, none now in heaven or hell, to whom you would bear yourself otherwise than you have done? Are there none among the dead whose memory stings you, and whose everlasting state fills you with anxiety? Did you never share in sins that may have proved their ruin? and never fail in faithfulness that might have saved their souls? Oh! if every thread of our web

were yet to weave, what man would make the future
a faithful,—I will add, fearful copy of the past? I
will venture to say that no man living would; and
that the Apostle has universal conscience on his side,
when he says, "If we say that we have no sin, we
deceive ourselves." Our sins are more in number
than the hairs upon our head; and I know no lan-
guage nor attitude so becoming us as those of Ezra,
when, rending his mantle, he fell upon his knees and
cried, "Oh, my God, I am ashamed, and blush to lift
up my face to thee; for our iniquities are increased
over our heads, and our trespass is gone up into the
heavens."

II. The guilt of these actual sins is our own.

"Hast thou eaten of the tree?" God puts the ques-
tion, and man replies, "The woman whom thou gavest
to be with me, she gave me of the tree, and I did
eat." Adam points an accusing finger at Eve, and
turning round to the woman, God says, "What is this
that thou hast done?" She in turn lays the blame on
the serpent, saying, "The serpent beguiled me, and I
did eat." And thus and thus they shift the sin. We
have "eaten of the tree;" and,—unless it be to roll
the guilt on Christ,—we attempt in vain to screen our-
selves behind another's back—to lay the burden on
any shoulders but our own.

There are strong pleas which the poor heathen may
advance in extenuation of their guilt; and, stepping
forward with some confidence to judgment,—may urge
upon a just and merciful as well as holy God.

They may say, we knew no better; no man cared
for our souls. Great God! when thy followers landed
on our happy shores, they brought no olive branch or

Bible, but fire, and sword, and slavery; and on the back of those who, bearing thy name, oppressed us robbed us, enslaved us, and left us to die ignorant of thy love, we lay our guilt. Let them answer for us: place these Christians at thy bar; ask them "where is thy brother Abel?" and on their heads, not on ours, let thy dread justice fall. This wretched, ragged child, the victim of cruelty and neglect, who leaves hunger and a bed of straw to stand at the bar of God, may lift up his head at that august tribunal, and stand on his defence with more certainty both of justice and pity than he has ever met here below. In cold and nakedness, in hunger and thirst, in rags and ignorance, he was left to wander our hard streets, and, among all the Christians of this city, there was not one kind hand to guide his naked feet to Sabbath church or infant school. Poor wretch! the house of God was not for him; and now that he addresses one who will not refuse to hear him—child of misfortune!—now may he say, Merciful Lord! my mother taught me to steal, my father taught me to swear. How could I obey a Bible which I never learned to read? How could I believe in thee, whom no one taught me to know? Saviour of sinners! condemn me not; how was I to avoid sins against which I was never warned? I did not know what I did. Seizing thy cross, I claim the benefit of its dying prayer, "Father, forgive them, for they know not what they do."

What value may be given to these pleas—what weight they may carry at a tribunal where much will be exacted of those who have got much, and little asked where little has been given—it is not for us to say. The Judge of all the earth will do right. But this we know, that we have no such excuse to plead no such plea to urge in extenuation of one of a thousand of our offences. Some, indeed, plead their natural proneness to sin; they excuse themselves to conscience on that ground, or on this, that the temptation before which they fell, fell on them with the suddenness and vehemence of a hurricane. The command, however, to watch and pray leaves you without excuse. You were fully warned, and should have been on the outlook for the white squall. The sentinel is righteously shot who allows himself to sleep upon his post. Supposing, however, that the plea were accepted; I repeat, enough, and more than enough, remains to condemn us, and leaves guilt no refuge out of Christ. We talk of the strength and suddenness of temptation; but how often have we sinned designedly, deliberately, repeatedly? We talk of our bias to sin; but who has not committed sins that he could have avoided— sins which he could have abstained from, and sins which he did abstain from, when it served some present purpose to do so? This reeling sot and slave of drunkenness keeps sober at a communion season; and the swearer, who alleges that he cannot refrain from oaths, puts a bridle on his tongue in the presence of his minister. It is useless for the sinner to say that he is swept away by temptation; "he conceiveth mischief, and he bringeth forth falsehood;" and if swept away, it is as the suicide, who seeks the river, stands on its brink, and, leaping in, is swept off to his watery grave. I know that Satan goes about seeking whom he may devour; but, while he tempts *us*, how often have we tempted him? Stealing on unawares, and, like a lion crouching to the leap, with sudden and unlooked for spring he may cast himself upon us; but how often have we cast ourselves in his way? We have gone down to Delilah, we have stood in the way of sinners, we have sinned when we knew that we were sinning; we have gone where we knew that we were to sin; and, in pursuit of its guilty pleasures—trampling conscience beneath our feet, and more than that, the body and blood of Jesus Christ—we have done what the heathen never did, what Sodom and Gomorrah never did, what Tyre and Sidon never did —we have rejected a Saviour, and madly refused eternal life. There is hope for us in the blood of his cross, but none in its prayer. We knew what we did.

Some years ago, on a great public occasion, a dis-tinguished statesman rose up in the presence of assem-bled thousands, and, in reply to certain calumnious and dishonorable charges, raised his hands in the vast assembly, exclaiming, "These hands are clean." Now, if you or I, or any of our fallen race did entertain a hope that we could act over this scene before God in judgment, I could comprehend the calm and unim-passioned indifference with which men sit in church on successive Sabbaths, eye the cross of Calvary, and listen to the overtures of mercy. Are these matters with which you have nothing to do? If, indeed, you have no sins to answer for—if before this world's great assize you are prepared not only to plead, but to prove your innocence—if conscience accuses you in nothing, and excuses you in every thing—then sleep on, in God's name sleep on, and take your rest. But when the heavens over men are clothed in thunders, and hell yawns beneath their feet, and both God's law and their own conscience condemn them, such indif-ference is madness! Beware! play with no fire; least of all, with fire unquenchable. Play with no edged sword; least of all, with that which Justice sheathed in a Saviour's bosom. Delay by the mouth of no pit; least of all, on the brink of a bottomless one, the smoke of whose torment goeth up for ever and ever. Think of these things. Incalculable issues are at stake; your everlasting destiny may turn upon this hour.

Do you feel under condemnation? Are you really anxious to be saved? Be not turned from your purpose by the jeers and taunts of the ungodly. It is a very common thing with scoffers, and with those who use their religion as a cloak always worn loosely, nor ever drawn closely round, save, so to speak, in inclement weather, when distress troubles, or death alarms them; it is no uncommon thing to eye all men of zealous duty with cold suspicion, and represent them as either rogues or fools, fanatics or hypocrites. In answer to the charge of weakness or folly, I think I could produce an array of brilliant and immortal names—names of men in whom duty has been associated with the highest intellect, the loftiest genius, the most profound and statesman-like sagacity—men besides whom most of your scoffers, skeptics, and worldlings were as dwarfs in the company of giants. Folly! if Christians really such are chargeable with any folly, it is with that of not being zealous enough —with that of being, not too much, but too little religious. In the name both of common sense and religion, I ask, is it possible, if there be a hell, to be too anxious to escape it? If men are perishing, how can I, with my children, brothers, sisters, friends in the burning, be too anxious to save them? The man who rises at mirk midnight to quench the flames in a neighbor's house, is no fool surely; but he who can coolly eat his meals beside the sea or go singing about his common avocations along the shore, when the wreck is in his eye, and the roar of the surf and the shrieks of the drowning are in his ear, he is a fool, or something worse.

As to the insinuation of general hypocrisy, the wretched charge got up against all religion, when some specious professor stands unmasked before the world, how absurd it is! Is there no grain in our barn-yards, because there is so much chaff? Are all patriots— Wallace and the Bruce, Tell, Russel, and Washington —deceivers and liars, because some men have villainously betrayed their country? Is there no honor in the British army, because some soldiers, the sweepings probably of our city streets, have left the lines, and leaped the trenches, and deserted to the enemy? Is there no integrity among British merchants, because now and then we hear of a fraudulent bankruptcy? Because some religious professors prove hypocrites, is therefore all ardent piety hollow hypocrisy? To reason so, argues either a disordered intellect or a very depraved heart—is a conclusion, indeed, as contrary to logic as to love. When were hypocrites ever known to suffer for their principles? Yet is there a country in Christendom that has not been strewed thick with the ashes and dyed red with the blood of martyrs? Have not their heads in ghastly rows stood on our city gates? Two hundred years ago, and the windows of the very houses still standing round this church were crowded with eager faces, taking their last look of men who went with firm step and lofty carriage to die for principle—loving Christ more than their lives, and ready, as one said before they threw him off—had they as many lives as they had hairs on their head, to lay them all down for Christ. Religion is an honest thing, and true wisdom. God working in you, work out therefore your salvation. The way to the refuge lies open; with the feet of an Azahel haste to Jesus. Once in him, you can turn on the avenger, saying, I fear thee not; here thou comest, but no farther; this blood-red line thou canst not pass,—"There is no condemnation for them who are in Christ Jesus."

Do you see that sin stains your holiest services, de-filing head, heart, hands, feet—the whole man? Haste to the fountain where sins are lost and souls are cleansed. With its base ingratitude to your heavenly Father—with the wounds it has inflicted on a most loving Saviour—with the grief it has caused, and the resistance it has made, to a most gentle and Holy Spirit—with the deep injuries it has done to your own soul, and souls which, loving, you should have sought to save—Oh, let sin be your deepest sorrow, your heaviest grief, the spring of many tears, the burden of many sighs, the occasion of daily visits to the cross of Calvary.

> ' Weep not for broad lands lost;
>   Weep not for fair hopes crossed;
>   Weep not when limbs wax old;
>   Weep not when friends grow cold;
>   Weep not, that death must part
>   Thine and the best-loved heart;
>   Yet weep—weep all thou can—
>   Weep, weep. because thou art
>   A sin-defiled man."

Man Suffering.

Wherefore I poured my fury upon them, and I scattered them among
the heathen, and they were dispersed through the countries. Ac-
cording to their way and according to their doings, I judged them.
EZEKIEL xxxvi. 18, 19.

IT appears a very easy thing to say what a plant or
animal is. It is not so. There are myriads of living
creatures that occupy the debatable ground between
the vegetable and animal kingdoms, and naturalists
have not yet determined on which side of the border
to assign them a place—whether to rank them among
plants or animals. What is man? You would think
it an easy thing to answer that question; yet I am not
sure that, even at this day, we have any correct de-
finition which—distinguishing him on the one hand
from the angelic race and on the other hand from the
higher orders of inferior creatures,—is at once brief
and comprehensive. Now, if we have such difficulty
in defining even ourselves, or those objects that, being
patent to the senses, may be made the subject of
searching and prolonged experiment, we need not
wonder that, when we rise above his works to their
Maker, from things finite to things infinite, it should
be found much easier to ask than answer the question
" What is God?" The telescope by which we con-
verse with the stars, the microscope which unvails the
secrets of nature, the crucible of the chemist, the knife
of the anatomist, the reflective faculties of the phi-

iosopher, all the common instruments of science avail
not here. On the threshold of that impenetrable
mystery, from out the clouds and darkness that are
round about God's throne, a voice arrests our steps;
and the question comes, "Who can by searching find
out God, who can find out the Almighty to per-
fection?"

Divines, notwithstanding, have ventured on a de-
finition of God; and, according to the Catechism of
the Westminister Assembly, "God is a spirit, infinite,
eternal, and unchangeable, in his being, wisdom, power
holiness, justice, goodness, and truth." A very com-
prehensive definition, no doubt; yet did it never strike
you as strange, that there is no mention of love
here, and that that is a very remarkable omission?—
an omission as remarkable as if a man who described
the firmament were to leave out the sun, or, painting
the human face, made it sightless, and gave no place
on the canvas to those beaming eyes which give life
and animation to the features.

Why did an assembly, for piety, learning, and
talents, the greatest, perhaps, that ever met in
England, or any where else, give us that catalogue of
the divine attributes, and deny a place among them
to love? We think the omission may be thus ex-
plained and illustrated. Take a globe, and observ-
ing their natural order, lay on its surface the colors
of the rainbow; gave it a rapid motion round its axis;
and now you no longer see blue, red, yellow, and the
others. As if by magic, the whirling sphere changes
into purest white, presenting to our eyes and under-
standing a visible proof that the sunbeam is not a
simple, but compound body, woven of various rays,
and forming, when blended into one, what we call

light. Now, may it not be, that these divines make no mention of love (otherwise an unaccountable omission) just because they held that as all the colors together make light, so all the attributes acting together make love; and that thus, because God is justice, is wisdom, is power, is holiness, is goodness, and is truth, God therefore of necessity, and in the express words of John, "God is love." This is the briefest and best definition of Divinity, and would have been John's answer to the question, "What is God?"

It may be said, and is no doubt true, that objects take a color from the eyes that look at them; all things—sun, and sea, and mountains, look yellow to the jaundiced eye; all things look gloomy to a gloomy mind; while a cheerful temper gilds the edges of life's blackest cloud, and flings a path of light across a sea of danger; contentment sits down to a crust of bread and a cup of water, and gives God thanks; and the plainest person is beautiful in the eyes of fond affection. Now it may be thought, to John's loving eye, his heavenly Father seemed so loving and so lovely, that it was very natural for him to give the color of his own eyes to this divine object, and say, God is love. But it is to be remembered, that when he gave this shortest, sweetest definition of divinity, he was not painting objects only as they appeared to him; he was a pen in the hand of inspiration;—like the keys of a musical instrument, he sounded to the movements of another's will, and the touch of another's finger; and that—one of the holy men of old, who spake as they were moved by the Holy Ghost—it was not he, but God himself, who thus described and defined himself, "God is love."

Assuming then that God is love, it may be asked,

how does that harmonize with the text? How is it to be reconciled with words where God represents himself as pouring down his fury like a thunder-shower, and scattering his people, in a storm of indignation, as light and worthless chaff blown away upon the wind. How, it may be asked, does this consist with God's love and mercy? Now, there is no greater mistake than to suppose that God, as a God of justice and a God of mercy, stands in antagonism to himself. It is not mercy, but injustice, which is irreconcilable with justice. It is cruelty, not justice, that stands opposed to mercy. These attributes of the Godhead are not contrary the one to the other, as are light and darkness, fire and water, truth and falsehood, right and wrong. No; like two streams which unite their waters to form a common river, justice and mercy are combined in the work of redemption. Like the two cherubims whose wings met above the ark—like the two devout and holy men who drew the nails from Christ's body, and bore it to the grave—like the two angels who received it in charge, and, seated, the one at the head, the other at the feet, kept silent watch over the precious treasure—justice and mercy are associated in the work of Christ; they are the supporters of the shield on which the cross is emblazoned; they sustain the arms of our heavenly Advocate; they form the two solid and eternal pillars of the Mediator's throne. On Calvary mercy and truth meet together, righteousness and peace embrace each other.

These remarks may prepare our minds for entering with advantage on the solemn subject of God's punitive justice; but, ere we open the prison, and look down into the pit, I would further bespeak your can

did and affectionate consideration of this very affect-
ing and awful subject, by remarking—

I. That God is slow to punish.

"He executeth not judgment speedily against the
workers of iniquity." He does punish; he shall pun-
ish; with reverence be it spoken, he must punish.
Yet no hand of clock goes so slow as God's hand of
vengeance. Of that, the world, this city, and this
church, are witnesses; each and all, speaker and hear-
er, are living witnesses. It is too common to overlook
this fact; and, overlooking the kindness, long-suffer-
ing, and warnings which precede the punishment, we
are too apt to give the punishment itself our exclusive
attention. We see his kindness impressed on all his
works. Even the lion growls before he leaps, and be-
fore the snake strikes she springs her rattle.

Look, for example, on the catastrophe of the De-
luge. We may have our attention so engrossed by
the dread and awful character of this judgment, as to
overlook all that preceded it, and see nothing but
these devouring waters.

The waters rise till rivers swell into lakes, and lakes
into seas, and along fertile plains the sea stretches
out her arms to seize their flying population. Still
the waters rise; and now, mingled with beasts that
terror has tamed, men climb to the mountain tops, the
flood roaring at their heels. Still the waters rise; and
now each summit stands above them like a separate
and sea-girt isle. Still the waters rise; and, crowding
closer on the narrow spaces of their lessening tops,
men and beasts fight for standing-room. Still the
thunders roar and the waters rise, till the last survivor
of the shrieking crowd is washed off, and the head of

the highest Alp goes down beneath the wave And now the waters rise no more; God's servant has done his work; he rests from his labors; and, all land drowned—all life destroyed—an awful silence reign-ing, and a shoreless ocean rolling, Death for once has nothing to do, but ride in triumph on the top of some giant billow, which, meeting no coast, no continent, no Alp, no Andes, to break upon, sweeps round and round the world.

We stand aghast at this scene; and, as the corpses of gentle children and sweet infants are floating by, we exclaim, "Has God forgotten to be gracious—is his mercy clean gone for ever?" No; assuredly not. Where, then, is his mercy? Look here; look at this ark which, steered by an invisible hand, comes dimly through the gloom. That lonely ship on a shoreless sea carries mercy on board; and within walls that are pitched without and within, she holds the costliest freight that ever sailed the sea. The germs of the church are there—the patriarchs of the old world, and the fathers of the new. Suddenly, amid the awful gloom, as she drifts over that dead and silent sea, a grating noise is heard; she has grounded on the top of Ararat. The door is opened; and beneath the sign of the olive branch, they come forth from their baptismal burial, like life from the dead,—like souls passing from nature into a state of grace,—like the saints when they shall rise at the summons of the trumpet to behold a new heaven and a new earth, and to see the sign, which these "gray fathers" hailed, encircling the head that was crowned with thorns.

Nor is this all. Our Heavenly Father's character is dear to us; and I must remind you that ere mercy flew, like the dove, to that asylum, she had swept the

world with her wings. Were there but eight, only
eight saved? There were thousands, millions sought.
Nor is it justice to God to forget how long a period
of patience, and preaching and warning, and compas-
sion, preceded that dreadful deluge. Long before the
lightning flashed from angry heavens; long before
thunders rolled along dissolving skies; long before
the clouds rained down death; long before the floo.
and solid pavement of this earth, under the prodigious
agencies at work, broke up, like the deck of a leaking
ship, and the waters rushed from below to meet the
waters from above, and sink a guilty world; long be-
fore the time when the ark floated away by tower and
town, and those crowded hill-tops, where frantic
groups had clustered, and amid prayers and curses,
and shrieks and shouts, hung out their signals of dis-
tress—very long before this, God had been calling
an impenitent world to repentance. Had they no
warning in Noah's preaching? Was there nothing
to alarm them in the very sight of the ark as story
rose upon story; and nothing in the sound of those
ceaseless hammers to waken all but the dead? It
was not till Mercy's arm grew weary ringing the
warning bell, that, to use the words of my text, God
"poured out his fury" on them. I appeal to the sto-
ry of this awful judgment. True, for forty days it
rained incessantly, and for one hundred and fifty days
more "the waters prevailed on the earth;" but while
the period of God's justice is reckoned by days, the
period of his long-suffering was drawn out into years;
and there was a truce of one hundred and twenty
years between the first stroke of the bell and the first
crash of the thunder. Noah grew gray preaching re-
pentance. The ark stood useless for years, a huge

laughing-stock for the scoffer's wit; it stood till it was covered with the marks of age, and its builders with the contempt of the world; and many a sneer had these men to bear, as, pointing to the serene heavens above and an empty ark below, the question was put, "Where is the promise of his coming?" Most patient God! Then, as now, thou wert slow to pun-ish—"waiting to be gracious."

As that catastrophe and many other judgments prove—he is slow to anger. God poured out his fury; but his indignation was the volcano that groans for days before it discharges the elements of destruc-tion, and pours out its lavas on the vineyards at its feet. Where, when God's anger has burned hottest, was it ever known that judgment trod on the heels of sin? A period always intervenes; room is given for remonstrance on God's part, and repentance upon ours. The stroke of judgment is indeed, like the stroke of lightning, irresistible, fatal; it kills—kills in the twinkling of an eye. But the clouds from which it flashes are slow to gather, and thicken by degrees; and he must be deeply engaged with the pleasures, or engrossed in the business of the world, whom the flash and peal surprise. The gathering clouds, the deepening gloom, the still and sultry air, the awful silence, the big pattering rain-drops—these reveal his danger to the traveler, and warn him from river, road, or hill, to the nearest refuge. Heeded or un heeded, many are the warnings you get from God. He has "no pleasure in the death of the wicked;" he is "not willing that any should perish, but that all should turn to him and live; and no man ever yet went to hell, but trampling under foot ten thousand warnings,—ten times ten thousand mercies.

Whatever injustice men may do themselves—however reckless they may cast away salvation and their souls, I demand justice for him whose ambassador I am—for these mysteries of salvation of which I am a steward. No doubt he says, "I poured out my fury upon them;" but when was this done? Not till divine patience was exhausted, and a succession of servants had been commissioned to warn, to preach, and plead with them. Remember the words of a weeping Saviour, as he looked on the city from the top of Olivet—"O, Jerusalem, Jerusalem, thou that killest the prophets, and stonest them which are sent unto thee, how often would I have gathered thy children together, even as a hen gathereth her chickens under her wings, and ye would not! Could language furnish terms more tender or pathetic than these? Or those, in which God pours forth his affection for this very people—"When Israel was a child, then I loved him: I taught Ephraim also to go: taking them by their arms, I drew them with the cords of a man, and with bonds of love?" This language carries us into the tenderest scenes of domestic life; it reminds us of a mother, who, when telling us how one child had been blighted in the bud, and how another had strayed from the paths of virtue, and how all the sweet flowers of her home had withered away, bitterly looked back on departed joys, and cried, as she wrung her hands in a lonely cottage—"Ah! these were happy days, when they were children at my knee." Like a father who hangs over some unworthy son, and, while his heart is torn by contending emotions, hesitates what to do—whether once and for ever to dismiss him, or to give him another trial—it is most touching to see God bending over sinners, and this

flood of melting pathos bursting from his heart--
"How shall I give thee up, Ephraim? how shall I
deliver thee, Israel? How shall I make thee as
Admah, how shall I set thee as Zeboim? Mine
heart is turned within me; my repentings are kindled
together. I will not execute the fierceness of mine
anger; I will not return to destroy Ephraim, for I am
God and not man."

Let us do the same justice to our Father in heaven
that we would render to an earthly parent. Would
it be doing a father justice to look at him only when
the rod is raised in his hand, and the child is on his
knees, and although the trembling lip, and weeping
eyes, and choked utterance of his boy, and a fond
mother's intercession also, all plead with him to spare,
he refuses. In this, how stern he looks! But before
you can know that father, or judge his heart aright,
you ought to know how often ere this the offence had
been forgiven; you should have heard with what
tender affection he had warned his child; and above
all, you should have stood at the back of his closet
door, and listened when he pleaded with God in his
behalf. Justice to him requires, that you should have
seen with what slow and lingering steps he went for
the rod, the trembling of his hand, and how, as the
tears fell from his eye, he raised it to heaven and
sought strength to inflict a punishment which, were
it to serve the purpose, he would a hundred times
sooner bear than inflict. When,—nursing his rage
for months, and coolly planning the atrocious murder,
—Absalom slew his brother, David was so shocked at
this horrible crime, that, although he permitted him
to return to Jerusalem, yet for two whole years he
refused to see him. His son, his eldest son, his

favorite son, he would hold no intercourse with Absa-
lom, nor speak to him, nor look on him. Would it
be justice to David to confine our attention to this?
Under that averted eye, and cold and stern aspect,
what a heart! Goaded on by ambition, this guilty
son next aims a blow at his father's life, and falls;
then the fountains of the great deep are opened, and
what a flood of feeling! What is it now to David,
his crown is safe, his throne secure? Absalom is
dead! "Oh Absalom! my son, my son Absalom!
would God I had died for thee, Oh Absalom, my son,
my son!" And, would we do our heavenly father
justice, we must look on Calvary as well as on Eden.
The Son of God indeed does not go up and down
heaven weeping, wringing his hands, and, to the
amazement of silent angels, crying, Would God that
I had died for man! A more amazing spectacle is
here. He turns his back on heaven; he leaves the
bosom and happy fellowship of his Father, he bares
his own breast to the sword of justice, and in the
depths of a love never to be fathomed, he dies on that
accursed tree, "the just for the unjust that we might
be saved!"

Through this vestibule of love, mercy, and long
suffering, we have thought it well to introduce you
into the scenes of God's punitive justice. It is on
iron, softened by the glowing fire, that impressions
are made and left; and expecting good only when
what is terrible is associated with what is tender, we
have thought it well that you should see at the very
outset how slow God is to smite, how swift to save.
Swift fly the wings of mercy. Slow goes the hand
of justice; like the shadow on the sun-dial, ever
moving, yet creeping slowly on, with a motion all but

imperceptible. Still let sinners stand in awe. The hand of justice has not stopped, although imperceptibly, it steadily advances; by and by, having reached the tenth, eleventh, twelfth hour, the bell strikes. Then, unless you now flee to Christ, the blow which was so slow to fall, shall descend on the head of impenitence with accumulated force. Let it never be forgotten, that although God's patience is lasting, it is not everlasting.

Observe—

II. How he punished his ancient people.

This is furnished to our hand in many portions of Scripture. For example, "Now, because ye have done all these works, saith the Lord, and I spake unto you, rising up early and speaking, but ye heard not; and I called you, but ye answered not; therefore will I do unto this house which is called by my name, wherein ye trust, and unto the place which I gave to you and to your fathers, as I have done to Shiloh. And I will cast you out of my sight, as I have cast out all your brethren, even the whole seed of Abraham. Therefore, pray not thou for this people, neither lift up cry nor prayer for them, neither make intercession to me; for I will not hear thee. The carcasses of this people shall be meat for the fowls of the heaven, and for the beasts of the earth; and none shall fray them away. Then will I cause to cease from the cities of Judah, and from the streets of Jerusalem, the voice of mirth, and the voice of gladness, the voice of the bridegroom, and the voice of the bride; for the land shall be desolate. And death shall be chosen rather than life by all the residue of them that remain of this evil family, which remain in all the places

whither I have driven them, saith the Lord of Hosts.
I will surely consume them, saith the Lord; there
shall be no grapes on the vine, nor figs on the fig-
tree, and the leaf shall fade; and the things that I
have given them shall pass away from them. The
Lord our God hath put us to silence, and given us
water of gall to drink, because we have sinned against
the Lord. We looked for peace, but no good came;
and for a time of health, and behold trouble! The
snorting of his horses was heard from Dan; the whole
land trembled at the sound of the neighing of his
strong ones: for they are come, and have devoured
the land, and all that is in it—the city, and those that
dwell therein. The harvest is past, the summer is
ended, and we are not saved. I am black; astonish-
ment hath taken hold on me. Is there no balm in
Gilead? Is there no physician there? Why, then,
is not the health of the daughter of my people recov-
ered?"

These were the children of Abraham, beloved for
the father's sake—the sole depositories of divine truth
—God's chosen people, through whose line and lineage
his Son was to appear. How solemn, then, and how
appropriate the question—"If such things were done
in the green tree, what shall be done in the dry?"
Look at Judah sitting amid the ruins of Jerusalem,
her temple without a worshiper, and her streets
choked with the dead: look at that bound, weeping,
bleeding remnant of the nation toiling, on its way to
Babylon: look at these broken, peeled, riven boughs;
and may I not warn you with the Apostle—"If God
spared not the natural branches, take heed lest he
spare not thee." We have seen an ancient mirror
from the sepulchers of Egypt, in which, some three

thousand years ago, the swathed and mummied form beside whose dust it lay looked upon her face, to nurse her vanity, or mourn her deformity. In the verses quoted we have a mirror well nigh as old, in which the prophet showed God's ancient people their like-ness and their sins; and when I take it from the dead man's hand, to hold it up before you, do not some of you recognize, in the features which it presents, those of your own state and character? Are they not to be seen in such words as these, for instance—"I spake unto you, rising up early, but ye heard not; I called you, but ye answered not:" or these—"The harvest is past, the summer is ended, and we are not saved." Are none of us the degenerate plants of a noble vine? Are there none of us who, although trained to respect the Sabbath, have forgotten the lesson of our child-hood? none with a picture of their early days yet fresh in memory, that exhibits a venerable father bending over the Bible, and, with his family around him, leading the domestic devotions, who have them-selves no altar in their homes;—who have a house, but no household God? Have none of us defrauded our children, not of ancestral lands, but of what is in-finitely more valuable, an ancestral piety? On the walls of many a house from which piety has been ex-pelled may we not read the words—"They did worse than their fathers?"

If we speak thus, it is for your good. We would not arm ourselves with these harsh thunders of the law, except, in the words of Paul, " to persuade you by the terrors of the Lord." We have no faith in ter-ror disassociated from tenderness. Trusting more to the process of drawing than driving men to Jesus, we pray you to observe that he who is the good is also a most tender Shepherd. Among the mins of our native land I have met a shepherd far from the folds, driving home a lost sheep—one which had "gone astray"—a creature panting for breath, amazed, alarmed, foot-sore; and when the rocks around rang loud to the baying of the dogs, I have seen them, whenever it offered to turn from the path, with open mouth dash-ing fiercely at its sides, and thus hounding it home. How differently Jesus brings home his lost ones! The lost sheep sought and found, he lifts it, tenderly lays it on his shoulder, and, retracing his steps, returns with joy, and invites his neighbors to rejoice along with him. The "green pastures" where he feeds his flock, the rocks under whose grateful shadows they repose in noontide of the day, the flowery and fra-grant banks of the streams where they drink, are dis-turbed by no sounds of violence nor voice of terror. Yes; Jesus rules his flock by love, not by fear; and amid the holy calm of sweet Sabbath mornings, gentle of countenance, he may be seen at their head, conduct-ing them forth to pastures sparkling with the dews of heaven, some sweet lamb in his arms, its mother at his side, and all his flock behind him; his rod their guard, and his voice their guide. Catching grace from his lips, and tenderness from his looks, I would speak to you as becomes the servant of such a gentle, lowly, loving Master. Yet, shall I conceal God's verity, and ruin men's souls to spare their feelings? Shall I sa-crifice truth at the shrine of a false politeness? To hide what Jesus revealed were not to be more tender, but less faithful than He. If the taste of these days were so degenerate as to frown down the honest preacher who should pronounce that awful word "Hell," and leave him to vacant pews, it were better,

far better, that he should be as "one crying in the
wilderness," and getting no response but the echo of
empty walls, than that he should fail in proclaiming
"the whole counsel of God." Apart from your inter-
ests, and looking only at my own, how could I other-
wise hold up these hands, and say, "They are clean
from the blood of all men?" How otherwise could
the preacher turn from his unhappy head the Bible's
closing curse—"If any man shall take away from the
words of this book, God shall take away his part out
of the book of life." Regard to myself, to you—re-
gard to a gracious God, to a blessed Saviour—regard
to all that is precious, solemn, sacred, eternal—these
now compel me, although with trembling hands, to
lift the vail.

If any are living without God, and hope, and Christ,
and prayer, I implore them to look here: turn to this
dreadful pit. How it gleams with fire! How it re-
sounds with woeful groans! Now, when we stand to-
gether on its margin, or rather shrink back with horror,
look there, and say, "Who can lie down in everlasting
burnings?"

It is alleged by travelers, that the ostrich, when
pursued by its hunters, will thrust its head into a bush,
and, without further attempt either at flight or resist-
ance, quietly submit to the stroke of death. Men say
that, having thus succeeded in shutting the pursuers
out of its own sight, the bird is stupid enough to fancy
that it has shut itself out of theirs, and that the dan-
ger, which it has concealed from its eyes, has ceased to
exist. We doubt that. God makes no mistakes; and,
guided as the lower animals are in all their instincts
by infinite Wisdom, I fancy that a more correct know-
ledge of that creature would show, that whatever stu-

pidity there may be in the matter, lies not in the poor
bird, but in man's rash conclusion regarding it. Man
trusts to hopes which fail him: the spider never; she
commits her weight to no thread which she has spun,
till she has pulled on it with her arms, and proved its
strength. Misfortune overtakes man unprovided and
unprepared for it: not winter the busy bee. Amid
the blaze of gospel light, man misses his road to
heaven: without any light whatever, in the darkest
night, the swallows cleave their way through the path-
less air, returning to the window-nook where they were
nestled; and through the depths of ocean the fish
steer their course back to the river where they were
spawned. If we would find folly, Solomon tells us
where to seek it:—" Folly," says the wise man, "is
bound up in the heart of a child:" and what is folded
up there, like leaves in their bud, blows out in the
deeds and habits of men. This poor bird, which has
thrust its head into the bush, and stands quietly to
receive the shot, has been hunted to death. For
hours the cry of its pursuers has rung in its startled
ear; for hours their feet have been on its weary track;
it has exhausted strength, and breath, and craft, and
cunning, to escape; and even yet, give it time to
breathe—give it another chance—and it is away with
the wind; and with wings outspread, on rapid feet it
spurns the burning sand. It is because escape is
hopeless and death is certain that it has buried its head
in that bush, and shut its eyes to a fate which it can-
not avert. To man—rational and responsible man—
belongs the folly of closing his eyes to a fate which
he may avert, and thrusting his head into the bush
while escape is possible; and, because he can put death,
and judgment, and eternity out of mind, living as if

there were neither a bed of death nor bar of judg-
ment.· Be wise: be men. Look your danger in the
face. Anticipate the day when you shall behold a
God in judgment and a world in flames; and now flee
to Jesus from the wrath to come. To come! In a
sense wrath has already come. The fire has caught,
it has seized your garments; you are in flames. Oh!
away then, and cast yourselves into that fountain which
has power to quench these fires, and cleanse you from
all your sins.

God's punitive Justice.

Wherefore I poured my fury upon them, and I scattered them among the heathen, and they were dispersed through the countries: according to their way, and according to their doings, I judged them.—EZEKIEL xxxvi. 18, 19.

THE dank mossy sward is deceitful: its fresh and glossy carpet invites the traveler to leave the rough moorland track; and, at the first step, horse and rider are buried in the morass. The sea is deceitful. What rage, what furious passions sleep in that placid bosom! and how often—as Vice serves her used-up victims—does she throw the bark that she received into her wanton arms, a wreck upon the shore. The morning is oft deceitful. With bright promise of a brilliant day it lures us from home; ere noon the sky begins to thicken, the sun looks sickly, the sluggish, heavily-laden clouds gather upon the hill-tops, the landscape all around closes in; the lark drops songless into her nest; the wind rises, blowing cold and chill; and at length—like adversities gathering round the grey head of age—-tempests, storm, and rain, thicken on the dying day. The desert is deceitful: it mocks the traveler with its mirage. How life kindles in his drooping eye, as he sees the playful waves chase each other to the shore, and the plumes of the palm waving in the watery mirror! Faint, weary, perishing with thirst, he turns to bathe and drink; and, exhausting his remaining strength in pursuit of a phantom, finds, unhappy man! that he has turned to die.

4

Deceitful above sward, or sea, or sky, or enchant
ed desert, is the heart of man; nor do I know a
more marked or melancholy proof of this than that
which our light treatment of such weighty matters
as sin and judgment affords. There is no exaggera·
tion in the prophet's language—"The heart *is* de·
ceitful above all things, and desperately wicked."
Put a case:—The flames have broken out in some
house, and the fire spreads fast; at midnight the roll
of the drum wakens the sleeping streets—a fearful
sound! soon followed by the hurried yet measured
tramp of armed men, and the rush of a crowd, who,
guided by a glare that illumines the sky, and turns
night into ruddy day, pour on the scene of danger;
and where the flames, bursting out from cellar to roof,
shed their lurid light on glancing bayonets, strong
arms below are working as for life, and daring men
above, ever and anon lost among clouds of smoke,
turn the stream upon the hissing fire. In this stirring
scene, where is the tenant of the house? How is he
engaged? They thunder at the door; they call his
name; they rear the ladder against the window; and
now they shout to him to wake, and haste, and flee.
leaving house and furniture to the flames. They listen,
but no answer. Alas! he has perished? Help has
come too late? No; he lives: he has heard all that
horrid din. He smells the smoke; he feels the floor
grow hot, and hotter, beneath his feet; and amid the
thick and suffocating air the man gasps for breath.
He has heard the cries of kindly neighbors; the glass
of the window, as a strong hand dashes it in, falls at
his feet, and he sees the very ladder resting on its sill.
Well; has some ruffian hand bound him neck and
heel, that he does not move? or gagged him, that he

gives back no answer? Not at all. The man is busy, very busy, ruminating on the question how the fire began; or with some pugnacious neighbor, as insane as himself, he is engaged in keen discussion about when and where it first broke out. Incredible! yet incredible as that appears, this heart is so deceitful, that something less excusable and more incredible still daily meets us in (what shall I call it?) the folly, the insanity, of thousands. God has sounded the alarum. Roused from sleep—in some sense convinced of sin—in some measure awake to danger—the dream of safety broken in upon—warned that there is no time to spare—with the flames of wrath above, beneath, around, blocking up all the common avenues of escape—the first, if not the only question, should be, "Oh, Sirs, what shall I do? Where shall I turn? Quick; say, this moment say, 'What shall I do to be saved?'" Yet, when the only question is, how to escape from impending, imminent danger, hours, days, years, are wasted in inquiries and discussions such as this—How the race came to be exposed to it.

Let theologians settle the metaphysics of the Fall; *their* business may be to know how we became sinners; *our* first business is to know how we are to be saved. Leave those who have reached the land to settle how and on what reef the vessel struck; the question with us, who still cling to the shrouds, or are battling with the surf, is, how to gain yon blessed shore. In God's name, and by God's help, get the fire put out; and then, when the flames are quenched, it will be time enough to consider how they were kindled. Tie the bleeding artery; and when life is saved, settle, if you can, how it was wounded. When you have plucked the drowning man from the water, and laid him on the bank, and the color flushes again on his cheek, and the pulse beats again at his wrist, and speech again returns to these blue and livid lips, then you may speculate on how he fell into the flood. When, in spite of Satan, and by God's help, we have wakened some careless one to care about his soul, it is one of the devil's wiles to distract his attention by such subjects, and amid the mazes of their inextricable labyrinths to bewilder him, who should be pressing on to salvation at the top of his speed. I would have the man who is engaged in such an enterprise to give these questions in the meanwhile the go-by—for once to apply well, words so often applied ill—"I will hear thee again on on this matter:" "when I have a more convenient season I will send for thee." These are profound subjects, worthy of the investigations of angels and exalted saints. We could not apply to their study the words of Nehemiah—"I have a great work to do; therefore I can not come down." But in saving ourselves and others, I am sure that there is enough to do, without occupying our attention with unsatisfactory speculations on moral evil, and the entrance of sin into our world. In the first place, few have time or talent for such studies. In the second place, although we had, we should find that, like going down into a coal-pit, or the depths of ocean, the further we descended the darker it grew: we should fare no better than the fallen intelligences described by Milton :—

> Others apart sate on a hill retired,
> In thoughts more elevate, and reasoned high
> Of Providence, foreknowledge, will, and fate—
> Fixed fate, free will foreknowledge absolute—

And found no end, in wandering mazes lost.
Of good and evil much they argued there—
Vain wisdom all, and false philosophy."

And in the third place, we may postpone these specu
lations till we enjoy the leisure of eternity, and can
examine subjects so obscure in the clear light of
heaven. Meanwhile, let it content us to be assured,
that the extent of our knowledge shall correspond to
the height of our elevation; and that, as a man, from
the bartisan of some lofty tower, or the summit of
some loftier mountain, commands a wider view and
broader landscape, and, in the course of rivers, the
ranges of hills, the outlines and indentations of the
coast, obtains a far more extensive view of objects,
and a much clearer conception of their relative bear-
ings, than he enjoyed in the plain below; so, while
some subjects, like the snowy summits of the Hima·
layas or Andes, may remain for ever inaccessible, yet,
once raised to heaven, we shall understand many
mysteries, and solve many questions, connected with
sin and its sorrows, of which it is best now to say,
"Such knowledge is too high for me; I cannot attain
unto it." A child seated on the shoulders of a giant
may see further than the giant himself; and an infant
standing on the top of a mountain very much further
than the giant at its feet: and even so, the lisping
babe, whom Jesus has taken from a mother's bosom
to his own, excels in knowledge the profoundest of
philosophers and the greatest of divines. In heaven
we shall see as we are seen—we shall know as we are
known: there "the light of the moon shall be as the
light of the sun, and the light of the sun shall be
sevenfold."

In considering at greater length the punitive justice

of God, I shall not attempt to offer any full or satis-
factory explanation of what is beyond our under-
standing. How a wise, holy, good, and gracious God
permitted what he certainly could have prevented—
permitted sin to exist at all—is at present a mystery,
and may for ever remain one. With others, I might
contribute some attempts to solve that difficulty; but
I believe that, like all preceding efforts, these would
throw no more light on this vast and mysterious sub-
ject than a candle sheds on a widely extended land-
scape clothed in mist or wrapped in midnight dark-
ness. Amid these awful and often painful mysteries,
we can only cling to the faith, and cherish an unshaken
confidence in this, that the Judge of all the earth doeth
right—that God at least is a King who can do no
wrong. To the man, then, who asks, Why am I born
with a bias to sin? Why has another's hand been
permitted to sow germs of evil in me? Why should
I, who was no party to the first covenant, be buried
in its ruins? if the Bible says in reply to the query—
" What mean ye, that ye use this proverb concerning
the land of Israel: the fathers have eaten sour grapes,
and the children's teeth are set on edge?" "As I live,
saith the Lord God, ye shall not have occasion any
longer to use this proverb in Israel," why, then, do I
suffer for Adam's sin? Why, most virulent of poisons!
should this sin infect the blood of a hundred gene-
rations? Why should I suffer for a crime committed
so long ago as six thousand years, and to which I no
more consented than to Cain's murder of Abel, or
Herod's massacre of the innocents? To these ques-
tions this is my reply: I shrink from sitting in judg-
ment upon my Judge. Clouds and darkness are
round about Jehovah now; but I am confident that,

when expiring Time cries, "It is finished," and the
vail of a present economy is rent, it shall be seen that
righteousness and judgment are the pillars of his
throne—that "there is no unrighteousness with God."
These questions open up an abyss respecting which
man's business is to adore, and not explore; and to
them, meanwhile, I have no other answer than the
great Apostle's, "Who art thou, O man! that repliest
against thy Maker? Shall the thing made say to him
who made it, why hast thou made me thus?"

But although the permission of sin is a mystery,
the fact of its punishment is no mystery at all; for,
while every answer to the question, How did God
permit sin? leaves us unsatisfied, to my mind nothing
is plainer than this, that, whatever was his reason for
permitting it to exist, God could not permit it to exist
unpunished. In proof of that, I observe—

I. The truth of God requires the punishment of sin.
"Take now thy son, thine only son Isaac, whom
thou lovest, and offer him for a burnt-offering on a
mountain that I will tell thee of." Startling announce-
ment!—so startling, that it is not possible to suppose
that the alarmed, amazed, confounded patriarch re-
ceived it at once—believed it without a dreadful
struggle. No; there never rung from mailed hand
or battle-axe such a stunning blow. What man, or
father, doubts that it made Abraham stagger, and
brought him to his knees? I think I hear him say-
ing, "Take Isaac—take my son, the son of my love,
the son of promise, the miraculous gift of heaven—
offer Isaac for a burnt-offering! Surely I dream.
What a dreadful fancy! Did my ears deceive me?
No: there was a voice; I heard it. It sounded like

the voice of God: could it be so? Was it for this that angels announced his birth? Was it to be thus rudely shaken off, that the old stock was made to blossom, and this sweet fruit to grow on a withered tree? Although this trembling hand could plunge the knife into Isaac's bosom, would it not be most honor to God to conclude that some demon, with false and wicked mimicry, had borrowed Jehovah's voice to lure me into a foul and monstrous crime, and, getting me to embrue these hands in Isaac's blood, by this horrid sacrifice to quench the light of heaven and the hope of earth—in this sweet bud to crush an un-blown salvation and unborn Saviour?" Now, what-ever room Abraham might have had for doubt—what-ever struggle faith had with unbelief in that father's heart—we have no room nor pretence to doubt that, however terrible its punishment, God has threatened to punish sin, and, true to his word, shall pour out his fury on the sinner's head. Christ is offered; and ye cannot escape, if ye neglect this great salvation.

Had that truth been written only in one solitary passage—within the whole compass of the Bible had there been but one line to that effect—we might have succeeded in persuading ourselves that its sense was mistaken, and its terms misunderstood. But is it so? Ah! no: there is letter upon letter, "line upon line, precept upon precept, here a little and there a little." God has recorded his irrevocable resolution, not in one, but in a hundred passages; and reiterated in a thousand ways the awful sentence—"The soul that sinneth, it shall die."

Some have fancied that they honor God most when, sinking all other attributes in mercy—indiscriminat-ing mercy—they represent him as embracing the

world in his arms—and receiving to his bosom with
equal affection the sinners that hate, and the saints
that love Him. They cannot claim originality for this
idea: its authorship belongs to the "father of lies."
Satan said so before them. It is the very doctrine
that damned this world. The serpent said to the wo-
man, "Thou shalt not surely die." Do you rest your
hope of salvation on such a baseless fancy? If so,
have you seriously considered in what aspect this
theory presents the God for whose honor you profess
such tender regard. We almost shrink from explain-
ing it. You save the creature, but at a price more
costly than was paid for sinners upon the cross of
Calvary. Is there something dearer than life to me?
—to God there was something more precious than
even the blood of Jesus. I can part with my life, but
not my honor;—and God could part with his Son,
but not with his truth. But let sin go unpunished,
either in person or substitute: this saves the sinner—
no doubt of that; but at what price? You save the
creature's life at the expense of the Creator's honor.
Your scheme exalts man; but far more than man is
exalted is God degraded. By this scheme no man is
lost; but there is a greater loss—something more
awful happens: the truth of God is lost; his crown
loses its topmost jewel, and the throne of the universe
is shaken to its foundations. It is as manifest as day-
light that God's truth and your scheme cannot stand
together. "Liar" stands against either God or you;
and, in the words of the Apostle, you "make God a
liar."

Nor is that all: my faith has lost the very rock it
stood on, and stood on—as I flattered myself—stead-
fast, immovable; for, however awful the threatenings

4*

in his Word may be, if God is not true to them, what security have I, or any man, that he will be true to its gracious promises? The rod which bends in one direction will prove as supple in another; and, since the truth of a Heaven stands upon the very same foundation as the truth of a Hell—the one upon the promise, the other upon the threatening, and both alike upon the simple word of God—why, then, the scheme which quenches the fears of the wicked extinguishes the hopes of the just. If he that believeth not shall not be condemned, farewell—a long and sad farewell —to my happy confidence that he that believeth shall be saved. I cannot consent that you should pull down my heaven, to build with its ruins, not a temple to justice, but an asylum for crime. Away with such a scheme. It is fatal to the peace of God's people. It is essentially blasphemous and dishonoring to their God. It makes God a liar. Making him do wrong, how can it be right? making him untrue, it must be itself untrue. We reject it with horror. It is a snare of the Evil One; and happy should we be to think that we had helped any of his captives out, and sent them singing, as on wings of faith they soared away to heaven, " My soul is escaped as a bird out of the fowler's snare: the snare is broken, and I am escaped."

II. The love of God requires that sin should be punished.

You may start at this. Love requires punishment? Had we said the justice, or holiness, or purity of God, we, no doubt, should have used an expression less startling, and more sure to command a ready assent. These attributes present strong positions, within which

it may be admitted that we could entrench this doctrine
—impregnable to all assaults. On that very account
it is that in this brief discussion we pass these by, and,
confident in the strength of our cause, select, of very
purpose, although some may think unwisely, what
they deem the weakest argument and point of de-
fence. Now I find one of the strongest and most af-
fecting proofs that the impenitent and unbelieving
shall not go unpunished, just in that tenderest of all
subjects, the love of God; and I think that I could
close with the man who uses this love to prove that
sin shall go unpunished; and having wrested that
weapon from his hand, take off the head of his ar-
gument with his own sword. I say of this love of
God, what David said of Goliath's sword, " there is
none like that—give it me."

Lend me your candid attention—open your minds
—and I think it will not be difficult to convince you,
that the love of God—which is a sevenfold shield to
the believer—not merely consents to, but demands,
the condemnation, as it aggravates the guilt, of the
impenitent. Let me at once prove and illustrate the
point by a piece of plain analogy:—This city, nay,
the whole land, is shaken by the news of some most
cruel, bloody, monstrous crime. Fear seizes hold of
the public mind; pale horror sits on all men's faces;
doors are double barred; and justice lets loose the
hounds of law on the track of the criminal. At length,
to the relief and joy of all honest citizens, he is caught,
He is tried, condemned, laid in irons, and waits but
the sentence to be signed. To save or slay—to hang
or pardon—is now the question with him whose pre-
rogative it is to do either; and by what motive is the
sovereign impelled to shut up his bowels of mercy,

and sign the warrant for execution? Is it want of pity? No; the pen is taken with reluctance; it trembles in his hand, and tears of compassion for this guilty wretch drop on the page he signs. Now it is not so much abhorrence of the guilty, as love of the innocent, and regard for their peace, purity, and honor, that dooms this man to die. If he were pardoned, and his crime allowed to go unpunished, neither man's life nor woman's virtue were safe; unless this felon dies, the peace and purity of a thousand happy families lie open to foul attack; and thus, love for those who have the best claim on a sovereign's protection, requires that the guilty die. That the community may live in peace, each man sitting beneath his own vine and fig-tree—that the citizen may feel himself safe in the bosom of his family—that streets may be safe to walk on—that beds may be safe to lie in—that our land may be a country fit to live in—crime must be punished. The magistrate who would reward obedience must punish rebellion; nor can he be a praise and protection to them that do good, but by making himself a terror to them that do evil.

There are scenes of domestic suffering which present another, no less convincing, and more touching analogy. I refer to those distressing cases where natural affection yields to the holiest parental duty; and where, although she thereby inflicts on her own bosom a wound time never heals, Love seizes the knife, and, lest the canker should extend to the other branches, lops off some once pleasant bough from the family tree. It has happened that, from love and regard to the interest of his other children—to save them from a brother's contamination—a kind parent has felt constrained to banish his son, and forbid him a father's

ι use. 't is sad to think that he may be lost; the
dread of that goes like a knife into the heart; yet,
bitter truth! painful conclusion! it is better that one
child be lost than a whole family be lost. These lambs
claim protection from the wolf; he must be driven
forth from the fold; weeping Love herself demands
this sacrifice; and, just because it is most lacerating,
most excruciating, to a parent's heart, it is in such a
case the highest and holiest exercise of parental love
to bar the door against a child. There have been pa-
rents so weak and foolish as to peril the morals, the
fortunes, the souls of their other children, rather than
punish one; and in consequence of this I have seen
sin, like a fever, infect every member of the family,
and vice ferment and spread till it had leavened the
whole lump. Divine Love, however, is no blind Di-
vinity: and that love being as wise as tender, sinners
may rest assured, that out of mere pity to them, God
will neither sacrifice the interests, nor peril the hap-
piness of his people. Love herself—bleeding, dying,
redeeming love—with her own hand will bar the door
of heaven, and from its happy, holy precincts, exclude
all that could hurt or defile. Stern words these! and
when Love puts on her armor, to fight against him,
what hope for the man who has compelled her to be
his enemy? Having armed Love against you, where
now are you flying? Look at this scene of judgment.
He who died on the cross occupies the throne. Love
incarnate presides at that august tribunal. The print
of the nail is on the very hand which waves away the
lost into perdition. The voice which so often invited
the impenitent is that which now condemns and com-
mands them to depart. Calmly, serenely anticipating
that day, Faith says, "It is God that justifieth; who

is he that shall condemn?" But oh! if Jesus Christ condemn, who shall justify? If He spare not, who shall save? From the wrath of the Lamb which impenitence has changed into the wrath of a Lion, despair turns away a face covered with the blackness of darkness, to cry as she wrings her hands, "The great day of his wrath is come, and who shall be able to stand?" If the Lamb of God—if the Love of God be our adversary, our case is desperate. Oh! take warning in Time, that you be not lost for Eternity. "Kiss the Son, lest he be angry, and ye perish from the way, when his wrath is kindled but a little." "Blessed are all they that put their trust in him."

III. Unless sin is to be awfully punished, the language of Scripture appears extravagant.

Next to the suffering is the sight of pain to a man of tender feelings: nor, but for your good, would I ask any one to cast even a hurried glance on those appalling pictures which the Bible reveals. But if men, for the mere gratification of taste—if the lovers of the fine arts—crowd to some picture of the damned —a scene of the last Judgment painted by a master's hand, where hideous demons torment shrieking victims, and drag the seven deadly Sins down into the gulf of fire—when, as far as the heavens do the earth, the preacher's object transcends the painter's, and the salvation of souls the gratification of taste—when my object is not to please your fancy, but profit your souls—shall that be condemned in the pulpit which is so much applauded in the painting? Where the highest interests are at stake, shall I be judged harsh, and showing no regard to feeling and propriety, because I ask you to turn your eyes on this spectacle—

on a worm that never dieth, and this fire that is never quenched? Oh! let me beseech, implore you, to read with tears and prayers those passages of Scripture that reveal the miseries of the lost. Blot not from your minds what you cannot blot out of the Book of God.

What is so sad—what so strongly and sadly illustrates the wicked deceitfulness of this heart—as the entertainment which men extract from the solemnities of judgment? Only think of those, who turn away with ill-disguised distaste from the very mention of such subjects in the house of God, crowding a brilliant saloon to hear this same judgment set to music, and listen with loud and rapturous applauses to the hired musicians, who give a bold (shall I say profane) imitation of the trumpet that rends the grave, of the thunders that announce the Judge, the song of adoring angels, the shouts of ransomed saints, and—for any thing I know—the awful shrieks of the damned! Think of this; think of criminals leaving the bar to set their sentence to music! When their life is a matter of hours, and its few remaining sands should be given to prayer and God's book of mercy, think of men, shut up in a cell, and drawing on its walls a wretched caricature of their judge, the gallows, the mighty crowd, the victim turning round on his cord, with eyeballs that protrude beneath the cap, and limbs convulsed in the very agony of death!

The sufferings and misery which awaits the impenitent and unbelieving, God has painted in most appalling colors. To save us from them, his Son left the heavens and died on a cross. When Paul thought of these, he wept like a woman. A dauntless man, who shook his chain in the face of kings—whose spirit no sufferings could subdue, and whose heart no dangers could appall—who stood as unmoved amid a thousand perils as ever rock amid a thousand billows—he could not contemplate these without the deepest emotion; his tears fell fast and thick upon the page where he wrote, "of whom I have told you often, and now tell you even weeping, whose god is their belly, whose end is destruction."

What horror did David feel at the sight and fate of sinners? With his blind face turned up to heaven, you see a man approach the edge of an awful precipice: every step brings him nearer—still nearer, the brink. Now he reaches it: he stands on the grassy edge. Oh for an arm to reach him—for a voice to warn him—for a blow to send him staggering back upon the ground! But he has lifted his foot; it is projected beyond the brink; another moment, a breath of wind, the least change of balance, and he is whirling twenty fathoms down. You stop your ears, close your eyes, turn away your head; horror has taken hold of you. And such were David's feelings when he contemplated the sins and fate of the wicked: "Horror hath taken hold upon me, because of the wicked that forsake thy law: rivers of water run down mine eyes, because they keep not thy law, O God." The wrath of God is the key to David's sorrow, to an Apostle's tears, to the bloody mysteries of the Cross. That was the necessity which drew a Saviour down. Had that wrath been tolerable or terminable, the sword of Justice had never been dyed with the blood, nor sheathed in the body of such a noble victim; and if there is a need be for the lightest cross that lies on a good man's lot, how great the necessity for that upon which the Saviour died! God is not willing that you should perish, and by

these terrors of the Lord we would persuade you.
Meditate on these words: pray over them—"Woe to
the man that striveth with his Maker!" "Who can
lie down in everlasting burnings?" "The wicked
shall be cast into hell, and all the nations that forget
God."

Rather than that you should perish, I would even
thus persuade you. Oh! there are terrors enough in
the Bible to make a man's hair stand on end. Surely,
were God but for one moment to let this world hear
the weeping and wail of the lost, that sound, more
terrible than Egypt's midnight cry, would rouse the
student at his books, arrest the foot of dancer in the
ball, stop armies in the very fury of the fight, and,
calling a sleeping world from their beds, would bend
the most stubborn knees, and extort from all the one
loud cry, "Lord, save me, I perish!" Still it is not
terror which is the mighty power of God. The
Gospel, like most medicines for the body, is of a com·
pound nature; but, whatever else enters into its com-
position, its curative element is love. No man yet
was ever driven to heaven: he must be drawn to it;
and I wish to draw you. The Gospel has terror in it,
no doubt. But it is like our atmosphere—occasionally
riven by the thunder, and illuminated by the fatal
flash—it is at times the path of the stealthy pesti-
lence—charged with elements of destruction, and
impregnated with the seeds of disease; but how
much more is not a great magazine of health, filled
with the most harmonious sounds, fragrant with the
sweetest odors, hung with golden drapery, the path-
way of sunbeams, the womb of showers, the feeder of
flowing streams, full of God's goodness, and the
fountain of all Earth's life! And, just as in that

atmosphere, which God has wrapped round this world, there is much more health than sickness, much more food than famine, much more life than death, so in the Bible there is much more love than terror.

The terror is not only subordinate to love, but subservient to it. God, indeed, tells us of hell, but it is to persuade us to go to heaven; and, as a skillful painter fills the background of his picture with his darker colors, God puts in the smoke of torment and the black clouds of Sinai, to give brighter prominence to Jesus, the cross of Calvary, and his love to the chief of sinners. His voice of terror is like the scream of the mother bird when the hawk is in the sky. She alarms her brood that they may run and hide beneath her feathers; and as I believe that God had left that mother dumb unless he had given her wings to cover her little ones, I am sure that He, who is very "pitiful," and has no pleasure in any creature's pain, had never turned our eyes to the horrible gulf unless for the voice that cries, "Deliver from going down to the pit, for I have found a ransom." We had never heard of sin had there been no Saviour; nor of hell had there been no heaven. "Sufficient for the day is the evil thereof;" and never had Bible light been flashed before the eyes of the sleeping felon to wake him from his happy dream, but that he might see the smiling form of Mercy, and hear her, as she says with pointing finger, "Behold, I have set before thee an open door."

God's Motive in Salvation.

I do this for mine holy name's sake.—Ezekiel xxxvi. 22.

THERE is a land lying beneath a burning sky, where the fields are seldom screened by a cloud, and almost never refreshed by a shower; and yet Egypt—for it is of it I speak—is as remarkable for the fertile character of its soil as for the hoar antiquity of its history. At least, it was so in days of old, when hungry nations were fed by its harvests, and its fields were the granaries of ancient Rome. Powers so prolific Egypt owed to the Nile—that river whose associations carry us upward to the beginning of all human history—upon whose banks, in the sepulchers of forgotten kings, stand the proudest monuments of human vanity—a river, the very name of which recalls some of the grandest scenes that have been acted on the stage of time. The Nile *is* Egypt; in the course of long ages it has deposited her soil, and by an annual overflow it maintains her fertility. The limits of that flood are the limits of life and verdure; and without her Nile —that great artery of vegetable life—she would be another Sahara—a vast expanse of burning and barren sands. Humbled as she now is, let this gift of heaven be improved, as of old, by the skill and industry of her inhabitants, and, vivified by a free and Christian government, Egypt would rise from the sepulchers of her kings, and take a place once more in the van of nations. The Truth shall prove her resurrection. The Gospel shall restore her to life and prosperity: and the day is coming when that land—rich now only in memories of the past, famous now only for her temples and gods, her pyramids and dusty tombs, for her throne of the Pharaohs, for her sacred stream, for the wonders God wrought of old in the field of Zoan, and, most dear above all to Christian hearts, for the asylum she opened to an infant Saviour—shall fulfill a noble destiny. Her day approaches. These prophecies regarding her wait their accomplishment—"The Lord shall be known in Egypt;" and, "Blessed be Egypt, my people."

From the earliest ages the source of this famous river was regarded with intensest interest. Whence it sprung, and how its annual flood was swelled, were the subjects of eager but ungratified curiosity. One traveler after another had attempted to reach its cradle, and had failed or fallen in the attempt; and when—forcing his way upwards through many difficulties, and traveling along its banks, from where, by many mouths, it disgorged its waters into the sea, till its ample volume had shrunk into the narrowness of a mountain stream—our hardy countryman at length stood beside the long sought for fountain, he won for himself, by the achievement, an immortal reputation. I can fancy the pride with which, first of travelers, he looked on that mysterious fountain. How sweet its waters tasted! How he enjoyed his triumph, as he sat down by the cradle of a river, which had fed the millions of successive generations, and in days long gone by had saved in famine the race which gave a Redeemer to the world!

Now, what this river, which turns barren sands into the richest soil, is to Egypt, the Gospel of Jesus

Christ is to the world. It flows through the earth, the "river of the waters of life." Whether they now bloom in heaven, or are still in the nurseries of earth, every plant of grace owes to the Gospel its existence and renown. Observe, however, that—although the parent of those harvests which angels shall reap and the heavens receive—no more in the case of the Gospel than of the Nile does the bounty of heaven suspend or supersede human exertions. No; but on earth's improvement of heaven's bounty the blessings of both are commonly suspended. "The hand of the diligent maketh rich:" and as it is according to the industry or indolence of the inhabitants, that the Nile flows through barren sands, or waters smiling fields, so is it with the Gospel. It is a blessing only where it is sedulously and prayerfully improved, and when, like the overflowings of the Nile, which are conducted along their channels to irrigate its shores, those living waters, through the use of means, are turned on our hearts and habits. "Not the hearers of the law are just before God, but the doers of the law shall be justified."

Now, if it is interesting to trace a Nile or Amazon to its source, how much more interesting to a Christian to explore the stream of eternal life, and trace it upward till we have reached the fountain. Bruce discovered—or thought he had discovered—the springs of Egypt's river: he found them away among cloud-capped mountains, at an elevation of many thousand feet above the plains they watered. Great men have been born in humble circumstances; but all great rivers boast of their lofty descent. It is when the traveler has left smiling valleys far beneath him, and toiling along rugged glens, and, pressing through deep mountain gorges, he at length reaches the chill shores of an icy sea, that he stands at the source of the Alpine river, which, cold as the snows that feed it, and a full grown stream at its birth, rushes out from the caverns of the hollowed glacier. But with that lofty birth place it is only a humble image of salvation. How high *its* source ! "He showed me a pure river of wa ter of life, clear as crystal, proceding out of the throne of God and of the Lamb." The stream of mercy flows from the throne of the Eternal; and here we seem to stand by its mysterious fountain : in contemplating the words of the text, we look upon its spring—"I do this for mine holy name's sake."

In now entering on the question, What moved God to save man? let us—

I. Attend to the expression, "my name's sake."

This is a most comprehensive term. It indicates much more than what, in common language, is in volved in a name. No doubt a name may sometimes convey much meaning. "Adam," for instance, means "clay;" made of earth, he receives a name that re minds him of his origin. "Isaac," again, means "laughter;" and in her son's name God rebuked Sarah for the merriment with which, when listening with a woman's curiosity behind the door, she heard of her coming child, and of fruit growing on such an old and withered stock as she was. "Moses," again, means "drawn from the water;" and his name reminded him, who was to deliver others, how he himself had been delivered from death. And in the name "Jesus," our Lord received a name that revealed his office and anticipated his work—the angel said, "Thou shalt call his name Jesus, for he shall save his people from their sins." Commonly, however, a man's name gives no idea of his properties, character, history, works, or life, and is nothing more than an appellation which he receives in infancy, and receives—since the flower is still in the bud—before his fortune can be told, or his character even guessed at. "What's in a name?" Its chief end is just to prevent confusion, and distinguish one person from another.

The name of God, however, as employed by the sacred writers, has many and most important meanings. In the 20th Psalm, for instance, it embraces all the attributes of the Godhead. "The name of the God of Jacob defend thee;" that is—if paraphrased—may his arms be around thee; may his wisdom guide thee; may his power support thee; the bounty of God supply thy wants; the mercy of God forgive thy sins; the shield of heaven be over, and all its blessings on thee. In the days of miracles, again, the name of Jesus carried with it the idea of his authority, and of the efficacy of his power. Uttered by the lips of faith, that name was a word of resistless might. It healed disease, shed light on darkness, and breathed life into cold death; it mastered devils, controlled the powers of hell, and commanded into immediate obedience the rudest elements of nature. Like Pharaoh's signet on Joseph's hand, he who used that name in faith, was for the time gifted with his Master's power; whatever he loosed on earth was loosed in heaven; and whatever he bound on earth, was bound in heaven. Standing over a cripple—one impotent from his mother's womb—Peter looked on his deformity, and said, "In the name of Jesus of Nazareth, rise up and walk." And, lo! he who had never stood erect till now, bounded from the earth, and, in the joyful play

of new-born faculties, walking, leaping, dancing, sing-
ing, he ushered the Apostles into the astonished tem-
ple. Powerful, like prayer, or any other means of
grace, as was this name when used by faith, yet on
the lips of the unbelieving no name more useless;
like a residuum from which the spirit had been evap-
orated, or a body bereft of life, it possessed no virtue
or power at all. There was no charm in the mere
name of Jesus, either to pour light on a blind man's
eyeball, or restore vigor to a withered limb. See how
Sceva's seven sons learn that to their cost! Profaning
this holy name, and employing it in their arts of
witchcraft, they use it to cast out a devil; and—
themselves Satan's servants—they find that "Beelze-
bub casts not out devils." "Jesus I know, and Paul I
know," says the Evil One, "but who are ye?" Hell
disowns their authority; the Demon defies them; he
leaps on them with the fury of a savage beast; and—
theirs the fate of the engineer who is hoised on his
own petard—they are driven off, disgraced and
wounded, from the field.

Again, in Micah, iv. 5, where it is said, "We will
walk in the name of the Lord," the expression assumes
a new meaning, and indicates the laws, statutes, and
commandments of God. Again, in the beautiful and
blessed promise, "In all places where I record my
name, there will I come unto thee and bless thee,"
the expression bears yet another meaning: it stands
for God's ordinances and worship—rearing, as it
were, by the hands of faith, a holy temple out of the
rudest edifice, and converting into heaven-consecrated
churches those rocky fastnesses and lonely moors
where our fathers worshiped in the dark days of
old. Contenting ourselves with these illustrations of

the various meanings of this expression in Scripture,
I now remark, that here the "name" of God compre-
hends every thing, which directly or remotely affects
the divine honor and glory; whatever touches, to use
the words of our catechism, "His titles, attributes,
ordinances, word, or works; or any thing whereby
God maketh himself known."

II. We are to understand that the motive which
moved God to save man was regard to his own glory.

"Where is boasting then?" we may ask with the
Apostle, and leave him to answer, "it is excluded."
If salvation is not of merit, but of mercy—not of
earth, but heaven—not of blood, nor of the will of
the flesh, nor of the will of man, but of God"—"Not
by might nor by power, but my Spirit, saith the
Lord of Hosts," it is beyond all doubt "excluded."
Grace glorifies man, no doubt; but for what purpose?
that he may glorify God. It saves man, but saves
him that he may sing, not his own praises, but a
Saviour's. It exalts man, but exalts him, that, like
an exhalation, sun-drawn from the ground, and raised
to heaven, each of us may form a sparkling drop in
the bow, which encircles the head that God crowns
with glory, and man once crowned with thorns.
Even our Lord himself, although in a sense the
"fellow" of his Father, and reckoning it no robbery
to make himself equal with God, kept his eye steadily
on that lofty mark. His Father's, not his own glory,
was the burden of Jesus' prayers and the end of Jesus'
sufferings: born for it in a stable, he bled for it on a
cross, and was buried for it in a sepulcher. When,
on the solemn eve of his last and awful sufferings,
our champion buckled on his armor for the closing

struggle, ere he joined battle with men, with death, and with him that had the power of death, that is, the devil, was not this his prayer—"Father, glorify thy Son, that thy Son also may glorify thee?" Dutiful Son! Pattern to all children of filial piety! Thou didst forget thine own sufferings in a mother's; and was more concerned for thy Father's honor than thine own.

This doctrine, that God saves men for his own glory, is a grand and very precious truth; yet there is a way of stating it which seems as offensive as it is unscriptural. Concave mirrors magnify the features nearest to them into undue and monstrous size; and in common mirrors, ill cast and of uneven surface, the most beautiful face is distorted into deformity. And, as if their minds were of such a cast and character, there are some good men who, not exhibiting Bible truth in its proper harmony and proportions, represent Jesus Christ in this matter of salvation as affected by no motive whatever but a regard to his Father's glory, and even God himself as moved only by respect to his own. Excluding from their view the commiseration and love of God, or reducing these into very shrunk dimensions, they magnify one doctrine at the expense of another, and, indeed, go to sever some of the most sacred and tender ties which bind a believer to his God. Now, it appears to us that this ill-proportioned theology—the doctrine that the only motive in redemption was a regard to God's glory—receives no countenance from the Bible. Does not God "pity us, as a father pitieth his children?" Taught to address Him by the endearing appellation of Father, Oh what affection, love, and loving-kindness, are expressed in that tender term! And if, on seeing some earthly father, whom a child's scream has reached and roused, rush up the blazing stairs, or leap into the boiling flood, it were wrong, it were cruel, it were a shame, to suspect him of being destitute of affection—of being moved to this noble act by no other motive than a regard to his own honor—and by no other voice than the calm command of duty—how much more wrong were it to harbor such suspicions of "our Father who is in heaven."

I know that we should approach so high a theme with the greatest reverence, and that it becomes us to speak on such a subject, and, indeed, on any thing that touches the secret movements of the Divine mind, with most profound humility. Yet, reasoning from the form of the shadow to the object which projects it—from man to God—I would venture to say, that it is with Him as with us, when we are moved to a single action by the united influence of various motives. To borrow an example from the place I fill:—The minister, worthy of his office, appears before his assembled people to preach; and, in doing so, he is moved by a variety of motives. Love to God, love to Jesus, love to sinners, love to saints, a regard to God's glory, and regard to man's good: these, like the air, water, light, heat, electricity, gravitation, which act together in the process of vegetation, may all combine to form one sermon. They are present, and act not as conflicting but concurring motives in the preacher's breast. This difference, however, there always is between us and God, that although our motives—like the Rhone, which is formed of two rivers, the one pure as the sky above it, the other turbid and discolored—are ever mixtures of good and evil, all the emotions of the Divine mind, all the influences that move God to action, are of the purest nature.

God cherishes, indeed, such respect to his own glory, that, had the salvation of the world been incompatible with that—this world had been left to perish. Dreadful thought! How should we adore and extol the wisdom which discovered a way to harmonize the glory of God, and the good of men. He was moved by regard to both. It is an imperfect vision that sees but one motive. This lofty subject resembles those binary stars which look to the naked eye as but one, but which, brought into the field of the telescope, resolve themselves into two orbs, rolling in their brightness and beauty around a common center. Blessed be his holy name! "He so loved the world, that He gave his only begotten Son, that whosoever believeth on Him should not perish, but should have everlasting life." "He commendeth his love to us, in that, while we were yet sinners, Christ died for us." Never, therefore, let us exalt this doctrine of the divine glory, at the expense of the divine love. God's love to sinners is his mightiest, his heart-softening argument; and it were doing Him, his gospel, and our own souls great injustice, if we should overlook the love that gives Divinity its name, and which, sending in his Son a Saviour from the Father's bosom, was eulogized by an Apostle as possessed of a "height, and depth, and breadth, and length, which passeth knowledge."

III. Observe, that in saving man for his "holy name's sake," or for his own honor and glory, God exhibits the mercy, holiness, love, and other attributes of the Godhead.

The truth is, that God saves man for much the same reasons as at first he made him. Why did God make man? What moved God to make him? The ball rolls forward over the ground, and the ship moves onward through the sea, by virtue of an external force—the hand projects the one, and the wind, caught in her sails, impels the other. But no foreign agent imparted an impulse to creating power; nor did any one command or compel God to make man. It is his prerogative to command—the creature's duty to obey. Why, then, did He make man? Did He need to make him? Was it with Him as with some lordly master, who depends for his comfort on his servants?—as with a king, whose glory lies in the numbers of his courtiers, or the brilliancy of his court?—as with the greatest general, who owes his victories to the bravery of his soldiers, and who, whatever his military skill, would win no battles and wear no laurels without an army at his back? Assuredly not. "Our goodness extendeth not to Thee;" our wealth makes God no richer, our praise makes Him no happier. "Hear, O my people, and I will speak. I will take no bullock out of thy house, or he-goat out of thy fold; for every beast of the forest is mine, and the cattle upon a thousand hills. I know all the fowls of the mountains and the wild beasts of the field are mine. If I were hungry, I would not tell thee, for the world is mine, and the fullness thereof."

What moved God, then, to make man? or, to enlarge the question so as to embrace creation, when there was neither world rolling, nor sun shining, nor angel singing—when there was neither life nor death, nor birth nor burial, nor sight nor sound, no wave of ocean breaking, no wing of angel moving—when, as in a past eternity, God dwelt alone in silent, solemn, awful, but happy solitude, what moved Him to make creatures at all, or with these worlds, suns and systems, to garnish the heavens, and people an empty universe? These are the deep things of God, and it becomes finite and fallible minds such as ours to approach them modestly. If the fabric of nature, if the machine of Providence, with its wheels rolling within wheels in many and complicated parts—if these, and the scheme of redemption, are full of inscrutable mysteries—how much more the vast mind that designed and executed them! The meanest of his works are full of Himself, and of mysteries which, when apprehended, are not comprehended. If I adore divinity in the humble daisy; and if in the creature, that lives for a day and dances in a sunbeam, I see the wisdom that made the sun—how can I lay aside the telescope by which I have held communion with the distant heavens, or the microscope that reveals a world of wonders in one drop of water, without concluding that, if the works of God are so wonderful, how much more wonderful his own infinite and eternal mind?

> "These are thy glorious works, Parent of good,
> Almighty! thine this universal frame,
> Thus wondrous fair: thyself how wondrous then
> Unspeakable! who sitt'st above these heavens,
> To us invisible, or dimly seen
> In these thy lowest works; yet these declare
> Thy goodness beyond thought, and power divine."

By turning the eye inward, however, on our own mind, we can form some conception of the divine mind, even as a captive child, born and retained in a dark dungeon, may learn some notion of the sun from the beam that, streaming through a chink of the riven wall, traves the gray lonely floor; or even as, although I had never walked its pebbly shore, nor heard the voice of its thundering breakers, nor played with its swelling waves, I could still form some feeble conception of the ocean from a lake, from a pool, from a little drop of water, even from this sparkling dew-drop, which, born from the womb of night, and cradled in the bosom of a flower, lies waiting, like a soul under the sun of righteousness, to be exhaled to heaven.

Look at man, then: be he a poet or a philosopher, a man of mechanical genius or artistic skill, a statesman or a philanthropist, or, better than all, a man who glows with piety: we see that his happiness does not lie in indolence, but in the gratification of his tastes and feelings, and the active exercise of his faculties Assume the same to be true of God—a conception which, while it exalts, endears our Heavenly Father. It presents Him in this most winning and attractive aspect, that the very happiness of Godhead lies in the forth-putting—along with other attributes—of his goodness, love, and mercy. Now, we may be mistaken, and I would not venture to speak dogmatically here; yet this does appear to shed a ray—a beam, if not a flood of light, on some mysterious passages in the providence of God. Shores on which man has never landed lie paved with shells; fields which his foot has never trod are carpeted with flowers; seas where he has never dived are inlaid with pearls; and caverns into which he has never mined are radiant with gems of the finest form and the fairest colors. Well, it may be, and has been asked, for what purpose this lavish expenditure of skill and beauty on

scenes, when there is neither an eye of intelligence
to admire, nor piety to adore the Maker? The poet,
lamenting genius unknown, unpatronized, sinking into
an ignoble grave, has sung of "flowers that waste
their sweetness on the desert air;" and up on the
unfrequented shelf of a mountain rock, or rooted in
the crevice of an old castle wall, I have found such a
flower, opening its modest beauty to the sun, and put-
ting to shame the proudest efforts of human skill.
Did you never sit down beside such a flower, and
courting its gentle company, ask the question, Fair
creature! for what end were you made, and made so
very beautiful? It certainly does look a waste of power
and skill divine. Yet may it not be, that angels, as
they fly by on their missions of mercy, have stayed
their wing over that lowly flower, and hovered there
awhile, to admire its colors and adore its Maker? But
whether or no, God himself is there. Invisible, He
walks these unfrequented solitudes, and with ineffable
complacency looks on this little flower as his own
mighty work, and as a mirror of his infinite perfec-
tions. "God," it is said, "shall rejoice in his work."
"He made all things for Himself—even the wicked
for the day of wrath."

The minnow plays in a shallow pool, and leviathan
cleaves the depths of ocean—winged insects sport in a
sunbeam, and winged angels sing before the throne;
and whether we fix our eye on the one or the other,
the whole fabric of creation appears to prove that Je-
hovah delights in the evolution of his powers, in the
display of his wisdom, love, and goodness; and, just
as it is to the delight which God enjoys in the exer-
cise of them that we owe this beautiful creation, so it

is to his delight in the exercise of his pity, love, and mercy, that we owe salvation, with all its blessings. Let us be humble and thankful. Man had as little to do with saving as with making himself: the creation of Eden and the cross of Calvary are equally the work of God; and Jehovah stands forth before the universe as not by one tittle less the Saviour than the Creator of the world. To display his glory in radiant efful·gence—to blaze it out on the eyes of delighted and adoring angels—to evoke the hidden attribute of mercy—to give expression to his love and pity—God resolved to save, and, in saving man, to turn this world into a theater for the most affecting tragedy and amazing love.

Salvation is finished. It is offered. Shall it be rejected? Take the good of it, and give Him the glory. "He is the God of salvation;" "in his name we will set up our banners." In that ladder whereby faith climbs her way aloft to heaven, there is not a round that we can call our own. In this ark which, with open door, offers an asylum in the coming storm, a refuge in the rising flood—from stem to stern and keel to deck there is neither nail, nor plank, nor beam, that we can claim as ours. The plan of redemption was the design of infinite wisdom; its execution was left to dying love; and it is Mercy, generous Mercy, whose fair form stands in the open door, bidding, entreating, beseeching you all to come in. Listen to the voice of Jesus, "Come unto me, all ye that labor and are heavy laden, and I will give you rest." And let his mother teach you how to speak, and learn from angels how to sing. With her—the casket of a divine jewel, who held the babe yet unborn in her virgin womb—with Mary say, ".My soul doth magnify the Lord; my spirit hath rejoiced in God my Saviour; for He that is mighty hath done great things to me, and holy is his name." Or, hark to the angels' song! glowing with seraphic fire, borrow seraphic words; and sing with them, ere they wheel their bright ranks for upward flight, "Glory to God in the highest; on earth, peace and good will to men."

Man an Object of Divine Mercy.

Therefore say unto the house of Israel, I do not this for your sakes, O house of Israel, but for mine holy name's sake.—EZEKIEL xxxvi. 22.

WE have seen a sere and yellow leaf, tenacious of its hold, hang on the tree all the winter through; and there it kept dancing and whirling idly in the wind, not beautiful or graceful, out of place and season, in humbling contrast with the young and fresh companions which budding spring had hung around it. Like that wrinkled and withered thing, some men (who were better in their graves) hang too long upon this world. They live too long; they die too late, for themselves at least. Half-dead and half-alive, mind and memory faded, surviving both their faculties and usefulness, and but mere wrecks of what once they were, they tax affection, to conceal from strangers' eyes the sad ravages of time, and do for them the tender office of the ivy, when she kindly hides beneath her green and glossy mantle the crumbling ruin or old hollow tree.

It was the happy fate of Moses—and one most singular at his age—neither to outlive his honor nor usefulness: the day he laid down his leadership saw him lay down his life: death found him at his post. Palinurus was swept from the helm. When Heaven saw meet to take Moses, he was one whom the earth and church would have gladly retained: but the time has arrived when the pilot, who, in calm and storm, through winter and summer seas, has steered the commonwealth of Israel for well nigh half a century. is to resign the helm into other hands. A faithful God calls a faithful servant to his reward and rest. He did not leave them, however, till these weary voyagers were brought within sight of land, and, indeed, to the mouth of the very haven they had so long desired and looked to see. The children of Israel have reached the banks of Jordan, and—grateful sight to eyes weary of these naked mountains and the dead flat level of barren sands—the people cluster with eager looks on every summit, and, scattered along the banks, they gaze across the flood on the Land of Promise. How they feed their eyes, and never weary looking on the verdant pastures, the golden harvests, the rocks clothed with vines, the swelling hills crowned with wood, the plains studded with villages and cities teeming with a population that told how rich the soil, and how well described, the land as one "full of corn and wine, and flowing with milk and honey." In this posture of affairs, before he ascends to his rest, Moses summons the tribes of Israel; and, like the members of a family who gather from their different and distant homes around a father's death-bed, they come to receive the old man's blessing, his parting counsels, and last, long farewell.

Propped upon pillows, bending on his staff, panting for breath, speaking in brief and broken sentences, by those groping hands that felt for Ephraim's and Manasseh's head betraying the stone-blindness of a great old age, Jacob gave his blessing to the twelve sons, who all—uncommon fortune in so large a family —survived their parent, and were themselves the fathers of the living millions now swarming beneath the eye of Moses. But how different the bearing and aspect of Moses from that of the hoary patriarch! An old man! if not as old a man, of age not much short of Jacob's! One hundred and twenty years had passed on his head, but they had neither blanched his beard nor thinned his locks, nor drawn a wrinkle on his lofty brow: that eye had lost none of its fire, nor that arm any of its force, since the day when, striking in for a brother's cause, he bestrode a prostrate Hebrew, and, parrying the blow of the Egyptian, gave it back, like a battle-axe, on his head. Nearly the same age as Jacob, whose bent and venerable appearance, as he entered leaning on Joseph's arm, led Pharaoh to ask, "How old art thou?" Moses bore himself erect, and looked the same as on the day, forty years before, when he strode into Pharaoh's hall, and demanded of an angry king that the Hebrews should go free. The sun that went down in the evening of summer's longest day, sunk as full and bright, as if it had set at noon; "his eye was not dim, nor was his natural strength abated." His life closed amid the rich glories of the noblest address that grace, genius, patriotism, and piety ever uttered.

Standing on some rocky platform, with his back to the sky, and his face to the people, Moses delivered an address never forgotten, and that for long ages continued to sound its trumpet echoes in the ears, and to breathe courage into the hearts of Israel. He blessed the tribes in succession, and—charged with inspiration, as a cloud with lightning—he burst forth at the close into these glowing exclamations—"There is none like unto the God of Jeshurun, who rideth upon the heavens in thy help; thy shoes shall be iron

and brass; and as thy days, so shall thy strength be.
The eternal God is thy refuge, and underneath are
the everlasting arms." Jordan gleamed in his eye,
and stretching out his arms to the land across its
flood, he cried—"Israel then shall dwell in safety
alone; the fountain of Jacob shall be upon a land of
corn and wine; his heaven shall drop down dew.
Happy art thou, O Israel: who is like unto thee, O
people saved by the Lord?"—Glorious words to the
Hebrews! and most gracious in Christian eyes. Faith
claims them as part of her inheritance, and looking
on that mighty multitude as the dying type of a
never-dying church, serves us heirs of entail to the
spiritual blessings which lay concealed beneath the
vail of these earthly promises.

It is not, however, so much of the close as of the
commencement of Moses' speech, that I would speak.
Their deliverer from the house of bondage, and leader
of their exodus to the promised land, he was a type
of Jesus. That host, supplied with streams from the
flinty rock, guided by the Shekinah, and fed with
manna from the skies, in its grievous bondage and
great deliverance, its pilgrim wanderings and hard-
fought battles, its trials and crowning triumph, was a
type of the Church of Christ. We are undoubtedly
heirs of all its promises; but as we cannot take the sweet
and reject the bitter, in serving ourselves heirs to
Israel's promises, we become heirs also to her chastise-
ments, her guilt and sin, her warnings and rebukes.
Now, listen to Moses as he addressed the very people
of whose coming fortunes he spoke such glorious
things:—"Hear, O Israel: Thou art to pass over
Jordan this day, to go in to possess nations greater
and mightier than thyself: Not for thy righteousness,

or for the uprightness of thine heart, dost thou go to possess their land. Understand, therefore, that thou goest not in for your own sakes. The Lord thy God giveth thee not this good land to possess it for thy righteousness; for thou art a stiff-necked people, and hast been rebellious against the Lord from the day that I knew you."

If there be a man still on earth, in a situation corresponding to theirs who stood on the brink of the flood, and saw Canaan's fair fields inviting them to cross, that man is a dying Christian. With life fast ebbing—his battle fought, the journey finished, the desert traveled, the world with its rough paths and vanities behind him, heaven opening its glories to his eye, and death's cold, dark stream rolling at his feet— he stands on the bank of the river and, ready to pass on when the High Priest has gone down to divide the flood, he waits but the summons to go. Well—I re- pair to the chamber where this good man dies, and, sitting down beside his bed, I open the Bible, and read these words in his listening ears, "Thou art to pass Jordan this day. Speak not thou in thine heart, saying, for my own righteousness the Lord hath brought me in to possess the land. Understand, that the Lord giveth thee not this good land for thy right- eousness and uprightness; for thou art stiff-necked, and hast been rebellious against the Lord." To some, who, taking compassion on our ignorance, might turn round to tell us, what a good man he had been, what an example of piety, how bright he had shone, how much the church would lament his death, and how much the poor would miss his charity, these words would sound hard and harsh, unseasonable and most uncharitable. But whatever harshness might appear to others in such an address, this, I am sure, would be that Christian's humble, prompt, hearty response:— How true! how characteristic! what a faithful picture! how descriptive alike of my original unregenerate state, and the many short-comings of my renewed nature! Raising his dying eye to heaven, and clasping his hands, he hushes into silence the ill-timed praise of his friends, and repeats as his own, the confession of Job,—"I have heard of thee with the hearing of the ear, but now mine eye seeth thee; wherefore I abhor myself, and repent in dust and ashes." He clings like Peter to the hand of Jesus. Mercy is all his prayer, and mercy all his praise; hopes of mercy in the future kindle in his eye, and grateful thanks for mercies in the past employ his latest breath, and dwell on his faltering tongue. His last conscious look turns away from his own works to fix itself upon the cross, and the last word that trembles on his quivering lip is, Jesus!

It were not easy to find a better example of this, than one which is recorded in the history of England's greatest apostle. When he lay on an expected death-bed (though God spared him some years longer to the world and church), his attendants asked John Wesley, what where his hopes for eternity? And something like this was his reply—For fifty years I have been traveling up and down this world, amid scorn and hardship, to preach Jesus Christ: and I have done what in me lay to serve my blessed Master. What he had done, how poor he lived, how hard he labored, with what holy fire his bosom burned, with what success he preached, how brilliantly he illustrated the character--"dying, and behold we live; unknown, and yet well known; poor, yet making many

rich; having nothing, yet possessing all things;"—
these things his life and works attest. They are seen
in his church's history, and in the crown he wears in
heaven so bright with a blaze of jewels—the saved
through his agency. Yet thus he spake, " My hopes
or eternity? my only hopes rest on Christ;" and as
he confession of his faith, he repeated these words:—

> " I the chief of sinners am,
> But Jesus died for me."

This confession, so redolent of Wesley's piety, and
honorable to his memory, and the words of Moses to
Israel, are in perfect harmony; and both are in har-
mony with this great truth of the text, that God saves
sinners, not for their sakes, or out of any regard what-
ever to their worth or merits. We have already
dwelt at some length on this truth. Why, then, it
may be asked, choose the same text, and expatiate
again on the same theme? If I needed apology or
defence for lingering on this humbling, but most sal-
utary and important subject, I would find it in a
high example. Observe how Moses, in his dying ad-
dress to Israel, repeats and repeats, iterates and re-
iterates, this very truth—" Speak not thou in thine
heart, saying, for my righteousness the Lord hath
brought me in to possess this land; but for the wick-
edness of these nations the Lord doth drive them
out from before thee." Again—" Not for thy right-
eousness, or the uprightness of thine heart, dost thou
go to possess their land." Again—" Understand,
therefore, that the Lord thy God giveth thee not
this good land to possess it for thy righteousness,
for thou art a stiff-necked people." Again—" Re-
member, forget not how thou provokedst the Lord

thy God to wrath in the wilderness; from the day that thou didst depart out of the land of Egypt, until ye came unto this place, ye have been rebellious against the Lord." Again—"In Horeb ye provoked the Lord to wrath, so that the Lord was angry with you, to have destroyed you." Again—"The Lord spake unto me, saying, I have seen this people, and behold, it is a stiff-necked people; let me alone, that I may destroy them." And again—"Ye have been rebellious against the Lord from the day that I knew you." Thus Moses. A master, who charges his servant with some important message, repeats, and reiterates it in his ear. The teacher, who communicates some leading rule in grammar to his pupils, or some fundamental truth in science to his students, comes over it again and again; just as a carpenter, by repeated blows drives home the nail, and fixes it firm in its place. For the same end we resume our study of the text. It divides itself into two branches; first, what does not; secondly, what does move God to save us.

To the first question our answer is—Not any thing in us; to the second—His regard to his own holy name. Now, in speaking on the first of these I remark—

I. The doctrine that God is not moved to save man by any merit or excellence of his, is a truth of the highest importance and consequence to sinners.

This is no doctrine—like our Lord's personal reign, or the question of adult or infant baptism, or the points of difference between Episcopalians, Presbyterians, and Independents—in regard to which it is not of vital importance which side of the controversy we espouse and advocate. This doctrine has a direct and most important bearing on the salvation of sinners. Like the rough and stern Baptist it prepares the way for Christ. Man must be emptied of self before he can be filled with grace. We must be stripped of our rags before we can be clothed with righteousness; we must be unclothed, that we may be clothed upon; wounded, that we may be healed; killed, that we may be made alive; buried in disgrace, that we may rise in grace. These words are as true of the soul as the body—"Sown in corruption, that we may be raised in incorruption; sown in dishonor, that we may be raised in glory; sown in weakness, that we may be raised in power." To borrow an illustration from the surgeon's art, the ill-set bone must be broken again, that it may be set aright. I would press this truth on your attention, because a soul filled with self has no room for God; and, like the inn of Bethlehem, given to lodge meaner guests, a heart full of pride has no chamber, within which Christ may be born " in us the hope of glory."

To tell man that he has no merit is, no doubt, a humbling statement, and one that lays the loftiest sinner in the dust. This doctrine is the true leveler, it puts all men on the same degraded platform before God; sets kings as low as beggars, and the strictest virtue—virtue which the breath of suspicion never sullied—with base and brazen-faced iniquity. I admit that, if we had no better righteousness than our own to rest on, we should do our best to establish its claims, and mayhap assert the right of decency to say to harlots, publicans, and sinners, " Stand aside, I am holier than thou." But why cling to that when we have a better righteousness in our offer? No wonder at all that the mendicant, whose timid knock has called us to the door, stands there shivering in filthy rags. Poor wretch! His crimes or misfortunes have reduced him to these; he has no change of raiment nor choice of clothing; and so,—with none kind or rich enough to help him,—he must make the best of what he has to robe his nakedness and protect an emaciated frame from the biting cold. No wonder also, that the prodigal, having spent all his portion in riotous living, in such dress—if dress it could be called—sought his father's house; nor any wonder that his father, so soon as the quick eyes of love espied him from afar, ran to meet the penitent, fell on his neck, and kissed him in that ragged and loath-some attire. To say nothing of those who have yearned over some unworthy child—every father understands *that*. But how had the wonder of the story grown, how had son, servants, and neighbors concluded that the wretched youth had drunk away his senses as well as money, had he so loved his rags, as to decline to part with them, and, clinging to these wrecks of better days—these sad memorials of his sin and folly—had he refused to put the foul rags off, that he might put the fair robe on! He did nothing so foolish; and why should we? Now since God pronounces our righteousness—observe, not our wickednesses, but our devotions, our charities, our costliest sacrifices, our most applauded services—to be "filthy rags," trust not to them. What man in his senses would think of going to court in rags? Nor think that the righteousness of the cross was wrought to patch up these; to make up, as some say, for what is defective and wanting in our own merits. Nor fancy, like some who would have a Saviour and yet keep their sins, that you may wear the rags beneath this righteousness. Put them away; not as a dress, which a man lays aside, to be afterwards resumed; but cast them away, like a beggar who, having got a better attire, flings his rags into the nearest ditch, and leaves them there in their foulness to rottenness and decay. God says of the soul which Faith has conducted to Jesus—"take away the filthy garments from him, Behold I have caused thine iniquity to pass from thee, and I will clothe thee with change of raiment."

If this doctrine is humbling to our pride, it is full of encouragement to a poor sinner's hope. It lays me down, but it is to lift me up. It throws me on the ground, that, like Antæus, the giant of fable, I may rise stronger than I fell. It is not for our sake that we are saved. If Mercy stoops to the lowest guilt, Oh then there is hope of salvation for me—for a man who has nothing that he can call his own but misery and sin; I will not sit here to perish; but following a Manasseh and a Magdalene, a dying thief, and a blood-stained Saul, I will join the throng that, called from highways and hedges, are pouring—a ragged crowd—into the marriage supper of the Lamb. Are any among you holding back, till, by this or that improvement in your habits, you consider yourselves fit to go to Christ? Fit to go to Christ!—fit to go to Christ you shall never be, but only by going to him. Your warrant lies in your wants; your plea for mercy in his merits; your plea for an interest in his merits in your own demerits. Hear and adopt the prayer of David—"For thine own name's sake, pardon mine iniquity;" that is his prayer; now what is his plea? "for it is little," "very little," or "less than others?" No. He adds and urges this, "for it is great."

Was there ever an invalid so senseless as to say, when I am somewhat better, when this fever burns less fierce, this pulse beats more calm, this running ulcer has a less loathsome and offensive discharge, I will repair to the hospital? Yet such is their folly who say, when I am holier, I will go to Jesus. Go to him as you are; show the physician your wounds, bruises, putrifying sores—how the whole head is sick, and the whole heart is faint. It is said of the disciples, that "they took in our Lord as he was into the boat;" now he is to take you in as you are—just as you are. You cannot be made holy till you go to him? And what hinders you to go and go now? What does he say? Hear him—"I came not to call the righteous, but sinners to repentance." And the worse your case is, the greater, in a sense, is your certainty of immediate salvation;—yours the hope of the maimed and bleeding soldier whom kind comrades bear from the deadly trench, and who knows that the worse his wound, the more sure is he of the surgeon's earliest care; and that from the very couch, where noblest birth or highest rank lies stretched under some less serious injury, that man of humanity —image of the great Physician—will turn away to kneel down by a poor orphan boy, the meanest private—aye, even a mutilated enemy, in haste to tie up the severed vessels, and stem the tide that pours his life's blood upon the ground. God help you to say with Paul—"It is a faithful saying, and worthy of all acceptation, that Jesus Christ came into the world to save sinners, of whom I am chief," and believing that, cry with David, "Make haste unto me, O God. O Lord, make no tarrying."

II. It is as important for the saint as for the sinner to remember, that he is not saved through personal merit, or for his own sake.

When age has stiffened its bark and fibres, if you bend a branch into a new direction, either turn that to the right hand which had grown to the left, or raise the bough to the skies which had been bent on the ground, it is long before it loses the tendency to resume its old position. And many years after its course has been changed, and the art, that conquers nature, has turned its waters into a new cut, the river needs careful watching; else, when swollen by winter snows or summer floods, it bursts our barriers, sweeps dyke and bulwark to the sea, and, in the pride of victory, foams, and roars, and rages, in its old accustomed channel. Even so, when God has laid hands upon us, and grace has given our earthly soul a heavenward bent, how prone it is to start back again! When he that sitteth upon the flood, and turneth the hearts of men like the rivers of water, hath sent the current of our tastes and feelings in a new direction, how apt are they, especially in some outburst of sudden temptation that comes down like a thunder-spout, to flow back into the old and deep-worn channels of a corrupt nature! Of this, David and Peter are memorable and dreadful examples. And who, that has endeavored to keep his heart with diligence, has not felt, and mourned over the tendency to be working out a righteousness of his own, to be pleased with himself, and, by taking some satisfaction in his own merits, to undervalue those of Christ. So was it with that godly man who, on one occasion—most rare achievement!—offered up a prayer without one wandering thought; and described it as the worst which he had ever offered, because, as he said, the Devil made him proud of it. So was it also with the minister, who, upon being told by one—more ready to praise the preacher than profit by the sermon—that he had delivered an excellent discourse, replied, "You need not tell me that; Satan told me so before I left the pulpit." Oh! it were well for the best of us that we could say with Paul, "we are not ignorant of his devices."

Step into this room, where the greatest Scotchman lies a dying, and see an example more striking, warning, alarming still. From the iron grasp of kings and princes, Knox has wrung the rights of Scotland. Ready to contend even unto the death, he had bearded proud nobles and prouder churchmen; he had stood under the fire of battle; he had been chained to the galley's oar; he had occupied the pulpit with a carabine leveled at his fearless head; and to plant God's truth, and that tree of civil and religious liberty which has struck its roots so deep in our soil, and under whose shadow we are this day sitting, he had fought many a hard-fought battle; but his hardest was fought in the solitude of the night, and amid the quietness of a dying chamber. One morning his friends enter his apartment. They find him faint and pallid, wearing the look of one who had passed a troubled night. So he had: he had been fighting, not sleeping; wrestling, not resting; and it required all God's grace to bring him off a conqueror. Till daybreak, Jacob wrestled with the Angel of the Covenant; and that long night Knox had passed wrestling with the Prince of Darkness. Like Bunyan's pilgrim, he met Apollyon in the valley, and their swords struck fire in the shadow of death. The lion is said to be boldest in the storm. His roar is never so loud as in the pauses of the thunder, and when the lightning flashes, brightest are the flashes of his cruel eye; and even so he, who, as a roaring lion, goeth about seeking whom he may devour, often seizes the hour of nature's distress to assault us with his fiercest temptations. Satan tempted Job when he was bowed down with grief. Satan tempted Jesus when he was faint with hunger. Satan tempted Peter when he was weary with watching and heart-broken with sorrow; and, reserving perhaps his grand assault on us for times that offer him a great advantage, it was when Knox was worn out, left alone, his head laid low on a dying pillow, that Satan, like a roaring lion, leaped upon his bed. Into that room the Enemy had come; he stands by his bed,—he reminds him that he had been a standard-bearer of the truth,—a reformer; a bold confessor; a distinguished sufferer; the very foremost man of his time and country; he attempts to persuade him, that surely such rare merits deserve the crown. The Christian conquered—but hard put to it—only conquered through Him that loved him. His shield was the truth of my text; he had been lost, wrecked at the mouth of the very harbor, had he lost sight of this beacon,—"I do not this for your sake, but for mine holy name's sake."

And seeing, as these cases show, there may be such danger lurking—like a snake among flowers—under our best attainments; seeing that, like the inflammatory attacks to which those are most liable who are highest fed, whose bones are most full of marrow, and whose veins are gorged with blood, we may be exposed to spiritual pride through the very fullness of our graces; seeing that he, who can twist the Bible into arguments for sin, can use our best works as fuel o the fires of vanity, let us watch and pray and learn to be humble. Oh, it is needful for the holiest to remember, that man's best works are bad at the best; and that, to use the words of Paul, it is "Not by works of righteousness that we have done, but according to his mercy he hath saved us, through the washing of regeneration. and the renewing of the Holy Ghost."

III. This doctrine, while it keeps the saint humble will help to make him holy.

Here—no ornament to park or garden—stands a dwarfed, stunted, bark-bound tree. How am I to develop that dwarfish stem into tall and graceful beauty—to clothe with blossoms these naked branches, and hang them, till they bend, with clustered fruit? Change such as that is not to be effected by surface dressing, or any care bestowed on the upper soil. The remedy must go to the root. You cannot make that tree grow upwards till you break up the crust—pulverize the hard subsoil, and give the roots room and way to strike deeper down;—for, the deeper the root, and the wider spread the fine filaments of its rootlets, the higher the tree lifts an umbrageous head to heaven, and spreads out its hundred arms, to catch, in dews, rain-drops, and sunbeams, the blessings of the sky.

The believer—in respect of character, ' a tree of righteousness of the Lord's planting," in respect of strength, "a cedar of Lebanon," in respect of fruitful-

ness, an olive, in respect of position, "a palm tree
planted in the courts of God's house," in respect of
full supplies of grace, a tree by the rivers of water
"which yieldeth its fruit in its season, and whose leaf
doth not wither"—offers this analogy between grace
and nature. As the tree grows best skyward that
grows most downward, the lower the saint grows in
humility, the higher he grows in holiness. The soar-
ing corresponds to the sinking. I wish you to think
little, very little of yourselves; but why? because
the less you think of yourselves, the more will you
esteem Christ; and the humbler you are in your own
eyes, the higher you will stand in God's. The guest,
who, coming modestly in, takes the lowest place at
the table, is called up to the seat of honor; and I have
always thought, that none are so sure to lie in Jesus'
bosom as those I have seen lying lowest at Jesus' feet.
Was it not over one, who content to be spoken of as
"a dog," held herself well served with crumbs, and
asked nothing but the sweepings of the table, that
Jesus pronounced this superlative eulogium—"I have
not found such faith; no, not in Israel." "God ex-
alteth the humble, and abaseth the proud." How im-
portant, therefore, the sentiment of my text? Re-
ceive it, "and the loftiness of man shall be bowed
down, and the haughtiness of men shall be made low;
and the Lord alone shall be exalted in that day."

Piety and pride are not less opposed to each other
than light and darkness. No doubt strange things—
singular conjunctions—are seen in grace as well as in
nature. Like an ill assorted marriage, you may find
a sour and ascetic temper allied to genuine faith.
Eminent piety has stood blushing in sackcloth on a
pillory of shame. The sun of saintship has undergone

a dreadful and unlooked for eclipse. Good and great men have fallen into gross sin, causing God's people to hang down their heads, and cry, as they wept in secret, "How are the mighty fallen!" In short, the grace of God has been found in such strange company as to give occasion for the remark of one, who said, "the grace of God will live where neither you nor I could live." But, among these anomalies, amounting sometimes almost to monstrosities, I will venture to say you never saw—no, nor the church, nor world, nor any eye nor age ever yet saw—a saint distinguished for his holiness, who was not also remarkable for his humility. The grandest edifices, the tallest towers, the lofties spires, rest on deep foundations. The very safety of eminent gifts and pre-eminent graces lies in their association with deep humility. They were dangerous without it. Great men need to be good men. Look at this mighty ship—a leviathan on the deep; with her towering masts, and carrying a cloud of canvas, how she steadies herself on the waves, and walks erect upon the rolling waters, like a thing of inherent, self-regulating life! Why—when corn is waving, and trees are bending, and foaming billows roll before the blast and break in thunders on the beach, is she not flung on her beam-ends—sent down—foundering into the deep? Why, because, unseen beneath the surface, a vast, well-ballasted hull gives her balance, and, taking hold of the water, keeps her steady under a press of sail, and on the bosom of the swelling sea. Even so, that the saint may be preserved upright, erect, and kept from falling, God gives him balance and ballast —giving the man, on whom he has bestowed lofty endowments, the grace of a proportionate humility.

We have wondered at the lowliness of a man, who stood among his compeers like Saul among the people —to find him simple, gentle, generous, docile, humble as a little child—till we found that it was with great men as with great trees. What giant tree has not giant roots? When the tempest has blown over some such monarch of the forest, and he lies in death stretched out at his full length upon the ground, on seeing the mighty roots that fed him—the strong cables that moored him to the soil—we cease to wonder at his noble stem, and the broad, leafy, lofty head he raised to heaven, defiant of storms. Even so, when death has struck down some distinguished saint— whose removal, like that of a great tree, leaves a vast gap below, and whom, brought down now, as it were, to our own level, we can measure better when he has fallen than when he stood—and when the funeral is over, and his repositories are opened, and the secrets of his heart are unlocked and brought to light, ah! now, in the profound humility they reveal—in the spectacle of that honored gray head, laid so low in the dust before God—we see the great roots and strength of his lofty piety.

Would you be holy? learn to be humble. Would you be humble? take my text, and, with a pen of iron and the point of a diamond, engrave it upon your heart; or rather pray—Holy Spirit, fountain of light, and giver of all grace, with thine own divine finger inscribe it there!

Would you be holy? you must be humble. Would you be humble? Oh! never forget that the magnet, which drew a Saviour from the skies, was not your merit but your misery. "Be clothed with humility," and ere long you shall exchange the sackcloth for a shining robe. What! although this grace may impart to your feelings a somber hue? Gray mornings are the precursors of brightest days; weeping springs are followed by sunny summers and autumns of richest harvest; and in the spiritual as in the natural kingdom—"They that sow in tears shall reap in joy."

God glorified in Redemption.

And I will sanctify my great name which was profaned among the heathen, &c.—Ezekiel xxxvi. 23, 24.

The character of a government may be read in the condition of its subjects. Are they turbulent—in their habits lawless, in their religion superstitious? with coasts full of harbors, and mountains rich in minerals, with a genial climate and a productive soil, are they yet clothed in rags, housed in cabins, steeped to the lips in poverty? These are the certain signs of bad government. Fields overrun with weeds—fences falling into ruins—the plough rotting in the flooded furrow—and hungry cattle bellowing on scanty pastures—these are the sure signs of bad husbandry. And yonder ragged family, who at school hours are roaming our streets—the unwashed face and tangled hair bespeaking no mother's kindness—hunger in the hollow eye, and pale, emaciated features—these are the sure and too common signs of an unhappy parentage. They suggest the picture of a home at the top of some filthy stair, or in some foul den of a cellar, where a miserable father, the neglected victim of disease and poverty, lies stretched upon the floor, or—as is still more likely—where a brutal drunkard lives, the tyrant of his children, and the terror of his wife. Thus we judge of a sovereign by his subjects, and thus we see the husbandman in his farm, and the father in his family.

It may be—it were indeed unfair—to apply this rule to our Faith and its Founder. Yet men have done so, and will do so; and thus the cause of God and religion is made to suffer grievous injury at the hand of its nominal friends. By their coldness, their worldliness, their selfishness, their open sinfulness, the little apparent difference between them and those who make no profession at all—nay, sometimes, by their glaring inferiority to the latter in the blow and fruit of the natural virtues—professing Christians—like venders of a bad coinage, have exposed genuine piety to suspicion, and inflicted its deepest wounds on the cause of Christ. Seeing how, in natural graces— kindness of heart—sweetness of temper—generosity— the common charities of life—mere men of the world lose nothing by comparison with such professors, how are you to keep the world from saying, "Ah! your man of religion is no better than others; nay, he is sometimes worse?" With what frightful prominence does this stand out in the answer—never to be forgotten answer—of an Indian chief to the missionary who urged him to be a Christian. The plumed and painted savage drew himself up in the consciousness of superior rectitude, and, with indignation quivering on his lip and flashing in his eagle eye, replied, "Christian lie! Christian cheat! Christian steal!— drink!—murder! Christian has robbed me of my lands and slain my tribe!" adding, as he turned haughtily on his heel, "the Devil, Christian! I will be no Christian." Let such reflections teach us to be careful how we make a religious profession; but having made it—cost what it may cost—to be careful in acting up to it. "It is better not to vow, than, having vowed, not to pay."

These remarks are suggested by the fact already adverted to in the previous discourses—that the interests of truth and the name of God suffered in Babylon, in consequence both of the miserable outward condition and still more miserable moral condition of the people of Israel. Reduced to bondage, sunk lower still—for, compared to a sinner, how free is a slave! —they exceeded their masters in crime, and went to greater excess of riot. The heathen—who overlooked the sins of which their misery was the righteous punishment—naturally enough concluded, that the God of a people so wretched and so worthless, must be a weak—perchance a wicked one. Thus God's name was profaned, and Jehovah himself dishonored, till the time arrived, when, arising to plead the cause that was his own, God sanctified his great name in the fortunes of his people, and in the sight of the heathen.

Passing over the special application of these words to the Jews, and looking at them in their prophetical connection with the scheme of redemption, I now remark—

I. That God might have vindicated his honor and sanctified his name in our destruction.

He sanctified his name in the emancipation of his ancient people. When by one blow he struck the fetters from a nation's limbs, baptized them with his Spirit, gave them favor in the sight of kings, and brought back these weary exiles, with songs and gladness, to Jerusalem, then God was sanctified in the midst of all the heathen. His power, wisdom, holiness, and goodness, were illustrated in the renewed character, joyous homes, and happy fortunes of his people. Now, God might undoubtedly have sancti-

fied himself in them otherwise—vindicating his char-
acter in such destruction upon Zion, as he here threat-
ens upon Sidon—"Behold, I am against thee, O Si-
don, and I will be glorified in the midst of thee, and
they shall know that I am the Lord when I shall have
executed judgment in her, and shall be sanctified in
her; I will send with her pestilence and blood into
her streets; and they shall know that I am the Lord."

Two methods of glorifying his name are open to
God. He is free to choose either; but by the one or
the other way he will exact his full tale of glory from
every man. In Egypt, for instance, he was glorified
in the high-handed destruction of his enemies; and, in
the same land, by the high-handed salvation of his
people. In the one case he proved how strong his
arm was to smite, and in the other how strong it was
to save. He gave Egypt's king—ere he was done
with him—a terrible answer to his insolent question,
"Who is the Lord that I should serve him?" God
was sanctified before Pharaoh, when, hurrying to the
banks of the Nile, and turning pale at the sight, he
saw them filled with blood—blood brimming in every
goblet, and blood flowing in every channel. God was
again sanctified before Pharaoh, when he saw the same
skies rain ice and fire. God was again sanctified be-
fore Pharaoh, when, startled at midnight by a nation's
wail, and summoned to the bed of his heir and eldest
born, he saw him, stiff and dead—smitten by the an-
gel of death. And God was again sanctified before
Pharaoh, when—as he looked along the watery vista—
he saw Moses come down in the grey of morning to
the shore, and watching the last Hebrew safe on
land, stretch his rod out upon the deep, whose waves,
roaring on their prey, now rush from either flank

on the power of Egypt, and bury pale rider and
snorting horse—all that bannered army—in their
whirling waters. The sea refused God's enemies a
grave. She flung them out upon her shore. Moses
stands over the body of the king; and as he gazes on
that glassy eye, which had lost its haughtiness, and
those lips, whose insolence the waters had washed
away, how might he stoop down, and say, Now you
know who is the Lord! Oh! Had the seal of death
been broken—removed from these blue, discolored
lips—theirs had been this solemn utterance, "Let the
potsherds strive with the potsherds of the earth; woe
to the man that striveth with his Maker."

In like manner, God sanctified his name on the
plains of Sodom. He sanctified it, on the one hand,
in the destruction of his enemies, and on the other,
in the salvation of Lot. Ah! then the world ceased
to doubt his character, and perhaps angels ceased to
wonder that such wickedness was allowed on earth.
The light of the city's conflagration illuminated his ho-
liness, and his throne rose up in dread and awful ma-
jesty amid the smoking ruins. And how was he
sanctified in that wretched fugitive, who has crossed
but half the plain! a wife, she comes not to a husband's
calls—a mother, she stirs not to her children's piercing
cry. Look at that spectral form with head turned on
the burning ruins—a woman, stiffened into stone, with
her cold grey eyes staring large on Sodom, and the
surprise—horror—that had seized her soul, as she felt
her warm flesh hardening into stone, carved on these
rigid features! "Remember Lot's wife." She stands
there an example of God's power to sanctify his name,
and an awful lesson to the end of time. Deep on the
statue's stony brow these words are engraven—"No

man having put his hand to the plough, and looking back, is fit for the kingdom of God."

Since there are two ways open to God, by either of which he may sanctify his great name, he might therefore, at the Fall, have vindicated his justice by swift and unsparing vengeance—by destroying the whole human family. He did so, in the case of fallen angels. Of these, there was no wreck or remnant saved. Not one escaped. No ark floated on the waters, to which, —like Noah's dove—a flying angel pursued by wrath might turn his weary wing. Can it be doubted, that the measure meted out to fallen angels, God might have meted out to fallen men?—sanctifying his great name in our ruin, rather than in our redemption. Now, before I show how he sanctifies himself in the redemption of his people, let me warn you, that what God might have done with all, he shall do with some —with all indeed who despise, or refuse, or neglect this great salvation. Yes; the trees shall burn that will not bear. Be assured, that God loses nothing in the end. He will make his own use of every man, extracting glory out of all—even from cumberers of the ground. If you are not good for fruit, you shall serve for fuel. God is not willing that any should perish; willing, most willing, rather that the sinner should live, he follows him to the very gate of hell, crying, "turn ye, turn ye, why will ye die?" Yet be warned in time; you cannot escape the alternative; this or that you must choose—to honor God by your active or your passive obedience. God help you, like Mary, to choose the better part! This day, I set before you "life and death." Will you do his will in heaven, or suffer it in hell? How terrible the words!

"God hath made all things for himself, yea, even the wicked for the day of wrath"

II. God sanctifies his name, and glorifies himself in our redemption.

It is easy to destroy—to destroy character, virtue, life, any thing. Falling with murderous strokes on yon noble tree, the woodman's axe destroys in a few hours, what it has required centuries to raise. Look at that beautiful gourd, under whose green and grateful shade the prophet sits! Emblem of all happiness that has its root in earth, it falls by means as weak as a worm's teeth; the poisonous east wind breathes on its leaves, the hot sun glares on them, and they wither away. An ounce of lead, one inch of steel, a drop distilled from a serpent's fang, even a grain of sand lodged in the passages of life—any one of these is fatal. They turn this living, delicate, wondrous fabric into a heap of undestinguishable dust—a handful of cold, black ashes. In the body man destroys what God only can make, and in this more precious and immortal soul, Satan destroys what God only can save. It needs but a devil to ruin the spirit, but it needs a Divinity to redeem it. It needs but a villian to steal virtue, it needs a divine power to restore the stolen jewel. How much easier is it to kill a man than cure him? To be an executioner than a physician? To sit robed on the bench of justice, and, assuming her fatal cap, to condemn a poor wretch to die; to draw the bolt and launch a soul into another world; to stand on the field of battle, and with leveled musket—by a motion of the finger—to dash a fellow creature into eternity—these are easier than to bless with one hour's sleep a bed of pain. It is easier to stop this pulse for ever, than bring down its death gallop to the calm and measured march of health. And as, in such cases, man's glory is more illustrated by curing than by killing, so God's glory is more pre-eminent in our redemption than it had been in our final and everlasting ruin.

Excepting of course the preacher's—for with Paul we magnify our office—of all earthly employments it appears to me that the physician's is the noblest, and that of all arts the healing art is the highest, and offers to genius and benevolence their noblest field. Casting no disparagement on the brave and gallant spirits who have guarded a country's shores—and some of whom falling in the ranks of battle have offered noble examples of soldiers, true both to an earthly crown and a Saviour's cross—yet we know that the aim of a warrior is ingeniously to invent, and his business effectively to use, instruments of destruction. His greatest achievements are wrought where deadly wounds are suffered; his proudest triumphs are won where burning cities blaze over blood-stained hearths, and, horrible to think of! where fields are fattened with human gore; his laurels are watered with tears; his course, like the hurricane, is marked by destruction; and it is his unhappy lot—perhaps the unhappiest view of arms as a profession—that he cannot conquer foes but at the sacrifice of friends. Now, in the eye of reason, and of a humanity that weeps over a suffering world, his is surely the nobler vocation—and, if not more honored—the more honorable calling who sheds blood, not to kill, but cure; who wounds not that the wounded may die, but live; and whose genius ransacks earth and ocean in search of means to save life, to remove deformity, to repair decay, to invigorate failing powers, and restore the rose of health to pallid cheeks. His aim is not to inflict pain, but relieve it—not to destroy a father, but—standing between him and death—to save his trembling wife from widowhood, and these little children from an orphan's lot. And if, although they be wove round no coronet, those are fairer and fresher laurels which are won by saving than by slaying; if it is a nobler thing to rescue life than destroy it, even when its destruction is an act of justice; then, on the same principle, God most glorified himself when revealed in the flesh, and speaking by his Son, he descended on a guilty world,—this his purpose—"I came not to judge the world, but to save it,"—and this his character—"The Lord God, merciful and gracious, long-suffering, and abundant in goodness and truth."

Apart, however, from this general consideration, I remark that the scheme of redemption is eminently illustrative of the attributes of Jehovah. For example—

I. His power is glorified in the work of salvation.

Its path is marked, and its pages are crowded with stupendous miracles. At one time God stays the waves of the sea, at another he stops the wheels of the sun, and, now reversing the machinery of heaven to confirm his word, he makes the shadow travel backwards on the dial of Ahaz. Heaven descends to earth, and its inhabitants walk the stage of a world's redemption. Here one angel speaks out of a burning bush, and there another leaps on a burning altar, and, with wing unscorched, ascends to heaven in its flame. Here a prophet, exempted from the law of death, goes up to glory in a fiery chariot, and there another in the belly of a whale goes down into the depths of ocean. In contradiction of the laws of nature, a body that should have gravitated to the earth, floats, from the top of Olivet, upward into the ambient air. Across a lake which frost never bound, and winter never paved with ice, walks a human form, stepping on from billow to billow. The tenant of the grave becomes its conqueror, and, laying by its cerements as night-clothes left in bed, he walks forth on the dewy grass at the break of day; the prisoner has bound his jailer and carried off the keys. Over Bethlehem's fields, angels with the light of their wings turn night into day, and shepherds, who watch their flocks, are regaled by voices of the skies—the song of heaven over a babe, who has a poor woman for his mother, and a stable for his birth-place. Nor less remarkable, the deaf are listening to the songs of the dumb, and the blind are gazing on the dead alive; a dumb beast takes human speech and rebukes the hoary sage; ravens leave their young to cater in the fields for man; and angels abandon heaven to hold sentinel watch by the grave of One whom God forsook, his country rejected, friends repudiated, and none but a thief confessed. And amid these wonders and thousands more, acted before men's eyes on the stage of redemption, and all so illustrative of the presence and power of God, the greatest wonder —the wonder of wonders—is He that works them; the Son of a virgin! dust and Divinity! Creator and creature! "the mystery of godliness, God manifest in the flesh." Truly, "This is the Lord's doing; it is marvelous in our eyes."

But to glance at the change wrought in redemption on man himself, what amazing power does it display! What a glorious combination of benevolence and om-

nipotence! Punishment is confessedly easier than
reformation. Nothing is more easy than to rid society
of a criminal by the hand of an executioner; but to
soften his stony heart, to get him to fall in love with
virtue, to make him an honest, honorable, kind, and
tender man, to guide his erring steps from the paths
of crime—ah! that is another thing. Hence, by men
callous of heart, and deaf to the groans of suffering
humanity, the preference given to prisons over schools,
to punishment over prevention. Well, then, since it
is confessedly easier—easier, not better; easier, not in
the end cheaper—to punish than reform, I say that
God's power is more illustriously displayed in par-
doning one guilty—in purifying one polluted man,
than if the law had been left to take her sternest
course, and our entire family had been buried in the
ruins of the fall. We honor justice when she holds
the balance even, and before a land that cries for blood,
brings out the murderer to hang him up in the face
of the sun: "whoso sheddeth man's blood, by man
shall his blood be shed." Yet, like the Romans, who
decreed a crown to him that saved a citizen, we would
hold him worthy of highest honors who brings forth
a criminal from his cell, so changed as to be worthy,
not only of being restored to the bosom of society,
but of holding a place in the senate, or some post of
dignity beside the throne. That were an achievement
of brilliant renown—a victory over which humanity
and piety would shed tears of joy.

To compare small things with great, something like
this—but unspeakably nobler and greater—God works
in salvation. For example—In John Bunyan, he
calls the bold leader of village reprobates to preach
the gospel; a blaspheming tinker to become one of

England's famous confessors; and from the gloomy portals of Bedford jail, to shed forth the luster of his sanctified and resplendent genius to the farther limits of the world, and adown the whole course of time. From the deck of a slave ship he summons John Newton to the pulpit; and by hands defiled with Mammon's most nefarious traffic, he brings them that are bound out of darkness, and smites adamantine fetters from the slaves of sin. In Paul, the Apostle of the Gentiles, he converts his Son's bitterest enemy into his warmest friend. To the man whom a trembling church held most in dread, she comes to owe, under God, the weightiest obligations. In Paul she has her boldest champion, her greatest logician, the most gallant of her defenders, her grandest preacher, the prince of Apostles, the largest contributor to this imperishable volume. How much better for these three stars to be shining in heaven, than quenched in the blackness of darkness. Better for the good of man—better for the glory of God. In them, and in all the sainted throng around them, has not God more illustriously displayed his power, than if he had crushed them by the thunders of his vengeance, and buried them in the depths of hell? The power of Divinity culminates in grace. Oh, that we may become its monuments, and be built up by the hands of an eternal Spirit, to the glory of the cross! And why not? Look at these men! Think what they were; behold what they are! and, addressing your prayers to him whose ear is never heavy that it cannot hear, nor his hand shortened that it cannot save, be this your earnest, your urgent cry, "Awake, awake, put on strength, O arm of the Lord. Awake, as in the ancient days in the generations of old."

The Wisdom and Holiness of God,

ILLUSTRATED BY SALVATION.

And I will sanctify my great name which ye have profaned.
EZEKIEL xxxvi. 23.

THE effect of the wind is visible, not the element itself. The clouds scud across the sky, the trees swing their arms wildly in the air, aerial waves chase each other in sport across the corn, and the boat, catching the gale in her flowing sheet, goes dancing over the billows. So—although in a sense infinitely higher— the Invisible is visible; and in his works we see a God, who, seeing all, remains himself unseen. He is lost, not in darkness, but in light; He is a sun that blinds the eye which is turned on its burning disc. Angels themselves are unable to sustain his glory. They cover their faces with their wings, and use them, as a man his hand, to screen their eyes from the ineffable effulgence.

Suppose that we ascend the steps of creation, from matter in its crudest form to nature's highest and most beautiful arrangements; from the lichen that clothes a rock to the oak that stands rooted in its crevices; from the dull coal to the same mineral crystalized in a flashing diamond; from a dew-drop, lying in the cup of a flower, to the great ocean that lies in the hollow of its Maker's hand; from a spark that expires in the moment of its birth, to the sun which has risen and set with unabated splendor on the graves of a hundred generations; from the instinct of the moth, that flutters round a taper, to the intellect of an angel, who hovers before the throne; from a grain of sand to this vast globe; from this world to a creation in extent, perhaps, as much greater than our planet as it is greater than the grain of sand: As we climb up wards, step by step, our views of God's glory enlarge. They rise with our elevation, and expand with the widening prospect. At length we reach a pinnacle where the whole heavens and earth lie spread out beneath our feet;—and reach it to fall on our knees, and, catching the strain of adoring seraphim, to exclaim, "Holy, holy, holy, is the Lord of Hosts, the whole earth is full of his glory!"

It is not given to man to discover all the works and ways of God. No; with our boasted discoveries and pride of science, perhaps these are as little known to us as the unbroken forest to the microscopic insect, whose life is a day, and whose world is a leaf—that little decaying leaf, the scene of its most distant journeys, its country, its cradle, its grave. With what modesty, then, should the highest intellect bow down and bear itself in presence of its Creator! Let the patriarch, in language worthy of so high a theme, describe his majesty. "He stretcheth out the north over the empty place, and hangeth the earth upon nothing. He holdeth back the face of his throne, and spreadeth his cloud upon it. He hath compassed the waters with bounds, until the day and night come to an end. The pillars of heaven tremble and are astonished at his reproof; he divideth the sea with his power, and by his understanding he smiteth through the proud; by his spirit he hath garnished the heavens; his hand hath formed the crooked serpent; lo, these are parts of his ways; but how little a portion is heard of him? but the thunder of his power who can understand?" Unbeliever as he was, the great Laplace echoed these sentiments of Job, in this, one of his last and not least memorable utterances—"It is the little that we know; it is the great that remains unknown." And in the confession of his ignorance, has not a Christian, and still greater philosopher, left us perhaps the finest illustration of his wisdom? Newton's most brilliant discoveries reflect no brighter luster on Newton's name than his well known comparison of himself to a little child—a child who had gathered some few pebbles on the shores of a vast and unexplored ocean.

Man, however—although comprehending but little of the ways of God—is privileged to contemplate, and is in himself honored to illustrate, the noblest of them all. He may be a beggar, but, if grace has made him a new creature, there is more of God seen beneath his rags than in the sun itself; nor does that brilliant sky studded thick with stars reveal the glorious fullness of Divinity that shines in the cross of Calvary and the face of Jesus. Bethlehem Ephratah was "little among the cities of Judah." Our world also seems little among the suns and systems of creation—a dark, dim, insignificant spot; yet the eyes of the universe have been turned on our planet. It has all the importance spiritually, which physically was attributed to it, when men supposed it to be the pivot and center of creation.

Man's world is the place in the great universe from which God and his attributes may be best beheld and studied. It corresponds to that one spot in a noble temple—lying right beneath the lofty dome—where the spectator, commanding all the grandest features of the edifice, is instructed to look around him, if he would see the monument of its architect. For where can we see God as we behold him on the cross and in the gospel? I scale bartizan or tower to embrace at one view the map of a mighty city. I climb the sides of some lofty hill to survey the land that lies in beauty at its feet. And had I the universe to range over, where should I go to obtain the fullest exhibition of the Godhead? Would I soar on angel-wings to the heights of heaven to look on its happiness, and listen to angel's hymns? Would I cleave the darkness, and—sailing round the edge of the fiery gulf—listen to the wail, and weep over the misery of the lost? No; turning away alike from these sunny heights and doleful regions, I would remain in this world of ours; and, traveling to Palestine, would stand beneath the dome of heaven with my feet on Calvary— on that consecrated spot, where the cross of salvation rose, and the blood of a Redeemer fell. Here I find the center of a spiritual universe. Here the hosts of heaven descended to acquaint themselves with God in Christ; here, in a completed arch, if I may so speak, locked fast by the key, all the properties of Divinity meet; here, concentrated as in a burning focus, its varied attributes blend and shine.

We had begun to show how these attributes were exhibited in the work of redemption; and having illustrated this in the power of God, we now remark that—

I. The wisdom of God is glorified in redemption.

The British Museum possesses in the Portland Vase one of the finest remains of ancient art; and it may be remembered how—some years ago—the world of taste was shocked to hear that this precious relic had been shattered by a maniac's hand. Without disparaging classic taste or this exquisite example of it, I venture to say, that there is not a poor worm which we tread upon, nor a sere leaf, that, like a ruined but reckless man, dances merrily in its fallen state to the autumn winds, but has superior claims upon our study and admiration. The child who plucks a lily or rose to pieces, or crushes the fragile form of a fluttering insect, destroys a work which the highest art could not invent, nor man's best skilled hand construct. And there was not a leaf quivered on the trees which stood under the domes of the crystal palace, but eclipsed the brightest glories of loom or chisel; it had no rival among the triumphs of invention, which a world went there to see. Yes; in his humblest works, God infinitely surpasses the highest efforts of created skill. "Wisdom is justified of her children;" nor shall our God be left without a witness so long as thunders peal and lightnings flash, and breakers beat upon the shore; so long as a flower blooms in the field, a fin cleaves the deep, or a wing cuts the air; so long as glowing suns blaze above, or dying glow-worms shine below. That man gave the Atheist a crushing answer, who told him that the very feather with which he penned the words, "There is no God," refuted the audacious lie.

In redemption this wisdom is pre-eminent. That work associates such amazing wisdom with love, and power, and mercy, that the Saviour of man is called "the wisdom of God." The Apostle selects the definite article, and pronounces Christ to be "*the* power of God and *the* wisdom of God." Can any doubt the propriety of the language, who reflects but for a moment on what a hard task wisdom was set—what a difficult problem she was called to solve—when man was to be saved? She had to forge a key that should unlock the grave; she had to build a life-boat that should live in a sea of fire; she had to construct a ladder long enough and strong enough to scale the skies; she was called on to invent a plan whereby justice might be fully satisfied, and yet the guilty saved. The highest intelligences had been at fault here—they might well have asked, who is sufficient for these things? "He saw that there was no man, and wondered that there was no intercessor." In such an emergency—for such a task—wisdom sufficient dwelt only with the Godhead—in him in whom "are hid all the treasures of wisdom and knowledge." "How shall man be just with God," is a mystery insolvable to all but Him in whom the most extraordinary and apparently conflicting elements have met;—who has a double nature in a single person—who has a divine Father and human mother, who is the only begotten of God and first-born of a virgin womb—who, being in one sense dust, in another sense Divinity, has a nature to satisfy and a nature to suffer.

Now, this wisdom of God in redemption is brought out in no aspect more strikingly than in the harmony which it has established among what appeared conflicting attributes. Here is nothing like the prophet's graphic picture of a city, where chariots jostle each other on the streets; nor like what happens even on the spacious ocean, when in the gloom of night bark dashes into bark, and foundering crews find in their ship a coffin, and in the deep sea their grave. Harmony, indeed, sits enthroned amid the order of the silent heavens. Flaming sun, and wandering comet, and rolling planets, move in their orbits without accident or collision; yet in the harmony established among the attributes of God, redemption illustrates a higher wisdom. There is one fact, which brings this out very palpably. With the deepest interests at stake—in circumstances eminently fitted to sharpen his ingenuity—man never approached, nor so much as guessed at, the only method of salvation. We can show how near preceding philosophers have been to the later discoveries of science. For many centuries before their practical application, China was acquainted with the properties both of gunpowder and the magnet; and have not we seen one astronomer get upon the track of a star, and start a thought, by which another—who pursued it to its ultimate conclusions—has been conducted to the brilliant discovery? Every one acquainted with the history of science knows that some of the greatest inventions of the nineteenth century were all but anticipated at former and even remote periods; another step—but another step—and the world had possessed them ages before,—and, centuries ago, man would have steered his way across the sea by the compass needle—yoked the spirits of fire and water to his triumphant wheels—and sent messages across oceans and continents on the wings of lightning.

The mystery of godliness, however—God manifest in the flesh—a Daysman such as the patriarch desired—with the right hand of Divinity to lay on God, and the left hand of humanity to lay on man, and thus the "fellow" and friend of both, to reconcile them—in short, a man to suffer and a God to satisfy, this was a thought which it never entered the mind of man to

7

conceive. We find nothing corresponding to this in the creeds and religions of a heathen world. There is neither glimpse nor glimmering of it in these. Every way but the right one was thought of. Here, the sinner seeks by his own works to work out redemption; here, by costly sacrifices, he attempts to appease offended justice: here, in children—whom he offers on the altar, or passes through the fire to Moloch—he gives the "fruit of his body for the sin of his soul;" here again—doing less violence to nature—guilty of a crime less contrary to reason and revolting to humanity, he courts death beneath the wheels of Juggernaut, and sheds the blood of his body to expiate the guilt of his soul. These were the sands on which man built his house. These were the straws drowning men caught at. There never entered into other mind than God's a plan, or shadow of a plan, by which sweet Mercy might be espoused to stern Justice, and God—in the luster of untarnished holiness, and the majesty of a vindicated law—might appear, as he appears in Jesus, the "just and yet the justifier of the ungodly."

II. The holiness of God is glorified in redemption.

The eyes are moved by the heart, as the hands of a time-piece are turned by the internal machinery. We turn them *to* what the heart loves, and *from* what the heart loathes. The most emphatic expression of dislike is a silent one—the closed eyes and averted head. Such an attitude as I can fancy Zedekiah's to have been, when they brought out his sons to slay them in their father's presence. And "to wound him that God had smitten," to add a crushing weight to his captivity and chains, to imprint a spectacle on his memory, that should haunt him like a horrid specter, when sight was quenched and hope for ever gone, his barbarous enemies put the sons to death before they put out the father's eyes. When you have in fancy imagined yourself in that father's place, imagining how, when you had implored them to begin with you, and save you this horrid sight, and they had refused the favor of these burning irons, how you would have closed your eyes, and turned shuddering away, you will be able in some measure to appreciate the abhorrence with which a holy God regards iniquity. Hear the prophet—"Thou art of purer eyes than to behold evil, and canst not look on iniquity."

Nothing might appear more strongly to express the holiness of God than this language, "Thou canst not look on iniquity;" and yet his hatred of sin is, beyond doubt, much more fully expressed by the very way in which he saves the sinner; more fully expressed in redemption, than if, executing relentless vengeance, with an eye that knew no pity, and with a hand that would not spare, he had made an utter end of sinners—such an end that, to borrow the language of the prophet, "there was none that moved the wing, or opened the mouth, or peeped." What man, what father, has not felt so on reading the story of the Roman judge? Had that stern patriot condemned common criminals enough to make the scaffolds of justice and the gutters of Rome run red with blood, that wholesale slaughter had been a weak expression of his abhorrence of crime, compared with the death of this solitary youth. When the culprit— his own child, the infant he had carried in his arms, his once sweet and beautiful boy, the child of his tenderest affections, who had wound himself round a

father's heart—rose and received the immolating sen-
tence at a father's lips, oh! that iron man offered the
costliest sacrifice man ever made at the shrine of jus
tice, and earned for Roman virtue a proverbial fame.

But that is nothing to the spectacle which redemp-
tion offers. Over what are these angels hovering?
On what do they bend a gaze so fixed, so intent, so
full of awe and wonder? Sons of the morning! they
had sung in their joy over a new-born world. Attend-
ants at the birth of earth! they now hail with intenser
wonder, and praise in loftier strains, the birth in a
stable, the appearance of a babe in Bethlehem. They
had seen suns blazing into light; they had seen worlds
start into being, and watched them as, receiving their
first impulse from the Creator's hand, they rolled away
into the far realm of space; but never had they fol-
lowed world or sun with such interest as they follow
the weary steps of this Traveler from his humble
cradle to the cross of Calvary. What draws all their
eyes to that sacred spot? what keeps them gazing on
it with looks of such solemn interest? The Son of
God dies beneath his Father's hand. Innocence bleeds
for guilt; divine innocence for human guilt; a spec-
tacle at which, in the mysterious language of the
Apocalypse, "There was silence in heaven." On the
night Daniel passed in the lion's den the Persian
would hear no music;—nor flute, nor harp, nor
psaltery, nor dulcimer, woke the echoes of his palace;
the daughters of music were all brought low. God's
Son is dying on the tree. I can fancy that during
these dread hours there was no music in heaven—
there was an awful pause; silent every harp, hushed
the voice of song; and when all is over, and the cry,
"It is finished," has been heard, and the last quiver

has passed from Jesus' lips, I can fancy how these angels broke the awful silence, and, turning round to the throne, with new, deeper, holier reverence, exclaimed, " Holy, holy, holy, Lord God Almighty."

This holiness, so glorified in redemption, appears still more plainly, when we consider how the eyes of Love both multiply and magnify beauties; and, over-looking all defects, reconcile us even to deformity. How beautifully, tenderly, touchingly, affection clings to an idiot child! and with what ingenuity does Love palliate in our children faults which are tolerable and tolerated in no one else. She flings a broad mantle over the shame of child and parent, brother, sister, and friend. See how Eli—a too indulgent parent—tolerates crimes in his sons, which it is only doing this holy man justice to believe, he would have died rather than have himself committed. Now, in our judgment, the holiness of God shines very conspicuously in this, that, even when sin was associated with his beloved Son, it appeared none the less vile in his eyes; perhaps viler, fouler, still more loathsome,—just as the churchyard mould, flung by the sexton from a grave upon winter's fresh fallen snow, looks the blacker for the contrast, Love would have spared the pains of a beloved Son, but it is met and mastered by God's hatred of sin. He looks on our sins as laid on Christ, and still he hates them with a perfect hatred, turning on him, that bare them on his own body on the tree, an unmitigated vengeance. To reach sin—to kill sin—he passes the sword through the bosom of his well-beloved Son; and if he did not spare even his own Son when he took our sins upon him, oh! what holiness in God! Whom will he spare? What will he spare? What a startling alarum is rung from Calvary in the ears of a drowsy world! With your eye on the cross, within sight of its agonies, within sound of its groans, I ask the question, and I wait for an answer, If he did not spare his own Son, how shall he spare the impenitent and unbelieving? "If they do these things in a green tree, what shall be done in the dry?"

III. The justice of God is glorified in redemption.

The prophet is perplexed. He strains his eye to penetrate a mystery. He says to God, "Thou art of purer eyes than to behold evil;" but then, as one unable to reconcile the character of God with the dealings of his providence, he asks, "Wherefore lookest thou upon them that deal treacherously, and holdest thy tongue when the wicked devoureth the man that is more righteous than he?" Now, although—as that question implies—clouds and darkness are round about Jehovah's throne, whatever shadow present events may appear to cast upon his justice, and to whatever trials, as in the wrongs of a Joseph or David, faith may be put, in believing that there is a just God upon earth, his justice is as conspicuous in redemption as the cross which illustrated it. Sinners, indeed, are pardoned, but then, their sins are punished; the guilty are acquitted, but then, their guilt is condemned; the sinner lives, but then, the surety dies; the debtor is discharged, not, however, till the debt is paid. Dying, "the just for the unjust, that he might bring us to God," Jesus satisfies for us; and, as we have seen a discharged account pierced by a nail, and hung to gather cobwebs on the dusty wall, he who paid our debt, nor left us one farthing to pay, has taken the handwriting that was against us and nailed it to his cross.

And now, I say, that justice is not only satisfied, but more than satisfied. She is better pleased to have her debtors free in heaven, than locked up in hell. It must be so. Is it better for the creditor to hold the money in his purse than the man that owed it in a prison? What man of common humanity or common sense does not esteem himself happier to have the debt paid, than the miserable debtor rotting in jail? Observe, I pray you, that in regard to the lost, and her claims upon them, justice, in a sense, is never satisfied. The pains of hell do not, can not exhaust the penalty. Dreadful sentence! Banishment for life, for life eternal, from the blissful presence of God. Mysterious debt! A debt ever paying, yet never paid. No wonder, in one sense, that Jesus died to save. The calamity is so incalculably tremendous, that the occasion was worthy of the interposition of God, and the salvation is most worthy of our grateful and instant acceptance. Embrace it; for no length of suffering discharges this debt—a truth established by the fact that the debtor is never discharged. Justice is never satisfied; and it is plain therefore, to say nothing of his mercy, that God's justice is more illustriously glorified, and more fully satisfied through the satisfaction rendered by our substitute, than it could have been by our everlasting sufferings.

Nor is that all. It is a mean and vulgar error to suppose that the only office of justice is to punish. She has higher and more pleasing functions. Sternly, indeed, she stands by the gallows tree; and, when she has drawn the bolt and launched her victim into eternity, she leaves the scene, sorrowing it may be, yet satisfied. It is a melancholy satisfaction. From that revolting spectacle, turn to this hall of assembled nobles. Amid the brilliant, flashing, gorgeous, magnificence of the scene, all eyes are fixed on one man. He comes red with the blood of a hundred battles, and crowned with the trophies of a hundred victories; he comes at the summons of a sovereign whose crown he has saved; he comes to receive the thanks of a country, grateful for his defence of its shores. Justice presides in that assembly. She was satisfied on the scaffold, here she is more than satisfied; pleasure and triumph light up her eye, as, with lavish hand, she dispenses titles and rewards, and on a head, so often covered by the God of battles, she places a laurel crown.

In fact, it is her noblest function to reward merit, to crown the brows of virtue or of valor, and send suspected innocence back to the world amid the plaudits, and flushed with the triumph of an honorable acquittal. Justice did a stern but righteous act, when she hung up Haman in the face of the sun, and before the eyes of the city—a warning to all tyrants, and a terror to all sycophants; yet it was a loftier and a happier exercise of her functions to call the Jew from obscurity, to marshal him along the crowded streets with a crest-fallen enemy walking at his stirrup, and royal heralds going before to blow his fame, and ever and anon to cry, " Thus shall it be done to the man whom the king delighteth to honor." Even so, shall the justice of God be glorified when heads, now lying in the grave, are crowned with honor. Believer! lift up thy drooping head. Thou shalt lift it up in glory from the dust. " He is faithful and just to forgive us our sion." In consideration of a Redeemer's righteous-ness, God shall crown thee; in the righteousness that is on thee, reward the work of his Son; and in the righteousness that is in thee, approve the work of his Spirit. The august assembly of the skies shall be a spectacle of glorified justice. In the Head with its members all exalted, the Captain and every soldier crowned, Jesus shall receive the full payment of His wages, and justice shall reward a Saviour in the saved. "He shall see of the travail of his soul, and shall be satisfied."

7*

The Mercy of God illustrated in Salvation

And I will sanctify my great name, which ye have profaned.

EZEKIEL xxxvi. 23

GRADUAL development appears to be the law of nature, or, to speak more correctly, the method of the divine government. The day does not rush into light, nor blaze upon a dazzled world with the flash of an explosion; but the sky brightens over-head, and the various features of the landscape grow more and more distinct below, as the first streaks of morning are developing into a perfect day. Nature never moves abruptly—by starts and sudden impulses;—the day bursts not into light, neither do the birds into song, nor buds into leaf, nor flowers into full-blown beauty. From her grave she comes forth at the voice of spring, but not all of a sudden, like the sepulchred Lazarus, at the call of Jesus. The season advances with a steady march—by gradual and graceful steps. From the first notes that break the long winter silence, till groves are ringing with songs; from the first bud which looks out on departing storms, till woods are robed in their varied foliage; from the first sweet flower—welcome harbinger of spring—that hangs its white bell beside the lingering snow, till gardens and meadows bloom, and earth offers incense to her God from a thousand censers; from summer's first ripe fruit, till autumn sheaves fall to the reaper's song, and ı. ds are bare, and stackyards are full, and every farm keeps "harvest home"— all is progressive.

Man himself presents no exception to this law. The cradle is shorter than the coffin; infancy outshoots its dress; the stammering tongue grows eloquent; the tottering foot follows the chase, or stands balanced on the rocking mast; and those feeble arms, which now clasp a mother's neck, shall ere long battle with difficulties, subdue the rugged soil, or lay groaning forests low.

Our minds also grow with our bodies. They open like a flower-bud; memory, fancy, reason, reflection, lie folded up in an infant's soul like the leaves of an unblown rose. Bathed by night in dews, and by day with light, these open out to show their colors and shed their fragrance; so those expand under the tender influences of a mother's culture, and the dawn· ing light of truth.

The law that reigns paramount in the worlds of mat· ter and mind—universal as that of gravitation—ex tends itself into the spiritual kingdom. The God of nature is the God of grace, and as he acts outside the church, he acts within it. In the first place, the gos· pel system itself was gradually developed. The Bible was once a very little book. It grew by degrees to its present size; and, as in a house, stone is laid on stone, and story built upon story, so book was added to book—history to history—prophecy to prophecy— gospel to gospel—and one epistle to another, till the hands of John laid on the copestone, and, standing on the pinnacle of this sacred edifice, he pronounced God's wide and withering curse on all who should im· pair its integrity. The temple, in which "the Lord of the temple" appeared, took forty years to complete, but the written word was a work of two thousand, and the revealed word of not less than twice two thousand years. It was a long way between Paradise and Patmos; and a protracted dawn from the first streak of morning that rose on the Fall, till the sun introduced the perfect day. A period of at least four thousand years elapsed between the curse of Eden and the cross of Calvary.

In the second place, while the truth was thus slowly developed and let in by degrees on a benighted world, the effect of that truth on a benighted soul is also gradual. No man starts up into a finished Christian. The very best come from their graves, like Lazarus, "clothed in grave clothes"—not like Jesus, who left his death dress behind him; and in our remaining corruptions, all, alas! carry some of these cerements about with them, nor drop them but at the door of heaven. The Christian is an example of gradual development. When our growth is quickest, how slow it is! As, from some fresh stain we wash our hands in the blood of Jesus; as, from the field of daily conflict we retire at evening to seek the healing of the balm of Gilead; as, with David, we eye some eminence from which we have fallen, or, looking back on some former period, measure the little progress we have made—how often are we constrained to ask in disappointment, "When shall I be holy?" How often are we constrained to cry in prayer, "How long, O Lord, how long?" At times it looks as if the dawn would never brighten into day. We almost fear that our fate shall have its emblem in some unhappy flower, which—withered by frost, or the home of a worm—never blows at all; but dies like an unborn infant, whose coffin is a mother's womb. This shall not happen with any child of grace. God will perform all things for his people, and perfect what concerneth them. Still, although He who has begun a good work in them will carry it on to the day of the Lord Jesus, all the figures of Scripture indicate a gradual progress. The believer is a babe who grows " to the stature of a perfect man in Christ," and "the path of the just is as the shining light, that shineth more and more unto the perfect day."

These laws of development have their limit in creation. They affect not God. He has made no progress. There was room for none. His maturity, eternally as well as divinely perfect, knows neither growth nor age. His wisdom, knowledge, goodness, love, justice, truth, and mercy, were always—millions of ages ago—were what they are now. Knowing no growth, he can suffer no decay. It is the sun which rises that sets; but it is the peculiar attribute of Divinity to be "the same yesterday, to day, and for ever." His being is as an infinite ocean, that holds within its bosom all that lives and is, that has neither shore nor bottom, beginning nor end, ebb nor flow, calm nor tempest; which no changes alter, nor tribu taries supply; and which, affected neither by tide nor time, has been, is, and ever shall be full. How adorable is God! He is great, and greatly to be feared. The attributes of God, however, have been gradually revealed to the knowledge of his intelligent creatures, and their light has risen on the universe like daybreak upon our planet. For example, when he created angels, suns, and worlds, God, in the first instance, displayed his being, wisdom, power, holiness, and goodness. Then came the first Fall. Its scene was laid in heaven, where a part of the angelic host committed sin; and this event called forth the exhibition of another attribute, or—to speak with more propriety—a new display of justice. Punitive justice was now revealed. She unsheathed her glittering sword, and it fell in vengeance on the workers of iniquity, and sheared their glory from angel's heads.

Time rolled on; how long we know not. At length our world was created—or rather brought into its present form—and became the scene of our parents' probation. Sin came; death trod on the heels of sin; for, as the Apostle tells, "Sin entered into the world, and death by sin, and so death passed upon all men, for that all have sinned." Now the culprits stand trembling before their Maker, nor is there an angel who looks on, but expects to see the sword once more unsheathed, and hear the thunders, that shook thrones and principalities in heaven, roll, and peal, and crash among the hills of earth. At this awful moment—at that eventful crisis—how unexpected the voice which came from the most excellent majesty—"Deliver from going down to the pit; I have found a ransom." To the surprise of angels, from out the light that vails the throne, a beautiful form steps forth, and Mercy, arresting the uplifted arm, turns its weapon from man on her own bared, spotless, loving bosom. In the Son of God about to become incarnate, she says—"Lo! I come to do thy will, O God.' Ready both to satisfy and suffer for them, Jesus interposes for his elect as he did for his disciples, when, stepping in between them and the armed band, he said—"I am he; let these go their way." This brings us now to remark--

I. The mercy of God is glorified in redemption.

To do justice to God, to the Saviour, and to our subject, we must be careful not to confound pity with mercy. This is no example of a distinction without a difference. Some time ago, upon a cold winter day, we passed the door of a humble abode. A venerable old woman stood in the open door-way, with a very wretched, ragged child before her. With one hand she offered a piece of bread—sharing her food with a poverty sorer than her own—while the other held up a bowl of milk to the lips of the sad, shivering, emaciated creature; and had you seen the benevolence that beamed in her aged face as she gazed on the orphan partaking of her bounty, you would have gone and done likewise—won over to humanity by such a lovely and living picture of the truth that charity is twice blessed—blest in those that give, and blest in those that get. Now, however beautiful that scene was to the eye of humanity, it was not a display of mercy. Not mercy but pity moved that kind hand and gentle breast; and there the aged matron stood, an example of what is not uncommon among the poor—lofty charity in lowly life. Take another example:—A man builds an asylum for the destitute— a harbor of refuge for the wrecks of fortune. This may be an honorable monument to his memory—it may be, perhaps, but a monument of his vanity; but, whether it be erected for the benefit of the poor, or to gratify the craving for posthumous fame, it is not a temple of mercy. The wandering mendicant, into whose hand you drop your money, as he begs his way on to a grave, where, with his head sheltered beneath the sod, he shall feel neither cold nor hunger, appeals to your compassion, not to your mercy. He has done you no wrong—he has not stolen your goods, nor traduced your character, nor inflicted injury on your person, nor in any way whatever disturbed your peace; and so it is but pity that is expressed in the charity which shares her bread with the hungry, and spares a corner of an ample cloak to cover the nakedness of the poor.

Mercy is a higher attribute—an act of mercy is a far nobler achievement. She sits enthroned among the divine Graces. On her heavenly wings man rises to his loftiest elevation, and makes his nearest approach and similitude to God. This distinction between compassion and mercy is clearly enunciated in the sacred Scriptures. We are told that "like as a father pitieth his children, so the Lord pitieth them that fear him;" but the Lord is merciful to them that fear him not. Not only did he so love the world as to give up his Son to die for it, but he commended his love to us, in that, while we were yet sinners, Christ died for us. We pity simple suffering; but let pity and love be extended to *guilty* suffering, and you have now the very element of mercy. Mercy is the forgiveness of an injury; mercy is the pardon of a sinner. Smiling when justice frowns, and extending her favors out and beyond those who are merely without merit, she bestows them on those who are full of demerit.

Leaving the priest and Levite to walk on in their cold and heartless indifference, look at this good Samaritan, as, bending over a bleeding form, he binds the wounds of a man whom robbers have assaulted, and whom these hypocrites have left to die. There, pity kneels beside suffering humanity, bears a brother's burden, and is afflicted in all his afflictions. Now from that beautiful spectacle turn to Calvary and the cross on which Jesus dies. Here,—herself wounded, and bleeding,—Mercy hangs over a wicked world, and with her tears sheds blessings on the head of murderers—"Father, forgive them ; they know not what they do." In fine, the objects of pity are sufferers who have been unfortunate; the objects of mercy are sufferers who have been guilty. And now understanding mercy to be the forgiveness of a wrong, the pardon of a sinner, the kindness of the injured to the injurer, where, as in redemption—where, indeed, but in redemption—is this crowning attribute of the Godhead to be seen? save for redemption, this fairest jewel in the crown of heaven had been concealed—unknown as a pearl still shelled in depths of ocean, or any diamond that still lies bedded in the dark mines of earth.

Guilty man embraced within her arms, how visible is mercy now! Where can we turn our eyes but she meets them? Pointing to the pit of perdition, do you say, look there! Well, we look there. We see mercy there: not mercy enjoyed, but mercy rejected. Turning with horror from the sight, do we look up? In every saint, robed in righteousness and reigning in glory, we behold a monument of mercy, and exclaim with David, "Thy mercy, O Lord, is in the heavens." And as to this guilty world, are not the arms of mercy around it? They preserve it and sustain it. Every sinner is a monument of sparing, and every believer is a monument of saving mercy. God's people in their creeds, catechisms, and confessions may differ in their mode of expressing some points of faith, but in this confession all concur—these words each and all adopt —"Great is thy mercy toward me, thou hast delivered

my soul from the lowest hell." There is mercy above
the ground, aye, and beneath it. There is mercy in
the very grave. You may see her form, and hear her
sweetly singing on a believer's tomb. To that quiet
harbor God has brought many a dear one before the
storm burst. There, earth, like a gentle mother, has
wrapped her mantle round a tender child ; and, when
the tempest was beating upon their own heads, have
not many been thankful that some, whom they loved,
were now beyond its reach—sleeping quietly in the
peaceful grave. Yes! and to believers themselves
there is the kindest mercy in the grave. How can
they doubt it? Were I the tenant of an old, crumb-
ling cottage, through whose chinks and rents the cold
rain was dripping, and frosty winds blew, it were, I
think, a kindness to pull down this crazy building
and build me a palace in its room. Quarrel not with
death's rude hand. It pulls to pieces this frail taber
nacle, that, on the day when mortal shall assume im
mortality, mercy may raise for me from its wreck, " a
building of God, an house not made with hands, eternal
in the heavens."

In short, on every thing I read the words, " The
earth, O Lord, is full of thy mercy." Mercies arrive
on the wings of every hour ; mercies supply our table ;
mercies flow in life's brimming cup. They fall in
every shower, and shine in every sunbeam. They lie
as thick around man's tent, as desert manna in the
days of old. Here, mercy runs to meet the returning
prodigal, and opens her arms to fold him to her bosom.
Here, she pleads with sinners, and pronounces pardon
over the chief of them. Here, she weeps with sufferers,
and dries the tear upon sorrow's cheek. And here,
eying the storm, she launches her life-boat through

foaming breakers, and pulls for the wreck where souls are perishing. It is her blessed hand which rings the Sabbath bell, and her voice which, on savage shores or from Christian pulpits, proclaims a Saviour for the lost. None she despises; she despairs of none; and, not to be scared away by foulest sin, she stands by its guilty bed, and, bending down to death's dull ear— when the twelfth hour is just about to strike—she looks into the glassy eye and cries, Believe, O believe, only believe, "whosoever believeth in the Lord Jesus shall not perish, but have everlasting life."

II. In redemption, God is glorified in the complete discomfiture of all his and our enemies.

He is glorified by Satan's defeat.

God made man in his own image, and put him on probation. But was he, could he, be indifferent to the issue? Assuredly not; for, although he does not will the death of guilt, he must, in a sense, have willed the triumph of innocence. What father ever saw his son leave for the field of battle, and did not follow him with wishes for his success? When the Spartan widow laced on the armor of her boy, and, kissing his cheek, sent him away to the fight, in handing him his father's shield, she bade him return with it or on it—dead, or a conqueror—in honorable life or not less honorable death. And I cannot but believe that the life and honor of our first parents were as dear to God —dearer, dearer far, than ever son's to mother; for, such was his love, that, even in our guilt he commended his love to us by giving up his Son to die for us.

Well; the hour of conflict came, and with it God's enemy and man's—the Adversary, the Devil, the Evil

One, Satan, Prince of Darkness, the Power and Po-
tentate of Hell.   A poor drowning man will seize the
swimmer's limb, clasp his arms, nor relax the death-
grasp, till, after a brief struggle, they go down to-
gether.   Thus it has often happened, most pitifully
and miserably, that the perishing has, in his unwise
attempts to save himself, been the death of a generous
friend.   But there is in sin a deep and damnable ma-
lignity, which, without any hope of personal advan-
tage, prompts the sinner to seize all within his grasp.
That he may drag others down into the same perdi-
tion with himself, he lays siege to honesty to conquer
it, to virtue to corrupt it; and hence the danger of
ungodly associates;—"A companion of fools shall be
destroyed."   It was this evil principle which we see
every day at work, that carried havoc into Eden; yet
not this alone.   Besides the inherent hatred that sin
bears to holiness, Satan was smarting under his wounds,
and, with a fire as unquenchable as that of his own
hell, he burned to be avenged.   Was there not a va-
cant throne in heaven?   Had it not once been his?
and still been his, but that God had hurled him into
perdition?   God was his enemy, and he was God's;
he would be revenged; he would defeat his purposes;
cross, thwart, disappoint him; and wreak his ven-
geance on God in the only way within a creature's
reach—he would wound a father's heart through the
sides of his children.

Placed on probation, man looked, lusted, ate, sinned,
and fell.   Satan triumphed.   With the ruins of Eden
around him, he stood above the grave of human hopes,
and, as it seemed also, of heaven's intentions.   He
contemplated with proud satisfaction the triumph of
his malignant subtilty.   As he wrung the first tears

from human eyes, I can fancy how he taunted his weeping victims with the question—"Where is now thy God?" Pharaoh, ere God had done with him, and he with God, got his question answered—"Who is the Lord, that I should obey his voice?" And the Devil got his answered, too. When the fullness of time has come, in a son of that woman Satan meets her God, to find in him not a match only, but a Master.

When his vessel has broken in the storm, and Ajax stands unsheltered on a rock in mid-ocean, he is represented as in anger with the gods, shaking his clenched hand at heaven. In Eden, for a time at least, Satan stands in a different and prouder position; he has conquered; he has won the victory; who shall pluck it from his grasp? He tramples on earth, and laughs at heaven. Although on a grander scale, and involving much grander issues, the scene reminds us of the day when—with the Philistines clustered on this mountain, and Israel on that—there stalked out into the narrow valley, Goliath, the pride of Gath, a moving tower, terrible to look on, in height six cubits and a span. High above his dancing plume, the giant shakes a spear, shafted like a weaver's beam, and thunders up this challenge to the trembling host— "Am not I a Philistine? I defy the armies of Israel this day. Give me a man that we may fight together."

So Satan stood, in bold defiance and unchallenged possession of the field; and now God might have left man to reap the full harvest of his sin and folly—to drink the cup which his own hands had filled. In the words of Scripture, He had entered into "a covenant with death;" he had been at an "agreement with hell;" --let him reap as he has sowed. But what then?

Why, Satan then would at least have seemed to have the advantage—would have seemed to be a match for God; and have boasted ability and skill enough, by his own wiles, to thwart the purposes of eternal wisdom. In that event, all men should have perished; but in that event, would Jehovah's power have stood out as unchallengeable, or his glory as clear, as at this day? No. God had another end in view in permitting this temporary triumph. Why does he permit it?

Observe yon skillful wrestler! He embraces his antagonist, and, with athletic power, lifting him from the ground, he holds him aloft; ah! but he raises, to dash him back on the earth with a more crushing fall. So fared it with the Evil One. God permits him to scale the walls, to carry the citadel by assault, and to plant for a time his defiant standard on the battlements of this world. He does this, that from his proud eminence he may hurl him into a deeper hell; and, angels rejoicing in man's salvation, and devils discomfited in their leader's defeat—both friends and foes—might be constrained to say, "Hast thou an arm like God, or canst thou thunder with a voice like his?" From this, believer! when providences are of darkest, and thou canst not trace the footsteps of thy God, learn to place unquestioning confidence in his ways and wisdom.

While God is glorified by Satan's defeat, he is glorified also by the very time and manner of it.

You ask, why did four thousand years elapse between the promise and the promised One? I may reply, by asking you, why does this accomplished racer, who stands abreast of his competitor, not start along with him? Why, lingering by the starting post, does he give his opponent a long advantage? and then, springing forward on the feet of the wind, approach him, pass him, leave him lagging far behind? Why, but to prove more plainly his own superiority, and embitter the bitterness of an antagonist's defeat. Or, we may ask you, why, when the news of his friend's illness was carried to Galilee, did our Lord tarry there, nor, hurrying through Samaria, hasten to the relief of Lazarus? He does not even arrive just when the breath has left, and ere the form of him he loved is yet stiff and cold in death. He leaves Lazarus to die. He leaves Lazarus to be buried. He leaves Lazarus to lie four days rotting in the grave. Why this strange delay? why, but that at the door of the dead man's tomb he might stand forth, not only the conqueror of death, but Lord also of the grave.

On the alarm of war, the news fly through the land, beacon fires are blazing on every hill and headland, and before one hostile foot has touched the soil, hurrying from shepherd's hut and peasant's cottage, lonely glens and crowded cities, freemen line the beach to fight a country's enemies on a country's shores. In the great battle of redemption there is no such haste. Not for four days, nor even four years, but for the long period of four thousand years, Satan is left in all but undisputed possession of his conquest. God leaves him ample time to entrench himself; to found, to strengthen, to establish, to extend his kingdom. And why? but that a Redeemer's power might be the more apparent in its ignominious and total overthrow. And in this, Christ glorified himself; just as we should do, were we to leave the sapling in possession of the soil until it grew into a tree, and then, bending on it more than a giant's strength, should lay its head, and pride, and glory, in the dust. As a Redeemer, Jesus

Christ was to show himself to be the "Power" as well as the "Wisdom" of God. This is the manner of redemption. And may I not take occasion from it to tell the oldest, hardest, most hoary sinner, to hope, and turn to God? He has left you long; He has left you till now; He has left you amid the infirmities of years to grow stronger in sin. Despair not! nor think that he has shut the door of mercy! What if he has left you so long, just to show how he can save at the very uttermost,—call at the eleventh hour,— and by the breath of his Spirit cause "dry bones" to live.

God is not only glorified in Satan's defeat, and also in the time and manner of it, but pre-eminently glorified in the instrument of it.

He was no veteran, the giant's match in years, experience, stature, or strength, who defeated Goliath. When the battle between the two nations was fought by their respective champions, fire flew not from opposing swords, nor were spears shivered on opposing shields; the valley shook not beneath the tread and collision of two giants; nor did victory hang in the balance, and anxious partisans endure the agony of suspense on confronting mountains, while the air resounded with the clash of arms, and blood gushed from gaping wounds. Never to appearance were there two men more unequaly matched. When the lines of Israel opened, and a youth, a beardless lad, clad in a shepherd's dress, with no weapon but a sling, and no confidence but God in heaven, stepped forth to measure his strength with the giant, loud laughed the Philistine, and wit ran merrily through his countrymen's ranks. Ere one brief hour had run its course, they wept that laughed, and they laughed that wept. He who guides the sun in his path in heaven, guided the stone as, winged with death, and winged by prayer, it shot from the whirling sling. It sung from the shepherd's hand; sank into the giant's brow; he reels, he staggers—and his armor making a mighty clash—he measures his long length upon the ground. Bounding like a young lion, David leaps upon his prey, and, leaving a headless carcass to feed the vultures, he returns to the ranks of shouting countrymen—in this hand, the giant's sword, in that other, his gory head. Old men bless the lad, and young men envy him, and happy mothers and laughing maidens sing his fame; and ere that day's sun has set, there is music, and dancing, and feasting in the homes of Israel.

That bright day was but the type of a brighter still, on which God glorified himself, mortified and scattered his enemies, and restored a fallen house to more than its ancient honors. Man falls; the world is lost; Satan triumphs. How does God pluck the victory from his hands? He might have discharged thunderbolts on his head; he might have overwhelmed this enemy by sending down upon him legions of embattled angels. It is not so. He meets him, matches him, masters him by a solitary Man. Beneath the heel of a Man of sorrows he crushes the serpent's head. A Son of man is the Saviour of man; a brother rises up in our house to redeem his brethren; a Conqueror appears in the conquered family. Out of the mouth of a Suckling—by One nursed on a woman's bosom, and carried in a woman's arms—he ordaineth strength. Never was the tide of battle so strangely, so completely, so triumphantly turned. The Babe of a cradle

8

wears the crown of the universe; and by One who died, God destroys "death, and him that had the power of death, that is, the devil."

"Give thanks then unto the Lord, for he is good; for his mercy endureth for ever. Oh give thanks unto the God of Gods; for his mercy endureth for ever. Oh give thanks unto the Lord of Lords; for his mercy endureth for ever; who remembered us in our low estate, and hath redeemed us from our enemies. Oh give thanks unto the God of heaven, for his mercy endureth for ever."

The Benefits flowing from Redemption.

I will take you from among the heathen, and gather you out of all countries, and bring you into your own land.—EZEKIEL xxxvi. 24.

MEN'S chief end is to glorify God; and God's chief end is to glorify himself. While that is an end worthy of the great Creator, it goes greatly to enlarge our interest in his works, and enhance their value in our eyes. That end gives loftiness to the humblest of them. When I know that for his own glory he paints each flower, gives the fish its silver scales, and sends forth the beetle armed in mail of gold, his creatures rise in my esteem. It may look a sickly fancy, but one almost feels reluctant to destroy the humblest flower or insect, lest we should silence one of the ten thousand voices which form the choir of nature, and swell the praises of nature's God. Is there a child whose heart does not warm towards him who praises an earthly father, or speaks honorably of the good man's memory? Now, the very same feeling inclines a child of God to love all the works that do his Father honor; and of all men he cannot fail to enjoy the most exquisite pleasure in the beauties of nature, who carries to her fields a pious spirit, and sees his Father mirrored in them all; hears his praise sung in the voices of groves, or pealed in the roar of thunder. Such was the spirit of one—a venerable patriarch—who shed on a very humble station the luster of bril liant graces. When the storm sent others in haste to their homes, he was wont to leave his own, and to stand with upturned face, raised eye, and with his gray head uncovered, to watch the flash, and listen to the music of the roaring thunder. How fine his reply to those who expressed their wonder at his aspect and attitude—"It's my Father's voice, and I like well to hear it." What a sublime example of the perfect love that casteth out fear! "Happy is that people that is in such a case, yea happy is that people whose God is the Lord."

Now, as it ennobles nature—so that the sun shines more bright, and the flowers look more beautiful, and there is a grander majesty in the rolling sea—when we know that God does all things for his own glory, it greatly enhances the preciousness of salvation to know, that in the kingdom of grace also he has the same end in view. If God saves—not because we deserve mercy—but that his own great mercy may be illustrated in saving, ah! then there is hope for me—Yes, although thou wert an adulterer, a thief, a murderer, the vile wretch who spit in Jesus' face, the ruffian who forced the thorny crown deep into his bleeding brow, although thou wert that very soldier who buried the lance in Jesus' side, and just returning from Calvary, with the blood of Christ's heart red on the spear head, I would stop thee in thy way to say, there is hope for thee. Oh, this has inspired with hope souls which had otherwise despaired, and gilded the edges of guilt's darkest cloud. In circumstances where we would have been dumb—opening not the mouth—when called to the dying bed of vilest, lowest sin, it has unsealed our lips, and lent wings to prayer. Of the preacher, whose walk lies among the most wretched, hopeless, and abandoned, this truth says, since God saves for his own glory, haste, "loose him, and let him go"—go to offer Christ (as I do to-day) to the chief of sinners; like a sunbeam passing undefiled through the foulest atmosphere, go in thy heavenly purity where the basest of thy race is perishing, nor shrink from this loathsome guilt, but with Jesus' pity and Jesus' tears, lift up her dying head, and in the mercy of God in Christ, let her drink this wine of love out of its cup of gold. If the worse a patient is, if the fiercer his fever burns, if the deeper his wound has penetrated, so much the greater is the glory of the physician who cures him; then the worse a sinner is, the greater Christ's glory when he saves him. But for this, that God in every case saves men, not out of regard to their merit, but his own glory, what could sustain the faith of him who, in preaching the gospel to unconverted men, has to run his horses on a rock, and ploughs there with oxen; to sow the seed of God's blessed word under the most unfavorable circumstances; to write sermons for dead men, and preach them to dry bones. Nothing but faith in this could carry us to the top of Carmel, not seven, but seventy times seven, to look out over the sea of God's mercy for the cloud of blessing, and wait till it rise, and spread over the heavens, and discharge its treasures on a barren land. "Seeing we have this ministry we faint not."

Having already attempted to show how God glorifies himself in redemption, we shall now address ourselves to the subject-matter of the text, where we are taught that redemption brings good to man as well as glory to God. And it appears from the text—

I In carrying out the work of redemption, God will call his people out of the world. "I will take you from among the heathen."

By nature his people are no better than other people. They were no better till grace made them so. The Apostle settles the point by the question, "Who maketh thee to differ from another?" and the confession, "By the grace of God I am what I am." And our Lord teaches the same doctrine in these brief but expressive parables—"Two women are grinding at the mill; one is taken, and another left." "Two men are in one field; the one is taken, and the other left." "Two men are in one bed; one is taken, and another left." Christ states the truth, and how often does Providence supply the commentary? Here are two children; they were born of one mother; nestled in one bosom; rocked in one cradle; baptized in one font; they were reared under the same roof; grew up under the same training; sat under the same ministry; and in death not divided, they are sleeping together in the same grave. But the one is taken, and the other left. This, a child of God, ascends to heaven; the other, alas! is lost. Who dare challenge the justice of God? Mysterious subject! He will have mercy on whom he will have mercy. The wind bloweth where it listeth, and thou hearest the sound thereof, but canst not tell whence it cometh, and whither it goeth; so is every one that is born of the Spirit.

The truth is, that by nature this world is sunk in sin, and all men are in a sense idolaters. In the days of old, it is said that Egypt had more gods than men. Elsewhere than in Egypt, every where, as the Bible says, "there be lords many and gods many." The Hindoo reckons his divinities by thousand and tens of thousands; but the world has a larger Pantheon—as many gods as it has objects, be they innocent or guilty, which usurp the place of Jehovah, and dethrone him in the creature's heart. Nor are men less idolaters if drunkards, though they pour out no libation to Bacchus—the god of wine; nor less idolaters, if impure, that they burn no incense at the shrine of Venus; nor less idolaters, if lovers of wealth, that they do not mold their gold into an image of Plutus, and, giving a shrine to what lies hoarded in their coffers, offer it their morning and evening prayers. He has been an idolater, who, rebelling against Providence, follows the hearse of a coffined god; he made an idol of wife or child; and now, when the robber of our homes has stolen them away, and bears them off to the grave, the feelings of that man's heart may be expressed in Micah's complaint to the Danite robbers, "Ye have taken away my gods which I made, and what have I more? and what is this that ye say unto me, What aileth thee?" Since man, therefore, in his natural state, is—although not in fact—in spirit as much an idolater as the pagans of any heathen land, may it not be justly said of all who have been converted by the grace of God, that he has "taken them from among the heathen?"

II. The power of divine grace is strikingly displayed in this effectual calling.

It is a remarkable fact, that while the baser metals are often diffused through the body of the rocks, gold and silver lie in veins—collected together in distinct metallic masses. They are *in* the rocks, but not *of* the rocks. Some believe that there was a time, long gone by, when—like the other metals—these lay in intimate union with the mass of rock, until, by virtue of some mysterious electric agency, their scattered atoms were put in motion, and, being made to pass through the solid stone, were aggregated in those shining veins, where they now lie to the miner's hand. Gold and silver are the emblems of God's people. And as by some power in nature God has separated these emblems from the base and common earths, even so by the power of his grace he will separate all his chosen from a reprobate and rejected world. They shall come at his call; He will "say to the north, Give up; and to the south, Keep not back; bring my sons from afar, and my daughters from the ends of the earth." The corruption of nature, circumstances of temptation, an evil world, the hostility of hell, all interpose between his purpose and the objects of his mercy. The difficulties in the way tower up into a mountain! Fear not. God will make up the number of his chosen ones. "Who art thou, O great mountain, before Zerubbabel thou shalt become a plain."

His grace shall prove sufficient for the work. No doubt it has a great work to do. Think from what an abominable life and from what abandoned company God calls some to grace on earth and glory in heaven. Look at this Manasseh or at that Magdalene. How different their Sabbaths now from what once they were! How different their society now from the associates with whom once, in mad and frantic dance, they went whirling round the mouth of the burning pit! Another, and another, and another plunge into the abyss, and they drown the lost one's perishing cry in louder music; and in giddier whirl they dance on, as little deterred by the fate of their fellows, as the in-

sects that on an autumn evening dash one upon an
other into the flame of our candle. Ah, when God's
saints look down from their elevation into the depths
where grace descended and found them, and from
whence it raised them, they are not satisfied to sing,
"He raiseth up the poor out of the dust, and lifteth
up the beggar from the dung-hill, to set them among
princes, and to make them inherit the thrones of
glory;" they tune their harp-strings to a higher
strain. Lost in wonder, love, and praise, they are
ready to adopt the words which a humble-minded but
eminent Christian insisted should be engraved upon
her tombstone—"How great is thy mercy toward
me." "Thou hast delivered my soul from the lowest
hell?" It is in a state of deep ungodliness—without
God, without the love of God, without the holiness
that shall see God, without true purity of heart or
peace of conscience—that grace finds all it saves.
Such is not the judgment of the world. And I do
not deny but that many are very lovely in the bloom
and beauty of natural virtue—so beautiful, that we
cannot help loving them. Is there sin in that? No;
for Jesus loved the young ruler who yet refused to
follow him. But then, with much that is attractive in
the graces of the natural man, they have the same
nature, and lie under the same condemnation, as a
world that liveth in wickedness, and lieth under sen-
tence of death. An old writer has said that "man in
his natural state is half a devil and half a beast."
How wonderful the grace which changes such a
monster into the image of God, and converts the
basest metal into the purest gold!

It is indeed amazing to see what grace will do, and
where grace will grow; in what unlikely places God

has his people, and out of what unlikely circumstances he calls them. I have seen a tree crowning the summit of a naked rock; and there it stood—in search of food sending its roots out over the bare stone, and down into every cranny—securely anchored by these moorings to the stormy crag. We have wondered how it grew up there, amid such rough nursing, how it could have survived many a wintry blast, and where, indeed, it found food or footing. Yet, like one familiar with hardship and adversities, it has grown and lived; it has kept its feet when the pride of the valley has bent to the storm; and, like brave men, who think not of yielding, but nail their colors to the mast, it has maintained its proud position, and kept its green flag waving on nature's topmost battlements.

More wonderful than this, however, is it to see where the grace of God will live and grow. Tender exotic! plant brought from a more genial clime! one would suppose that it would require the kindliest nursing and most propitious circumstances; yet look here—A Daniel is bred for God, and for the bravest services in his cause, in no pious home of Israel; he grows in saintship amid the impurities and effeminacy of a heathen palace. Paul was a persecutor, and is called to be a preacher—was a murderer, and becomes a martyr; once, no pharisee so proud, now no publican so humble. Like those fabled monsters, which, sailing on broad and scaly wings, descended on their helpless prey with streams of fire issuing from their formidable mouths, he set off for Damascus, "breathing out threatenings and slaughter against the disciples of the Lord." Jesus descended in person to meet this formidable persecutor, and selected him for

his chiefest apostle. He bids him wash the blood of
Stephen from his hands, and go preach the gospel.
And where afterwards has this very man some of his
most devoted friends? where, but in Cæsar's house-
hold. What can more strikingly express the power
of all-sufficient grace than the words of John Newton?
One asked him whether he thought the heathen could
be converted. "I have never doubted," he said,
"that God could convert the heathen, since he con-
verted me."

"Never despair" should be the motto of the Chris-
tian; and how should it keep hope alive under the
darkest and most desponding circumstances, to see
God calling grace out of the foulest sin? Look at
this cold creeping worm! Playful childhood shrinks
shuddering from its touch; yet a few weeks, and with
merry laugh and flying feet, that same childhood,
over flowery meadow is hunting an insect that never
lights upon the ground, but—flitting in painted beauty
from flower to flower—drinks nectar from their cups,
and sleeps the summer night away in the bosom of
their perfumes. If that is the same boy, this is no less
the self-same creature. Change most wonderful! yet
but a dull, earthly emblem of the divine transforma-
tion wrought on those, who are "transformed by the
renewing of their minds." Gracious, glorious change!
Have you felt it? May it be felt by all of us! You
have it here in this woman, who, grieved in her mind,
lies a-weeping at the feet of Jesus. She was a sinner.
Her condition had been the basest; her bread the bit-
terest; her company the worst. She is casting off her
vile, sinful slough. She leaves it. She rises a new
creature. The beauty of the Lord is on her; and
now, with wings of faith and love wide outspread, she

follows her Lord to heaven. How encouraging the wonders of converting grace! Let us despair of none —neither of ourselves nor any one else.

III. God will make up the number of his people. "I will gather you out of all countries." There are some gatherings in this world which are largely alloyed with pain. Christmas or some birthday season comes round, summoning the members of a scattered family. The circle is again formed; but, like that of men who have been standing under fire, and closing up their ranks, how is it contracted from former years! There are well-remembered faces, and voices, and forms, that are missing here; and the family group, which looks down from the picture, is larger than the living company met at table. Some are dead and gone—"Joseph is not, and Simeon is not;" and a dark cloud hangs on a mother's brow, for on the cheek of yet another her anxious eye, quick to see, discovers an ominous spot that threatens to "take Benjamin away."

There is a gathering, also, when, at the close of a hard-fought day, the roll of the regiment is called, and to familiar names there comes back no answer. How small the band who meet at night compared with the morning muster! As the day wore on, and the ranks grew thinner, and the "red line" grew less and less, they came back from each charge like a wave broken on an iron shore, and every shock they stood, and charge which they repelled, left broad gaps to fill. And so, now when the fight is over, and the broken hosts muster on the field, to many a gallant man in vain the trumpet sounds, or war-pipe blows the gathering of the clan. Alas, for the day! They shall answer no trumpet but that which calls a world to judgment.

When daylight breaks on the shore of the ship-wreck, there is also a mustering and reckoning of numbers. There, a mother clasps and kisses the living babe which the waves had plucked from her arms, and she never thought more to see; and here, a true brother cheers the boy whom he held in a grasp strong as death, while, with the other hand buffeting the billows, he bore him safely to the beach. But others, less fortunate, are wringing their hands in the wildness of their grief. Distracted mothers cry, " Where is my child?" Some, with the dead on their knees, sit stunned by sorrow; frightful to look upon! speechless, tearless, motionless, as if turned into stone; while others, wild, raving, frantic, stand on the shores of the 'devouring sea, and, stamping on its sands, demand back their dead.

These are mournful musterings; and in striking contrast to them is this gathering on Melita's shore :— It was a frightful storm; the coast unknown; the ship grounds in deep water, with nigh three hundred souls on board; the night before, the boats had been cut adrift, and now not a boat—if boats could live in such a swell—to save them. The swimmers, who strip and plunge into the sea, may perchance reach the shore, but none else shall cheat the deep of its prey. Yet, when there is not another head among the billows— when the last surviver has climbed the beach—they muster; and soldiers, sailors, and prisoners—all are there. Paul got their lives, and not one has gone amissing. "Some on boards, and some on broken pieces of the ship;" but, by whatever way it came to

pass, it did come to pass, as the narrative tells—
"they escaped all safe to land."

Even so shall it be with those of whom Jesus says,
" I give unto them eternal life, and they shall never
perish. My Father that gave them me is greater than
all, and no man is able to pluck them out of my
Father's hand." Happy those who sail in the ship,
and have embarked in the same cause with Christ.
What they have committed to him, he will keep until
the great day. And when all earthly schemes are
foundered, and life itself becomes a wreck—plunging
us amid the billows of eternity's shore—and this old
world itself is broken up like a worn out and stranded
ship—then, at the last day's muster, all who are
Christ's shall be there, not one of them shall be amiss-
ing; sooner or later, all shall reach the heavenly
coast. "The Lord knoweth them that are his;" and
"all that his Father hath given him he shall keep."

But my text tells us not only that He will gather
his people, but gather them "out of all countries." Let
those mark that, who, indulging an extravagant pa-
triotism, or in the narrow spirit of bigotry, allow them-
selves to "limit the Holy One of Israel," and are ready
to say with the Jews of old, "We are the people of
the Lord; the temple of the Lord are we." "We have
Abraham to our father." Alas! we are all too prone
to think that we stand allied to Jesus in closer rela-
tionship than others, even as Benjamin to Joseph
others may be brothers, ours is a closer brotherhood;
we are not only father's but mother's sons. Now, we
are patriotic enough to hope much for our country—
for a land like ours, which has been crimsoned with
precious blood, consecrated by prayers, and whose
almost every mountain, as Rutherfurd said, "has been

flowered with martyrs." We sympathise, also, with
domestic affection; and the hope that families—so dear
to us as our own—shall rise from the place of many
graves to dwell together in the house of many man-
sions. Still, heaven, like the starry firmament which
encompasses our globe, is as near other countries as
our own. God has people where we look not for them,
and know not of them. A hundred prophets are se-
creted in Obadiah's cave; and when Elijah, wrapped
in his mantle, stands before the God of the storm and
calm, and the "still small voice," complaining, "they
have slain thy prophets, and I, even I only am left,'
he is surprised to be told of seven thousand in Israel,
as true men as he, who have not bowed the knee to
Baal. We may be astonished to miss some in heaven
whom we calculated on meeting there, we shall be
astonished to see some there whom we never expected.

The gospel belongs to no country, but to all. Every
sea is not paved with pearl shells; nor does every
soil grow vines and palms, nor does every mine sparkle
with gems, nor do the streams of every land roll
their waters over golden sands. These symbols of
grace have a narrow range; but not grace herself.
She owns no lines of latitude or longitude. All cli-
mates are one to her. She wears no party badge; and
belongs neither to class nor color. She takes no ob-
jection to a negro's skin. He, whom his white op-
pressor refused to worship with, eat with, sail with,
or dwell with on earth, shall dwell, and worship, and
reign where his master may never be; and when—
as may often happen—the white skin is shut out,
and the black man, now and for ever free, passes in
at the celestial gate, it shall furnish but another illus-
tration of the truth, that salvation is "not of blood,

nor of the will of the flesh, nor of the will of man,
but of God."

With this truth, as by a zone of love, elastic enough
to be stretched round the globe, we would bind man-
kind together.   Let it awaken in Christian hearts an
interest and an affection for every land.   Humanity
rejoices with piety in the prospects that it opens.   The
distant natives of the Poles and Equator shall be asso-
ciated in heaven ; they who have never met on earth
shall meet there ; and they who never could agree on
earth shall agree there ; the desire of our hearts shall
be accomplished there ; and there those who, scowled
at by bigots, and pitied by many as amiable vision-
aries, have sought a closer union among God's children
here, shall have their fondest wishes gratified.   From
the dreadful wars that now shake the earth, and the
hardly less painful battle-fields of churches, it is a
pleasant change to contemplate this general assembly,
where—Jesus himself presiding—the representatives
of all nations, tribes, languages, sects, and parties, are
met to sing the jubilee of universal peace, and cele-
brate the funeral of all their differences.   Over that
grave no tears are shed ; beside it no pale mourners
stand ; all quarrels and controversies, with their wea-
pons of war, are now for ever buried—buried without
fear of resurrection, and above it heaven rises, a temple
dedicated to eternal concord, "whose builder and maker
is God."

Dishonored often in the present time by their quar-
rels, and always by their separation, Jesus shall then
be glorified in all his saints.   It is the dust and the
rust which the liquid mercury has contracted that im-
pair the beauty of its luster, and prevent the union of
its divided globules.   And what is it but earthly con-

taminations and unworthy passions that keep true Christians apart. From these let them be purified by the genial fires of love, or the sharp fires of suffering, and union will follow—follow as when the purified globules of quicksilver, brought into contact, run into each other's embraces to form one shining and brilliant mass. May God give his divine Spirit of love and unity for such a blessed end—a consummation so devoutly to be wished for. The prophecy fulfilled which foretells such an union, then, the redeemed of the cross, and elect of God, shall make up a countless company, one which no man can number—multitudes and myriads—offering such a contrast to the handful who follow the steps of the Man of sorrows, that we shall hear these words no more—"Ye are a little flock."

"He cometh, he cometh to judge the earth;" and how? after what manner? in what royal state? "Behold he cometh with clouds"—clouds, that on their nearer approach to earth, when the general mass shall resolve itself into individual objects, may be found to consist of innumerable hosts of winged and shining angels. On that great occasion, the saints—countless as the atoms that float in the vapors of the sky, or the drops that fall in its showers—shall also form, to use Paul's expression, "a cloud of witnesses." Already they form a cloud in heaven; and to the eye of faith it is as those nebulous spots, which, by their great distance, shine only with a faint luminosity far away in the depths of the starry firmament, but which, under the eye and instruments of the astronomer, are resolved into a countless aggregate of burning suns.

IV. We are assured that God will bring all his peo

ple to glory, by the fact that his own honor, as well as their welfare, is concerned in the matter.

In that lay the salvation of ancient Israel. "How long will this people provoke me? I will smite them with the pestilence, and disinherit them; and I will make of thee a greater nation and mightier than they." Thus spake the Lord to Moses, and how did he reply? He had certainly a great temptation to make no reply and let things take their course, since the issue would bring him and his such great advantage. Type of the Saviour, he flung himself between justice and her culprits. He ventures to remonstrate with God. He sets himself to show, that the destruction of Israel—although the just punishment of their sins—might militate against God's declarative honor, and expose it to suspicion; and that, therefore, although he could not spare them for their sakes, he should spare them for his own. Moses was concerned for the fate of his countrymen. Like a true patriot, he declined to rise on their ruins; but more deeply concerned still for the honor of God, he takes courage to reply, "Then the Egyptian shall hear it, and they will tell it to the inhabitants of this land. Now if thou shalt kill all this people as one man, then the nations which have heard of thee will speak, saying, Because the Lord was not able to bring this people into the land which he sware unto them, therefore he had slain them in the wilderness."

As it was then, so is it now. God's honor, and truth, and covenant, are all concerned—are, so to speak, compromised to make good the promise, that he will bring his redeemed to glory. It is, indeed, no easy work to bring believers safe to glory. When I think of the sins to be forgiven, and the difficulties to be overcome, the wonder seems not that few get to heaven, but that any get there. We have read of voyages, where for nights the sailors enjoyed no sleep, and for days saw no sun. Lying at one time becalmed beneath a fiery sky, at another time shivering amid fields of ice; with sunken rocks around them, and treacherous currents sweeping them on dangerous reefs; exposed to sudden squalls, long, dark nights, and fearful tempests, the wonder was that their battered ship ever reached the port. I select a case of recent occurrence. Some while ago a vessel entered one of our western harbors, and the town poured out to see. Well they might. It had left the American shore with a large, able-bodied crew. They have hardly lost sight of land when the pestilence boards them; victim falls after victim; another and another is committed to the deep, as from deck to deck, and yard to yard she pursues her prey; nor does she spread her wings to leave that ill-fated ship, till she has left but two to work it over the broad waters of a wintry sea. And when, with Providence at the helm, these two men, worn by work and watching to ghastly skeletons, have brought their ship to land, and now kiss once more wives and little ones they never thought more to see, and step once more on a green earth they never more hoped to touch, men run to see the sight, and hear the adventures of a voyage brought against such dreadful odds to such a happy issue.

Yet there is never a bark drops anchor in heaven, nor a weary voyager steps out on its celestial strand, but is a still greater wonder. Save for the assurance that what God hath begun He will finish—that what concerns his people He will perfect—Oh, how often would our hope of final blessedness altogether expire.

Well might David say, "I had fainted unless I had believed." And knowing what we know, and feeling what we feel, how entirely may we acquiesce in the old remark, that the greatest wonder we shall see in heaven, shall be to see ourselves there.

Yet let Christians take comfort. Your good and God's glory ever run in the same direction. They are the parallel rails on which the chariot of salvation rolls. They shall bring you to the Jerusalem above. To compare small things with great, our journey there, with its dangers and changes, has sometimes appeared to me like that of a passenger to our own city. On these iron roads he now travels along rich and fertile plains; now, at a dangerous and dizzy height he flies across intervening valleys; now, he rushes through a narrow gorge cut in the solid rock, with nothing seen but heaven; now, boring into the earth, he dashes into some gaping cavern, for a while losing sight even of heaven itself, and then again he sweeps forth and on in sunshine, till at length the domes, and towers, and temples of the city burst on his view. And, these close at hand, he concludes his journey by passing through an emblem of death. He enters a gloomy arch, advances in darkness through a place of graves, and then, of a sudden, emerges into day, to feast his eyes on the glorious scenery, and receive the congratulations of waiting friends, as he finds himself safe "in the midst of the city."

Man Justified.

Then will I sprinkle clean water upon you, and ye shall be clean: from all your filthiness, and from all your idols, will I cleanse you.— Ezekiel xxxvi. 25.

In the earliest peopled regions of the world, there still stand some ancient monuments, bold in plan, and colossal in dimensions, defying both time and change. Raised, as these rude structures were, in the very infancy of art, and ere the giant arms of machinery had grown into their present strength, they are objects of deep interest, both to the architect and antiquary. How came these great stones there? By what means or machinery did man, in days so rude, raise such ponderous masses?

Science has questions as inexplicable to put regarding the works of nature. We climb a mountain range, and, standing on its apex, see valley and plain stretching far away to meet the ocean, that lies, gleaming, like a silver border, on the dim and distant horizon. After expatiating on the beauties of the scene around us, our eye turns downwards, and lights on a very extraordinary object—a shell—a plant—a zoophite, whose proper *habitat* is the low sea-shore—or, lower still, down in the dark depths of ocean—embedded in the rock. How came it here? what business has it here? We find, in fact, that, although now raised some thousand feet above the sea, the platform on which we stand had once been an ocean's bed. And he would be a stupid man, in whose mind the question would not rise, what agent, of tremendous power was that, which, upheaving the crust of earth, has turned the floor of a sea, where corals grew, and fish swam, into a mountain crag whereon eagles build their nests.

In the Providence which determines the lot of man, history presents subjects not less interesting. It is a curious thing how a sea shell came to be embedded in the summit of a mountain crag. It is even a curious thing to watch the progress of a worm, as it climbs up tree or wall to the place of its apparent death and beautiful resurrection. It is still more interesting to see a man fighting, toiling, tearing his way up from the bottom, to the sunny but often cold and stormy pinnacles of society; so that, perhaps, when dead, he, whose birth a cottage saw, lies in state within a palace. There are all manner of ways by which men rise in the world. Some, flung up by national convulsions, rise like the fire stones shot from a volcano's mouth; they flare for a little, and then are lost in night. Some, like sea-weed or an empty shell, are thrown up by the wave of popular agitation, only by its reflux to be swept back again into oblivion. Some rise in times of trouble and of turmoil, like the dust and light straws of the whirlwind; the lighter they are the more sure are they to rise. Some ascend by the foul and slippery path of crime, rising on other men's shoulders, and building dishonest fortunes on honest men's ruin. While some,—being amid all the mysteries of Providence, witnesses that there is a just God upon earth,—illustrate the adage of the world, "Honesty is the best policy," and the still better saying of Scripture, "Godliness is profitable unto all things, having promise of the life that now is, and of that which is to come." But there is no rising so interesting to study, or by those who are fired with a holy ambition, so blessed to emulate, as that of a sinner into a saint—of a soul to glory. That man, however, enjoys one of the charms of history, and reads one of the strangest chapters in the book of Providence, who traces the successive steps by which great actors in the theatre of this world have mounted to fame and fortune out of the deepest obscurity.

To us there are inquiries of greater interest than any of these. Few rise from cottages to be kings— nor are such giddy elevations desirable ; most men fall and are crushed before they reach the top of their ambition, and the few who have reached it have learned that " uneasy lies the head that wears a crown." It is of little moment to me, how this base-born but brave peasant reached a throne ; but to me it is every thing to know how this sinner became a saint, and from being the slave of Satan and very drudge of sin rose to a crown in heaven—to be a king and priest to God. If I am engrossed with the momentous interests of eternity, and have not yet made my calling sure, but am still lying in the anxieties and darkness of spiritual distress, it will be of little importance to me, how the shell, which once lay in the depths of ocean, has been raised into the light and regions of the sunny air, but to me it is every thing to know, how I, lying buried beneath the wrath of God, can be raised to the sunshine of his peace and favor. To me the question is of the highest importance, which the elder put to John, when, pointing to the multitude whom no man can number, " who stood before the throne and before the Lamb, clothed with white robes,

and palms in their hands," he said, " who are these,
and whence came they?" I am deeply interested to
know by what means these, each one—originally like
myself—a being of sin and guilt, escaped the wrath
of God, and rose to such lofty favor? Recognizing
in that company, one, and another, and yet another—
who were the chief of sinners, I take heart to say, if
they got up there, why should not I? The door that
was wide enough and high enough for them, can not
be too strait or low for me. These questions, in other
words, how does God save the sinner? and what am
I to do to be saved?—questions, the most important
which you can ask, or I can attempt to answer, are
those at which, in the progress of these discourses, we
are now arrived.

I intend, God helping me, to set forth the means by
which He who is most willing to save sinners, accom-
complishes his generous and gracious purpose. I am
now to show you that famous breach by which the
soldiers of the cross, led on by their Captain, with
banners flying and sword in hand, have taken the
kingdom, and, trampling under foot the body of sin,
have entered into glory with holy violence. We are
now to look upon that famous ladder which the hand
of God has let down from heaven, and by which Abel,
and Adam, and Enoch, and Noah, and Abraham, and
Jacob, and Daniel, and Peter, and Paul, and the
Marys, and Dorcas, and Phœbe—martyrs and confess-
ors, prophets and saints—pressing on each other's
heels, have scaled the walls of glory, and entered into
possession of the celestial city. And now, as the angel
who had blown the coal and baked the bread beside
the lonely sleeper—for such things angels will do for
saints—woke Elijah and said to him, "rise and eat;"

with this ladder within your reach—you at its foot, and heaven at its top—I say, rise and climb. What meanest thou, O sleeper? What do you sleeping there? The slightest turn, and you roll over into the pit, on whose dreadful edge sinners make their bed Rouse up, look up, rise and climb; God helping you by faith, lay hold of Him who says—"I am the Way, the Truth, and the Life."

In entering on the subject of a sinner's justification, I remark—

I. God's people are not chosen because they are holy.

They are chosen that they may become holy, not because they have become so. It is after God elects that God justifies, as it is after he has justified that he sanctifies. This appears—stands out—most visibly in the very terms of the text, "*then* will I sprinkle clean water upon you." Do not, I pray you, suppose that we disparage holiness. In the doctrines of grace holiness holds a most important place; a place so important—so prominent and conspicuous—that the notion, once current, that the doctrine of a free salvation through the mercy of God and the merits of Christ alone is unfavorable to the interests of morality, can only be ascribed to the malice of the natural heart, or the grossest ignorance. These doctrines set forth the love of Christ as a believer's great motive power, and it might be a sufficient refutation of the calumny to quote the glowing exclamation of the poet—

> "Thou bleeding Lamb !
> The best morality is love of Thee."

But what place in the scheme of grace do we assign

Q

to holiness? what language do we hold regarding it? We say that without holiness no man shall see God. Could more be asked or said than that? We say so to all men—to the sovereign on his throne we say, Without holiness thou shalt never wear a crown in heaven; to the minister in his pulpit we say, Without holiness thou shalt never minister before the Throne—thou mayst save others, but shalt be thyself a castaway; to the communicant at the Lord's table we say, Without holiness thou shalt never sit at the marriage supper of the Lamb; thou mayst drink of the juice of the grape—but shalt never drink the new wine of his "Father's kingdom;" we say to all, "If any man have not the spirit of Christ, he is none of his." You may have his name; but that is worth nothing; unless with the name you have the nature of Him who was holy, harmless, and undefiled. Grace may make you his; but whatever you may become, you are not so now, unless there be germinating in you the mind of Him who was holiness in the flesh—incarnate virtue. We ever echo the exhortation of the Apostle, "Be careful to maintain good works."

This is surely no lax or immoral creed. So far from holding good works cheap, we say that by them God is glorified, by them faith is justified, and, by them on the great day of judgment shall every man be tried. You are not to be justified by your works, but you are to be tried by them. The rule of that day shall be this—"the tree is known by his fruit." "Every tree which bringeth not forth good fruit is hewn down and cast into the fire." Are any of you, then, living in sin—known, habitual, cherished sin—and yet in hope? Oh, how great is your mistake! You may be saved *from* your sins, you cannot be

saved *in* your sins. One sin, even one! is the "dead
fly, that maketh the apothecary's ointment to stink;"
is the leak, however small and concealed from the
public eye, which, if not stopped, fills and sinks the
ship. Men talk of poverty, misfortune, disease, be-
reavement, as evils! There is no radical evil in this
world but sin; if you still persist in calling other
things evils, remember sin is their mother—these her
hateful progeny. No sin, no suffering; no sin, no
sorrow; no sin, no sting, no death, no grave, no hell.
We change the saying of Paul, and, so changed, apply
to sins what he spoke of the sailors. He said of the
seamen, *Except* these abide in the ship ye cannot be
saved. To prevail on you to abandon and cast your
sins—these Jonahs—overboard, we say, *If* these abide
ye cannot be saved.

Now, while maintaining, to the utmost, that holi-
ness is essential to salvation, we nevertheless regard
it as of the highest importance that holiness should
have a right and not a wrong place in our system.
Should earthquakes shake the ground, or even rude
storms the air, that pyramid must stand unsafely
which, according to the poet,

> "Like an inverted cone,
> Wants the proper base to stand upon."

That body would be a monster in nature, hideous of
aspect, and happily of brief existence, which should
have its organs and members so misplaced, that the
hands should occupy the place of the feet, and whose
heart should beat in the cavity of the brain. The
fruitfulness, beauty, the very life of a tree, depends
not only on its having roots and branches, but on
these members being placed in their natural order.

Let a tree be planted upside down—the roots in the air and the branches in the earth—and I need not ask how much fruit it would yield, nor how many seasons the unhappy plant would survive such barbarous and blundering treatment.

Well, if it be of such consequence in these things not to depart from the order established in nature, it is of no less consequence not to depart from the order established in the kingdom of grace? It is not enough that men hold right doctrines,—nay in a sense hold all the doctrines. The right doctrines must be in the right places. Your astronomy may include all the bodies that enter into our solar system, but if it give a satellite the imperial position of the sun, your system passes into inextricable confusion. The machine may have all its parts, but, if the great wheel that moves them, or the balance-wheel that regulates them, revolve on any shaft but its own, the entire mechanism stops, or flies round in furious and destructive disorder. Even so, although all the doctrines of the gospel be present in our creed, we may commit a great, a dangerous—possibly a fatal mistake —by any mal-arrangement that would put these out of their proper place. And such is their mistake who build election upon holiness—not holiness upon election; who regard good works, not as the result, but the cause of God's mercy; and who, mistaking the root for the fruit, think that God adopts men because they are holy; when, in point of fact, he makes them holy, just because he has adopted them.

This, believe me, is not an example of the nice and fine distinctions which theologians sometimes spin, nor of the matters about which bigots may contend, but good men need give themselves no trouble. Some small things have great effects. A slight wedge of wood or small pebble lying upon the slip, prevents the vessel from being launched on the bosom of a tide that swells to receive her in its arms. The full tide of love flows in Jesus' heart, his bosom is open to receive the sinner, every thing conspires to his salvation, and yet in such happy circumstances, we have seen the notion, that a man must be holy before he goes to Christ, arrest a soul that had already moved, advanced, got some way in its course, and as we thought, was off for heaven. This is a delusion of the enemy of souls. I believe it to be a common wile of Satan. When conscience gets so uneasy, that for all the devil's rocking it won't sleep, and men grow anxious about their eternal interests, and will be out of the "City of Destruction," it is no uncommon thing with him to send them away in a wrong direction. Would you make yourselves more pure and more penitent, that you may have some right to divine mercy? You are trying to weave ropes of sand, and he who has set you to a task so impracticable knows well that you will by and bye abandon it in despair; and then, perhaps, returning to your old favorite sins, like a drunkard to his cup after a season of sobriety, you will furnish another illustration of the saying—"The last state of that man is worse than the first."

With God's help I would endeavor to disabuse your minds of such an error. For that purpose, let me borrow an illustration from an asylum, which, in the form of a ragged school, opens its loving arms to the outcast, like the Gospel which it teaches, and seeks to train up to God and glory the poor children whom its piety and pity adopts. On entering these blessed doors,—the gate of hope to many,—your attention is

caught by a child, who is supported there by the
bounty of some generous Christian. The boy now
can spell his way through a bible—once a sealed book
to him; he knows now, and, in tones fitted to melt
any heart, he sweetly sings of a Saviour, of whom
once he knew not even the name. These little hands
are now skillful to weave the net or ply the shuttle,
which once were alert only to steal, or held out in
their pitiful emaciation to plead for charity; and there
is such sharp intelligence in that bright eye, and such
an open air of honesty in his beaming face, and such
attention to cleanliness appears in his dress and person,
and such buoyancy in his whole bearing, as if hope
hailed a brighter future for that poor child, that these
bespeak your favor. But do you conclude that they
were the child's passport to this asylum? Do you
suppose, that when he wandered, an outcast upon the
winter streets, shoeless among the snow, shivering in
the cold, it was what now so interests you that caught
the eye of pity, or that to these habits and accomplish-
ments, learned under a parental roof, the child owed
his adoption? How great your mistake. This were,
indeed, to turn things upside down. He was adopted,
not for the sake of these, but notwithstanding the
want of them. It was the very want of them, which,
if I may so speak, carried his election. It was his
wretchedness that saved him. It was his very misery
—when he stood there with beggary on his back and
hunger in his looks, cold, naked, wicked, wretched—
which pleaded for him, and, with more power than elo-
quence, melted men's hearts and gained his cause.
The clean hands, and rosy cheek, and lighted eye,
and decent habits, and arts and knowledge, and all
which now wins our regard are the consequences of

his adoption, and never were nor could be its cause. Even so is it with holy habits and a holy heart in the matter of redemption—

"Ye have not chosen me, but I have chosen you," says God. Blessed truth! Glad tidings, indeed, to sinners! for, since God chooses his people, not because they are holy, but to make them so, who may not be chosen? and who should not hope? To my eye hope, in that truth, bends her bright bow on life's blackest cloud, and sends a beam of light down into the guiltiest heart.

II. In redemption, the saved are not justified by themselves, but by God.

This is no recondite truth—one which we need to dig or dive for. The pearl lies in the dark depths of the sea, but gold commonly lies near the surface of the earth. Like the precious ore gleaming from the naked rock, this truth shines on the face of my text; a child's eye can catch it there, and a child's mind comprehend it. For how is a sinner made clean? but through the application of what is here called clean water; and by whom, according to the text, is that water applied? It is applied *to* the sinner, but not *by* the sinner.

Elisha remained in his house, nor accompanied Naaman to the banks of Jordan. Commanded by the prophet to wash, and—when pride was ready to revolt from so mean a remedy—persuaded by his servants that it were a foolish thing not to try so small a remedy for so great a cure, the Syrian descended into the water; and, going down a leper, rose at the seventh dip with a skin fresh as a new born child's. A type of salvation in one respect, that case is not so in another. It is not so in this, that Naaman bathed himself;—the sinner does not. Here, as in the sacrament of baptism, there are two parties. The baptized and the baptizer are not one. Whether that ordinance be administered to infant or adult, the water is applied by another's hand; and, as no man baptizes, so no man saves himself, no man justifies himself, no man ever sprinkled himself with that atoning blood, which we shall show to be symbolized by this "clean water." The bloody baptism is administered by the hand which kindled the sun, stretched out the curtain of the heavens, and sustains the universe. To God, as Author and Finisher of our faith, the whole glory of salvation belongs; for, observe how he says in my text—" *I* will sprinkle clean water upon you, and ye shall be clean."

Job inquires, " How should man be just with God?" A great question—one in which we have the deepest interest—one for which the Gospel was revealed, and the cross of Calvary raised to answer—and one to which our own merits and works furnish no satisfactory solution. It is natural, most natural, for us to trust in these. I do not deny it. Observe what happens when the cry rises at sea—" A man overboard!" You rush to the side of the vessel; you watch the place where the rising air-bells and boiling deep tell that he has gone down. After some moments of breathless anxiety, you see his head emerge from the wave. Now, that man is no swimmer—he has never learned to breast the billows; yet, with the first breath he draws, he begins to beat the water; with violent efforts he attempts to shake off the grasp of death, and, by the play of limbs and arms, to keep his head from sinking. His struggles may only exhaust his strength, and sink him all the sooner, nevertheless, that drowning wretch makes instinctive and convulsive efforts to save himself. So, when first brought to feel that we are perishing—when the horrible conviction rushes into our mind that we are lost, and we feel ourselves oing down under a load of guilt into the depths of .vrath, our first effort, also, is to save ourselves. Like a drowning man, who clutches at straws and twigs, we seize on any thing, however worthless, that promises salvation. Thus, alas! many toil and spend weary, painful, unprofitable days in attempting to establish a righteousness of their own, and to find in the deeds of the law protection from its curse.

There was a time, no doubt, when man had his fortunes in his own hand; but that time is gone —our power passed away with our purity. Impotence has followed the loss of innocence, and we have nothing now left us but a wretched pride. Amid the changes which this world presents, I have seen a man who had known better days—who had been nursed in luxury, and reared in the lap of fullness— outlive his fortune, and sink into the baseness and meanness of the deepest poverty. It seems to be in such circumstances with men as with plants. Naturalists say that it is much more difficult to get a mountain plant to accommodate itself to a low locality, than to get one, which by birth belongs to the valleys, to live and thrive at a lofty elevation. So, there seems nothing more difficult to men than to descend gracefully, and for those who have been accustomed to a high position in society to reconcile themselves to a humble one. And thus I have seen such an one as I have described, when he had lost his wealth, retain in his vanity what he should first have parted with, and continue proud even when he had become poor. So is it with us in our low and lost estate. Spiritually poor, we are spiritually proud—saying, " I am rich and increased in goods, and have need of nothing," while we are " wretched, and miserable, and poor, and blind, and naked." Even when we are in some degree sensible of our poverty, and know we can not pay, we are yet like the unjust steward, ashamed to beg. With a pride that assorts ill with the rags we wear, we will not stoop to stand at God's, door, poor mendicants, who ask for mercy. We will work out our own salvation—nor be beholden to another. Nor, sometimes, if not always, till the sinner learns, by prolonged and painful trials, that he can not be his own saviour, does this proud heart of ours allow us to stand suppliants at the gate of Mercy—our plea for pardon not our own merits,—nothing, nothing whatever but Jesus' merits and our own misery. Yet thus and there we must stand if we would be saved. Jesus is the Saviour of the lost, and of none but the lost.

Now, to bring us down to this conviction, and to draw from our lips the cry, " Lord save me, I perish," God in mercy often leaves those, whom he calls, to try their hand at working out their own salvation, and of the rubbish and untempered mortar of their own works and vows to build up a righteousness of their own. They toil and labor at the Babel tower —a tower to reach to heaven. It rises imposingly. It grows lofty, and looks strong; until some day, conscience awakens, and there follows an earthquake of the soul which shakes it to its foundation; or some sudden gust of temptation strikes it, and lays the labor of years in ruins upon the ground. This ruin proves their redemption : for—first step in a right direction—they at least come to feel, that, notwithstanding their utmost efforts to live holily, holy they are not.

God deals with them as Jesus did on Galilee with Simon Peter. Impetuous, self-satisfied, puffed up with vanity, Peter will walk the sea to show off his power and prove his superiority to the other disciples. His Master lets him try it. Jesus bids him come ; not that he may drown Simon, but drown Simon's pride. Boldly he ventures on the water. He begins to walk ; but, alarmed at his new position as he rises and falls with the swell of the waves, he begins to fear, and, like a cause which is lost for want of courage, he begins to sink—lower and lower still he sinks, till the cold water rises to his heart, and kisses his drowning lip. Painful but profitable lesson ! His danger and failure have taught him his weakness ; terror masters shame, and, stretching out his arms to Christ, he cries, " Lord, save me, I perish." Now, to this state, and this very confession, all who are to be saved must first be brought. " I perish," is a saving word. " I perish," like the cry of the child in the natal chamber, is the first utterance of a new existence. He who raises his eyes to heaven to cry, " I perish," " Lord, save me, I perish," has planted his foot on the first round of the ladder that raises man from earth to heaven. Have you got your foot there ? from lips pale with terror, have you ever cried " Lord, save me, I perish."

This confession and this petition will, sooner or later, rise to God from every man, who, through the influence of God's grace and spirit, is intelligently, seriously, resolutely, bent on salvation. We say so, because no man ever yet tried to live without sinning and succeeded. Who that ever tried it has not failed? Who has not found, that it were as easy for a man of mortal mold and weight to walk the water, as to walk this world one day without sin? Oh, has not He who is angry with the wicked every day, reason to be angry every day with the best of us? "In many things we offend."

Imagine not by your vows, and engagements, and promises, and resolutions, to restrain the corruption of your nature—to bind the limbs of "the old man." That "old man," although old, is ever young. To him age brings no infirmities. He grows in strength with increase of years. Vulnerable to no weapon but the "Sword of the Spirit," and, entrenched within your heart, he is immortal till you pierce him there. This terrible "old man" laughs at your strongest bonds, and snaps them on his giant arms, as Samson in the days of old the green withes of the Philistines.

Time is precious, and you waste it in attempting to work out a righteousness of your own. In you I see a negro, black and tawny, seated by a running stream, a laughing stock to some, an object of pity to others, who labors and toils to wash himself white, and remove the dark pigment of his skin. Rise up, throw soap and nitre into the stream, and, turning your back on these, go, seek the blood that cleanseth from all sin. Are you engaged in the attempt to work out a righteousness of your own? Leave that loom. Are the gossamer threads of your own vows and promises ever snapping in your hand, and breaking at every throw of the shuttle? The robe of righteousness, a raiment meet for thy soul, and approved of by God, was never woven there. It was wrought upon the cross; and, of color more enduring than Tyrian purple, it is dyed red in the blood of Calvary.

Come away, and come to Jesus. Come as you are. There is neither time nor need for delay. Imagine not that you have to do what Joseph did before he was ushered into Pharaoh's presence. The Hebrew lies immured in a foul and lonely dungeon, when to a thundering at the gate, and the cry of " a message from the palace!" the ponderous bolts are drawn. The door is thrown open, and, guided by the jailer, the royal messengers hurry along the dreary passages and enter Joseph's dungeon. Pale, sad, disconsolate, far from his father and a father's love, a slave, a captive, neglected in dress and person, the Hebrew lies before them. They strike the fetters from his limbs, and hurry him off, for Pharaoh with royal impatience frets and grieves till his dream is read ; and yet, with all their haste, Joseph is not ushered into the presence of royalty till the marks of the prison are removed, and in attire and appearance he is made like one who is fit to walk the floor of a palace, and stand before a king. We are told that " he shaved himself, and changed his raiment, and came in unto Pharaoh." I have to tell the sinner that, although he lies in a deeper and darker dungeon, although he is covered with fouler and filthier rags, and although the presence of Jesus is infinitely more august, and venerable, and exalted, than that of any mortal king, he stands in no need of preparatory holiness, of even one short hour's delay. You have neither to change a rag, nor remove a stain. He is ready to receive you as you are. Come then as you are. Here, this hour, the bridegroom stands by the marriage altar. It is not your wealth nor your beauty which has won his heart. He loves you; he has shed his blood to wash you; at great cost he has purchased the wedding garment, a robe of righteousness, and the crown of glory. The romance which relates how a peasant maid was united to a great prince, and the turn in fortune's wheel which gave the honors of a queen to some female slave; these but dimly shadow what thy fate might be. Why, when Christ seeks you, should you hang back? He is ready to espouse you to himself in the marriage bonds of an eternal covenant—"The mountains shall depart, and the hills be removed, but my kindness shall not depart, neither shall the covenant of my peace be removed, saith the Lord that hath mercy on thee."

Man Justified

THROUGH THE RIGHTEOUSNESS OF JESUS CHRIST.

Then will I sprinkle clean water upon you, and ye shall be clean.
EZEKIEL xxxvi. 25.

THE dinner was to prepare, the rooms were to be made ready, there were servants to direct, and guests to accommodate; there was the character of the house to maintain, and its whole machinery to keep oiled and in good working order—with these things Martha was busy. Not only busy, but, like many others, she was so intently engrossed with household cares, that, in a tone which had the sound of a gentle rebuke, our Lord said, "Martha, thou art cumbered about many things; but one thing is needful." That observation applies as much to men as to women; more so, perhaps.

Furnished with clasping tendrils, and strong by the attachments which they form, the woodbine and ivy wind their arms round the tree, embrace it closely, and rising to its lofty boughs, and clinging to its rough bark, they give ornament and beauty—a vesture of soft green spangled with flowers—in return for the support they get. Like these, woman, with her strong and warm affections—gentle, loving, confiding—is prone to attach herself to a nature stronger than her own, and to lean on it for support. And, whether it be that she is from this peculiar disposition less op-

posed to the faith which looks to another's righteous-
ness and leans on another's strength, certain it is there
is more religion among women than men. If, on ac-
count of the elevation and high position which it has
given her in Christian countries, woman owes most to
religion, religion in turn owes most to her. You tell
me that "by woman came sin?" I know it; but I
set off this against the fact—by woman came the
Saviour. Jesus was a virgin's child. And, more
than that, in those days when he walked this world,
women were his trustiest, kindest friends. Whoever
betrayed, denied, deserted him—they never did. The
nearest to his cross, and earliest at his sepulcher, they
were faithful when others were faithless, and gave
early promise of that devotedness to his cause, which
their sex in all ages have honorably and pre-eminently
displayed. Go through our Christian households, and
I will venture to say, that you will find more women
than men, more wives than husbands, more sisters
than brothers, who are living under the influence of
religion. Many more children are to be found, who
refer their earliest, deepest religious impressions to a
mother's than to a father's piety.

But, be we men or women, "One thing is needful."
Yet how sad and strange it is, that this one needful
thing, which, for that very reason, should be the most,
is often the least sought after; which, for that very
reason, should be the first, is often the last sought
after; and sometimes, alas! never sought after at all.
It is the brightest feature in man's sad and sinful lot,
that while amid the business and anxieties, and toils,
and cares, and keen competitions of a world, which
has so many blanks and so few prizes, there is, after
all, but one thing needful. And especially blessed is

·t, that the only thing we really need is the only thing we are sure to get. Sought in sincerity, it was never sought in vain. Other gifts may be asked and re· fused ; but it is true of this as of nothing else what ever, "Ask and ye shall receive, seek and ye shall find, knock and it shall be opened to you."

Need I say that the one thing needful is salvation— that it must be *that*—can be nothing else than *that* To a man, the conscious possessor of a never-dying soul, who is burdened with a heavy load of guilt, and who, in an eternity which he is nearing every hour, descries a throne of rigid and righteous judgment, Oh, what has this wide world to offer comparable to sal· vation ? What profit would it be to me, though I gained it all, if I lost my soul ? All those other things which we seek, all that we toil and travail for, all for which we daily fret and vex ourselves, nay, all for which some are fools enough to barter away their souls, compared to this are but mere spangles and tinsel, dross and dust—bubbles colored with rainbow hues that break at a touch, and, bursting, smart the eyes of the child who blows them. When a man lies stretched out on a bed of death, ah! he sees objects then in their due proportions. From that point of view the highest objects of earthly ambition, the loftiest pinnacles of wealth, of power, of fame, dwindle down into littleness, and look as far beneath salvation as the loftiest Alp beneath the sun. Yet, strange to tell— incredible, did we not know it to be true—many, as if there was neither God in heaven, nor fire in hell, nor soul in man, feel no anxiety about the matter. They live and die like the beasts that perish. Is it otherwise with you ? Anxious about what alone is worth your anxiety, are you pressing on the preacher the jailer's question, "Oh, sir, what shall I do to be saved?"

That great question—the greatest of all questions—is one which admits of a very short and intelligible answer. Capable of being much expanded, it can yet be brought within a very narrow compass. The river, which there flows between distant banks, and yonder expands itself out into a lake, reflecting on its mirror-face the bright heavens above and the dark hills around, is here brought—where its foaming waters flash past, loud as thunder, and quick as lightning, or creep sullenly along at the bottom of the deep, dark gorge—within narrow bounds; bounds so narrow, that with nerve enough, by one brave leap from rock to rock, I could clear its breadth. Even so all the wide expanse of doctrines to be believed, and duties to be done, which might be expatiated over in reply to the question, What shall I do to be saved? is contracted, compressed, comprehended in the Apostle's brief speech, "Believe in the Lord Jesus Christ, and thou shalt be saved." Bring out from the dust of six thousand years the old covenant of Eden, and on that soiled and torn banner, you read the fading motto, "Do and live." But what read we on the folds of this banner, which, defiant of hell and the world, waves above Calvary, and under which believers march to crowns and victory? The eye of a sinner's hope kindles at the sight of another and better motto; for there, inscribed in the blood of Jesus, like red letters on a snow-white ground, we read, "Believe and live." Salvation is the one thing needful for man, and faith is the one thing needful for salvation.

Like other things, however, that are one in the aggregate, this one thing consists of many parts. My hand, for instance, is one, yet it has five fingers. This body is one, yet it has many organs. The Nile or Ganges is one river, but one which is fed by many tributaries, and disgorges its waters into the sea by the channels of many mouths. A tree is one vegetable form, but one that has many roots below, and many branches above; and even so, to leave the other figures, and select the last, is that "Tree of Life," which has Christ for its root, and for its fruit holiness and heaven. I have seen a tree which, after rising in a single stem, divided itself into two great boughs, which, stretched out to the air and light, and dews and heat, were afterwards divided and subdivided into innumerable branches. So with redemption. The subject presents itself to our eye under two grand divisions. First, the remission or pardon of sin; and secondly, the renovation of the soul. While salvation is the one thing needful, the two things needful to it are sin pardoned and the soul renewed. For, suppose that your sins were pardoned, but that your heart remained in its corruption, the door of heaven remains shut; because, "Without holiness no man shall see the Lord." Then, again, although your hearts were renewed, unless your sins also were pardoned, that door stands shut; because of the sentence, "The soul that sinneth shall die." The door of heaven, like that of some treasure-chest or gate of citadel, guarded with jealous care, is thus barred by two strong bolts; "There shall in no wise enter into it any thing that defileth, neither whatsoever worketh abomination, or maketh a lie; but they which are written in the Lamb's book of life." Both bolts must be drawn before we can enter; we must be pardoned as well as renewed, and renewed as well as pardoned.

Leaving the renovation of the soul to be afterwards considered, I resume my observations on the pardon of sin, and justification of the sinner, as expressed and promised in these words: " I will sprinkle clean water upon you, and ye shall be clean." Having endeavored to prove, first, that God's people are not chosen because they are holy, but that they may become so; and, secondly, that man does not justify himself, but is justified by God, I now remark—

III. That we are not justified or cleansed from the guilt of sin through the administration or efficacy of any outward ordinance. " I will sprinkle clean water upon you, and you shall be clean."

Now, since the cleansing is accomplished through the application of water—and water sprinkled—surely, some may say, this refers to baptism. The element used in that ordinance is water, and the common method of using it is by sprinkling. And seeing that God says, " I will sprinkle clean water upon you, and ye shall be clean;" and by that, certainly, means that he will cleanse his people from sin; and seeing that he thus appears to connect the forgiveness of sin with the sprinkling of water, is there not something—if not much—in these words, favorable to the views of those who maintain that baptism, when duly administered, removes original sin, and confers on its recipients the grace of regeneration? No; nothing of the kind, as we shall prove.

Three hundred years ago, our church, with an open Bible on her banner, and this motto, " Search the Scriptures," on its scroll, marched out from the gates of Rome. Did they come clean out of Babylon? Experience shows, that it is much easier to leave our mother country than drop our mother tongue. Across the seas which they sail, and to the lands which they settle on, the emigrants carry their prejudices, passions, and even superstitions. They people the glens and valleys of the new world with the fairies that dance on the green, and the specters that walk by night among the haunted ruins of the old country. So I fear that, on departing from the Church of Rome, we carried into our Protestantism—as was not unnatural —some of her ancient superstitions; just as our fathers carried into their practice some of her intolerant principles. We can not approve of their intolerance, yet it admits of an apology. They had been suckled by the wolf, and it was no great wonder that, with the milk of the wolf, they should have imbibed something of her nature.

It is not the privilege and happiness of man to pass through his changes like the Saviour. When Jesus rose, a conqueror from the grave, he left the dead-clothes behind him; but look at this apparition, from which sisters and friends shrink back. Some scream with terror, and all afraid to touch him, they leave him to stand in the dark mouth of his grave, till the word is given, " Loose him, and let him go." Lazarus comes forth alive, but he is bound hand and foot; he leaves the sepulcher, but with his grave-clothes on. And prone, as we of Scotland are, to boast that our fathers, with Knox at their head, came forth from Rome with less of her old superstitions about them than most other churches, to what else than some lingering remains of popery can we ascribe the ex-treme anxiety which some parents show to have bap-tism administered to a dying child? Does not this look very like a rag of the old faith? It smells of the sepulcher.

Summoned once, and in haste, to the dying bed of a mother, who was anxious to see her child baptized ere she herself expired, I found that with her I could sympathize. The last act of sinking life—the last effort of her throbbing heart—was to give her infant to God. With her dying arms she laid the new-born lamb on the Shepherd's bosom, and as the babe slept, unconscious of the affecting scene, it received a double baptism. Ere the water was sprinkled by our hands on its face, the mother had breathed her last. She left the babe motherless, to be baptized by the water that fell from our agitated hand and by the big bitter tears that rolled down on its sweet face from a father's cheeks. There was sorrow—bitter sorrow there; beside that dead mother deep solemnity, but no superstition; and if there was a mother's weakness in the wish, it was one which we felt it no sin to sympathize with and comply with. But sympathize with those we can not, who, when death has stamped his seal on an infant's brow, hurry off for a minister that he may baptize the dying. I cannot believe that there is any virtue in water to save its soul. I recoil with horror from the thought that a God of mercy would suspend its salvation on a mere outward ordinance. Is there not reason to suspect that at the root of this anxious and unnecessary haste, there lies some lurking feeling that baptism—if not essential—is at least serviceable to salvation, and has some connection, near or remote, with regeneration and the remission of sins?

Now, with all respect and due regard to the feelings of others, so far as they are conscientious, we can not look upon such notions as else than the rags of an old superstition. We acknowledge no authority in these matters but the word of God. And there I can see no foundation for the idea, that baptism and salvation —baptism and regeneration—are necessarily linked together, or are in any respect inseparably connected. Were it so, baptism were the highest, holiest ordinance in the universe of God. Had it been so, it is not reasonable to suppose that our Lord would have left a rite of such transcendent importance to be administered in every case by inferiors—by the hands of his servants. Were baptism thus identified with regeneration and the "new creature," would the Apostle Paul, who gloried in preaching, have spoken of it as an inferior ordinance? He declared with manifest satisfaction that he had not been sent to baptize but to preach; and, leaving the administration of the rite to his inferiors, he even thanked God that he had baptized none of them. Then, do the cases, for instance, of Simon Magus and the Ethiopian give any sanction to this theory of baptismal power? Assuredly not.

Look at Simon Magus! He was baptized by apostolic hands; and in his case the ordinance, beyond all doubt and controversy, was duly administered. Does his conduct warrant us to believe that his sins were pardoned, or his heart renewed? By no means. On the contrary, this man is declared, on apostolic authority—by the voice of Simon Peter himself, to be still, although baptized by that Apostle's hands, "In the gall of bitterness and the bond of iniquity." Shocked to find a baptized man, offering with money to buy the Holy Ghost, Peter, bursting with indignation, said, "Thy money perish with thee, because thou hast thought that the gift of God may be purchased with money. Thou hast neither part nor lot in this matter;

for thy heart is not right in the sight of God. Repent, therefore, of this thy wickedness, and pray God if perhaps the thought of thine heart may be forgiven thee, for I perceive that thou art in the gall of bitterness and the bond of iniquity." Surely it is much more reasonable to believe that Simon Magus, although baptized, was not regenerated, than to believe that an inspired Apostle would speak in such terms of a regenerate man. How could he be regenerate when we hear heaven itself pronouncing him by the lips of its messenger to be still "in the gall of bitterness and bond of iniquity."

Look next at the Ethiopian eunuch. Was he not *baptized* and *regenerate?* True; but observe that that order should be reversed; he was *regenerate* and *baptized*—regenerate before he was baptized—not born again in his baptism, but born again before it. Why did Philip baptize him? He granted him baptism, because he believed with all his heart. But can a man believe till he is renewed! In other words, can a dead man move, or cry, or wish, or walk? This stifled shriek, this awful sound within the coffin, these struggles to force up the lid and throw off the cerements, prove that the dead has come to life—that he has passed "from death to life." And did not the Ethiopian give proof of spiritual life previous to his baptism? Ere he had left the chariot, ere his feet had been dipped in the stream, ere one drop of its water had fallen on his bended head, the Spirit of the living God had fallen on his heart. Hear the narrative:—"And, as they went on their way, they came unto a certain water; and the eunuch said, See, here is water; what doth hinder me to be baptized? and Philip said, If thou believest with all thine heart, thou mayest." And he answered and said, "I believe that Jesus Christ is the Son of God." These cases are not reconcilable with the notion that baptism has any necessary connection with the forgiveness of sin, and the renewing of the Holy Ghost. They prove that baptism and regeneration do not, and can not stand to each other in the relation of cause and effect. Otherwise, the case of the Ethiopian were an illustration of what the world never saw—would be an example of what were a contradiction and an absurdity—of something far more wonderful than a miracle—of such an impossibility as a son older than his father, or as a thunder-peal that preceded the flash in which it originated—of, in short, an effect in the order of time preceding its own cause.

Besides, does not the sad and melancholy history, alas! of thousands prove that the outward ordinance is often administered without any corresponding administration of renewing grace? The altar and the offering are there, but no fire descends from heaven on the sacrifice. Grant that in our case, and in that of any other such church as ours, the cause of the failure is to be found in our lack of apostolic succession; grant that in our case the water, if not actually polluted by unconsecrated hands, is deprived of all its virtue by the channel through which it flows; grant that we have no commission to baptize, and that therefore what we do in such holy offices is null and void; grant the relevancy of all these allegations (each and all of which we deny)—is it not an undeniable and melancholy fact, that the lives of persons in all churches—even of the most transcendental in their claims—demonstrate that many are baptized with water who have never been baptized with the Holy

Ghost. The question, therefore, that we would urge on your most serious consideration, does not concern the sign, but the thing signified. If you have got the living element, I care little, or, rather, nothing, through what church, or by what channel it may flow. Have you got the grace of God? In the words of an apostle, "Have ye received the Holy Ghost?"

IV. We are justified, or cleansed from the guilt of sin by the blood of Christ. "Without the shedding of blood there is no remission;" and none we may add, without its application.

Where do we find this doctrine in the text? By what process of spiritual chemistry can this truth be extracted from it? There is water, and clean water, and sprinkling of water, it may be said, but no word of blood; there is neither sign nor spot of blood upon the page. True; so it looks at first sight; but without the hand of Moses we shall see this water turned into blood. It may appear difficult, without Moses' rod, to repeat the miracle of Egypt; yet this is plain, that here, as elsewhere, water is but the sign of spiritual blessings. And a most expressive symbol we shall find it, if we but think of the important part that this element plays in the economy of nature. It covers more than two thirds of the entire globe; it is universally diffused through the ambient air; by the clouds it forms it tempers the force of a fiery sun; it drapes the heavens with curtains of the most gorgeous colors, dyed in the rosy tints of morn, or in evening's golden hues; and it fills the floating reservoirs of the sky, to descend, when burst by lightning, or breaking by their own weight, in refreshing showers on the thirsty ground. The circulation of water is to the world what that of blood is to the body, and that of grace to the soul. It is its life. Withdraw it, and all that lives would die; forests, fields, beasts, man himself would die. This world would become one vast grave. Water constitutes as much the life as the beauty of the landscape. It is true both in a spiritual and in an earthly sense, that the world lives because heaven weeps over it. It was Christ's choicest figure of himself, when, turning on his own person the eyes of thousands, as on a perennial fountain—one never sealed by winter's frost, nor dried by summer suns—free, full, patent to all, he stood up on the last and great day of the feast, and cried, "If any man thirst, let him come unto me and drink." And in case any of you should be thirsting for eternal life, let me say, that thus Jesus now addresses us. Would God, he were as precious to us as water in the sight of him who is dying of thirst! With blood-shot eyes, his throat black as coal, his tongue cleaving to the roof of his mouth, the desert reeling round him, Oh! what will the traveler not give for one cup of water? Fill it with water, he will give it back to you filled, twice, ten times over with gold. Would to God that our thirst for Jesus Christ were as ardent; that in like manner He were all our salvation, and all our desire.

The property of water, however, to which reference is made here, is a different one from any of these. It is not the property by which it sustains or revives life, yet it is one for which this element is as well known, and as universally used. All the world wash with water, as well as drink water; and the reference here is to that solvent power, by virtue of

which water dissolves impurities—turning white what
is black, and cleansing whatever is foul. It stands
here, therefore, the figure of that which cleanses.
The object to be cleansed is the soul; the defilement
to be cleansed away is sin; and we now, therefore,
address ourselves to the all-important question—Of
what is this water the figure? The key to the ques-
tion lies in the epithet *clean* water. Let us analyse
this water. It is not water in the state in which it
descends from the skies, or flows in rivers, or may be
drawn from a common well; for, observe, it is not
said, then will I sprinkle water, but "*clean* water on
you, and ye shall be clean." The water is such as the
Jews understood by *clean* water—not free from im-
purity, and in itself clean, but water that maketh
clean—in the words of the ceremonial law, "water of
purifying." This was prepared according to a divinely
appointed ritual. Look how it was prepared, and you
shall see it reddening and changing into blood.

Gathering the lowing herds from their different pas-
tures, they sought up and down among them, till a red
heifer was found—red from horn to hoof, and mottled
by no other color—one all red, and on whose free
neck yoke had never been. Separated from the herd,
she is led by priestly procession, accompanied by the
people outside the camp; and there, struck by a mor-
tal blow, she falls under the hands of the priest. As
the blood gushes to the knife, he catches it in his
hand, and seven times casts it in a bloody shower to-
wards the tabernacle. So soon as the victim is dead,
it is heaved on the burning pile, and, while the smoke
of the sacrifice floats away to heaven, horn and hoof,
skin, flesh, and bone, are all reduced to ashes. These
ashes, carefully collected, are mixed with pure water

in a pure vessel—and that water is the *clean* water of
my text. See now how plainly—when understood
aright—this expression refers to a vicarious sacrifice,
and the merits of an atoning death. What was that
heifer? Spotless and separated from the herd, she is
a type of Him who was without spot or blemish, holy,
harmless, undefiled, and separate from sinners. With
neck on which yoke had never lain, she is a type of
Him, who said, " The prince of this world cometh,
and he hath nothing in me." Red in color, she is a
type of Him, whose feet were dipped in the blood of
his enemies, and, as seen coming from Bozrah, was
"red in his apparel, traveling in the greatness of his
might." And what is this public procession, which
conducts the heifer without the camp, but a figure of
the march to Calvary? And what is her bloody
death, but a type of that which Jesus suffered amid
the agonies of the cross? And what are these fires
that burn so fiercely, and consume the victim, but a
faint image of the wrath of God, under which his soul
was " withered like grass?" And what was the water
mingled with this heifer's ashes, but a type of the
righteousness, which, imputed and applied to sinners,
makes sinners just? For, as the Jew on whom that
water was sprinkled became ceremonially clean, so
guilt of original and actual sin—all guilt is removed
from him (much the happier man) whom God sprin
kles with the blood of Calvary—and to whom sove
reign mercy imputes the merits of a Saviour's sacrifice.

Let me further illustrate this. There was another
method of preparing this *clean* water, which, although
in some respects different, was the same in this, that it
also implied the death of a vicarious sacrifice. The
leper, a mass of sores from crown to heel, a banished

man—banished from city, synagogue, the dwellings
of men, and the house of God—the victim of a loath-
some disease, which made his presence an offense to
others, and his life a burden to himself, was a hideous,
doleful, revolting emblem of a sinner. Now let us
see how—when God was pleased to cure him—his
ceremonial uncleanness was removed. On the happy
occasion, which was to restore him to the arms of his
wife, the sweet society of his children, the brotherhood
of men, and the presence of God—two living birds
were taken. They must be doves or turtles—the
gentlest of all God's creatures, and therefore the more
fitting emblems of his Son. They are held over a
vessel, already filled with running water. One is
slain. The blood, as it flows over the snowy plumage
of the fluttering bird, falls into the water; and that,
dyed by the crimson stream, now becomes " water of
purifying"—the clean water of the text. With this
sacred lavation the priest sprinkles the man who had
been a leper, and now ceremonially clean, that blessed
moment he is folded in the embrace of his wife;
kisses his children, and walks with them, a happy
man, at the head of a happy family, into the house of
God.

But there were two birds. We have seen one dis-
posed of. What has become of the other ? With
beating heart it is still a prisoner in the hands of the
priest; and the close of this ceremonial offers us a
beautiful and most vivid picture of the removal of
guilt. The living bird, type of a sinner to whom a
Saviour's merits are to be imputed, is dipped head, feet,
wings, and feathers—plunged overhead—into the
blood-dyed water. It is "baptized unto death." And,
brought out before the people—all crimsoned with

blood—the priest opens his consecrated hand, and restores the captive to liberty. Image of a pardoned one on his path to glory, it spreads out its wings, and, beating the air with rapid and rejoicing strokes, flies away to its forest or rocky home.

You will now understand the nature of this clean water; and cannot fail, I think, to see, that although clothed in a Jewish dress, justification by faith in the righteousness of Jesus—that paramount article of our creed which Luther called the test of a falling or standing church—is the doctrine of my text. Thus understood, my text sheds, we think, a valuable light on one of the most prominent, and best known and most important passages in the word of God. When Nicodemus, not yet prepared to confess Christ before the world, muffled himself up in his cloak, and, stealing forth under the cloud of night, sought an interview with our Lord, Jesus said to him—"Except a man be born again, he cannot see the Kingdom of God," adding, by way of explanation, the no less memorable words—"Except a man be born of water and of the Spirit he cannot see the Kingdom of God." Now, as commonly understood, these words refer only to the renewing of the Holy Ghost. It is generally thought that the water there is but an emblem of the Spirit, and that our Lord just meant to say—"Except a man's soul is purified by the Spirit's regenerating influence, as his body is by water, he cannot be an heir of grace and an heir of heaven.

We venture to think, that on that occasion, and in these words, our Lord preached the Gospel more fully. Turn the light of my text upon them, read them in connection with it, understand by the water of Christ's address the water of my text, and his language to

Nicodemus expands into a full Gospel. If the wate. in his address meant only the Holy Spirit, he told a truth, but not the whole truth. Are not more than regenerating influences needed, that a man may enter the kingdom of heaven? For that end, is not the blood of the Saviour as necessary as the renewing of the Holy Ghost? But let our Lord, in speaking to Nicodemus—who as a Jew would at once catch the allusion—have an eye to the clean water of the ceremonial law; let the water there refer, like the water here, to an atoning sacrifice, and the Gospel in that celebrated passage shines forth in its effulgent radiance. Our Lord tells him what I preach, and pray you to ponder on, that except you are washed in his blood, as well as renewed by his Spirit, you cannot see the Kingdom of God.

The doctrine of my text, and, indeed, of all Scripture is, that nothing saves but blood. In that, as in other senses, "the life is in the blood." There may be the sprinkling of water, but without the shedding and sprinkling of blood, there is no remission—no remission, though the water fall from the holiest hand, and be itself the purest that ever dripped from mossy well or mountain spring. It is what came from the bosom of the upper heavens, of which that visible firmament is but the starry floor, that takes sin away. It is not the tears that fall from weeping heavens, but those that fell from Jesus' eyes; it is not the rain that drops from dissolving clouds, but the blood that dropped from a wounded Saviour; it is not what falls when lightnings flash, and thunders roll along shaking skies, but what fell when the sword of justice was flashed in his dying eye, and the law pealed its loudest thunders on his bleeding head—it is that which brings peace and pardon to the guilty soul, and fills to the brim this crimson fountain, which is opened for all uncleanness.

"I," not my ordinances, not baptism, nor the supper, nor preaching, nor prayer, not these, but "I," says Jesus, "am the way." Not *a* way, but *the* way. There is but one way. Let me warn you, that although there is but one way of getting to heaven, there are two ways of missing it; and what—at first seems strange—these two ways go off in opposite directions; the one to this side and the other to that. Yet, as one man traveling due westward, and another due eastward, at the same rate of so many miles a day, would meet again face to face somewhere on the opposite side of the globe, beneath our feet, the travelers by the two opposite paths I speak of meet again—meet in perdition. This doctrine of salvation by the blood and righteousness of Christ will—God blessing and enabling you to believe it—guard you against both errors—on this side against presumption, and on that against despair. Some—and of these the Pharisee is a type—believed that they are not sinners; or, if sinners, that God is not angry with them, and will not punish them. What an exposure of the delusion is that cross! The Son of God dies there. Unless he dies, your sin is not forgiven. Others—and of these Iscariot is the type—turning away from God, believe that he is so angry with them that he will not pardon. They look on God as a stern, austere, vindictive, and implacable Divinity; in whom the hatred of sin, like a roaring whirlpool, has swallowed up all other feelings—in whom the love, kindness, and pity of the Father is lost in the sternness of the Judge. And so—nor any wonder when such is their belief—they shun God, they hate God, they try to shut him out from their thoughts and wish —how vain the wish !—that there were no God at all. But where, let me ask, do we find this implacable God? If I ascend into heaven, he is not there ; there God sits enthroned, the father of a happy family—like an effulgent sun, pouring gladness and glory upon all. I return to this earth—go up and down the world—seek him, but he is not here ; I can not find a trace or footprint of him here. I see God's sun shining without distinction on the evil and the good, and his rain falling with the same affluent abundance on the fields of the just and the unjust. Fields, forests, mountains, smiling valleys, and sunny seas, are not more full of creatures than of happiness ; and from the deep bass of ocean to the ringing carol of the lark, nature forms one choir, and chants her hymns to God. I open the Bible, but he is not here. Gift of our heavenly Father, dying legacy of an incarnate Son, revelation of a kind and winning Spirit! love shines on thy every page, and in thy very name thy loving mercy is proclaimed—Gospel, glad tidings, good tidings, of good. Of this God, this appalling specter, whom Despair eyes with a dark and horrid scowl, Heaven says, he is not in me ; Earth says, he is not in me ; the Bible says, he is not in me.

Where is he, then ? With head averted, hair standing on end, and stony horror in her looks, Despair points to the pit, saying—look there! What have you to say to that ? In the first place, I have certainly not to say that that hell is but the dream which haunts a guilty conscience—nor yet to deny that there is a hell. No: nor, further, to conceal it although I could. It were no kindness to spread a covering over the pit; that is the cunning hunter's business; and the business of him who hunts the world for souls. It is an awful thought, that pit; it is an awful reality, that pit; it is an awful abode, that pit; and this is an awful declaration, " The wicked shall be cast into hell, and all the nations that fear not God." But over against these stern declarations, and between the pit and you, a high red cross is standing. Mercy descends from heaven, lights upon its summit, and preaches hope to despair, pardon to guilt, salvation to the lost. Free as the winds that fan her cheek, free as the sunbeams that shine on her golden tresses, she invites all to come, opens her arms to embrace the world, and in a voice that rings like a silver trumpet, cries, " O, Earth, Earth, Earth, hear the word of the Lord." A beautiful vision! Her eye, so pitiful, swims in tears as she looks on poor sinners, and, not willing that any should perish, she bids you read on that cross, where it is written, not in letters of gold, but blood, this greatest oath—these blessed words :—" As I live, saith the Lord, I have no pleasure in the death of the wicked." As *I live*, says God, I have no pleasure in the death of the wicked. By my cross and agony, by this thorny crown and bloody tree, as *I die*, says Jesus, I have no pleasure in the death of the wicked. Holy Spirit! Dove of heaven! hovering over us, staying, lingering, refusing to be driven away, thou sayest, as I now plead, entreat, implore, " I have no pleasure in the death of the wicked."

Man Converted.

A new heart also will I give you, and a new spirit will I put within you; and I will take away the stony heart out of your flesh, and I will give you an heart of flesh.—EZEKIEL xxxvi. 26.

IT is a happy thing that baptism is not the door of heaven;—happy for millions, who, dying in earliest infancy, never pass that way. Dying unbaptized, we hold that they die not on that account unsaved; for whoever dare hang God's mercy on any outward rite, we do not, and although we believe that this interesting ordinance is also, when engaged in with faith, an eminently blessed one, we dare not. Thousands go to heaven without baptism. Thousands, alas! perish with it. Heaven is greatly made up of little children —sweet buds that have never blown, or which death has plucked from a mother's bosom to lay on his own cold breast, just when they were expanding, flower-like, from the sheath, and opening their engaging beauties in the budding time and spring of life. "Of such is the kingdom of heaven." How sweet these words by the cradle of a dying infant! They fall like balm drops on our bleeding heart, when we watch the ebbing of that young life, as wave after wave breaks feebler, and the sinking breath gets lower and lower, till with a gentle sigh, and a passing quiver of the lip, our child now leaves its body, lying like an angel asleep, and ascends to the beatitudes of heaven and the bosom of God. Indeed, it may be that God does with his heavenly garden as we do with our own gardens. He may chiefly stock it from nurseries, and select for transplanting what is yet in its young and tender age—flowers before they have bloomed, and trees ere they begin to bear.

In the words of the Westminster Catechism, " Baptism is a sacrament, wherein the washing with water in the name of the Father, and the Son, and the Holy Ghost, doth signify and seal our ingrafting into Christ, and partaking of the benefits of the covenant of grace, and our engagement to be the Lord's." Baptism attaches us to the visible church; admits to *that*, and is its door of entrance; but, while it unites to the body of professing believers, it does not of necessity form any living attachment between us and the Saviour. Let us see what is done in these ordinances.

Years ago a man stood up in the house of God, and in his arms there lay a sleeping child. Dipping his hand into a laver, the minister sprinkled some drops on the infant's face, and over the unconscious creature pronounced the names of Father, Son, and Holy Ghost. That child was you. By hands, now moldering in the grave, your father then tied you—so to speak—to Christ. Well, time rolls on, and infants grow into children, children shoot up into youths, and youths change into bearded men; and then there comes another day. A table is spread in the house of God. Like the shroud in which kind women swathed his sacred body, a linen cloth covers the memorials of Christ's death. The broken body is un covered, the commemoration begins; and, amid the stillness of that solemn scene, with thoughtful countenance, a man leaves his seat, and taking the bread, and raising the wine-cup in his hand, he dedicates him self to the Saviour. That man again is you. And now awake, not asleep, conscious of what is done, not passive but active now, with your own hands you cast another knot upon the cord by which your father years ago bound you to Jesus. You are now tied— doubly tied—yet it does not follow that you are yet engrafted into him.

I have seen a branch tied to the bleeding tree, for the purpose of being engrafted into its wounded body, and that thus both might be one. Yet no incorporation had followed; there was no living union. Spring came singing, and with her fingers opened all the buds; and summer came, with her dewy nights and sunny days, and brought out all the flowers; and brown autumn came to shake the trees and reap the fields, and with dances and mirth to hold "harvest home;" but that unhappy branch bore no fruit, nor flower, nor even leaf. Just held on by dead clay and rotting cords, it stuck to the living tree—a withered and unsightly thing. So alas! is it with many; "having a name to live they are dead." They have no faith; they want that bond of living union between the graft and what it is grafted on—between the sinner and the Saviour. And, therefore, in quitting this part of our subject for another, let me ask, "believest thou;" and if thou dost not, O, let me urge you to pray with the man in the Gospel, "Lord, help mine unbelief?"

Do you say, I cannot believe? In one sense, that is true; in another, it is not. It is not true in the same sense as it is true—that a man who has no eyes in his head—nothing but empty sockets—can not see. All men are born with faith. Faith is as natural to a man as grief, or love, or anger. One of the earliest

flowers that springs up in the soul—it smiles on a
mother from her infant's cradle; and living on through
the rudest storms of life, it never dies till the hour of
death. On the face of a child which has been left for
a little time with strangers, and may be caressed with
their kisses, and courted with their smiles, and fondled,
and dandled in their arms, I have seen a cloud gather-
ing, and growing darker, till at length it burst in cries
of terror and a shower of tears. The mother returns;
and when the babe holds out its little arms to her, I
see in these the arms of faith; and when, like a be-
liever restored to the bosom of his God, it is nestling
in a mother's embrace, and the cloud passes from its
brow, and its tears are changed into smiles, and its
terror into calm serenity, we behold the principle of
faith in play. This is one of its earliest, and—so far
as nature is concerned—one of its most beautiful de-
velopments. So natural, indeed, is it for us to con
fide, and trust, and believe, that a child believes what-
ever it is told, until experience shakes its confidence
in human veracity. Its eye is caught by the beauty
of some flower, or it gazes up with wonder on the
starry heavens;—with that inquisitiveness which in
childhood, active as a bee, is ever on the wing, it is
curious to know who made them, and would believe
you if you said you made them yourself. Such is the
faith which nature gives it in a father, that it never
doubts his word. It believes all he says, and is con-
tent to believe where it is not able to comprehend.
For this, as well as other reasons, our Lord presented,
n a child, the living model of a Christian. He left
Abraham, father of the faithful, to his repose in
heaven; he left Samuel, undisturbed, to enjoy the
quiet rest of his grave; he allowed Moses and Elias,

after their brief visit, to return to the skies, and wing their way back to glory. For a pattern of faith, he took a boy from his mother's side, and, setting him up, in his gentle, blushing, shrinking modesty, before the great assembly, he said, "Whosoever shall not receive the kingdom of God as a little child, shall in no wise enter therein."

Paul said, "When I was a child I spake as a child, I thought as a child; but when I became a man, I put away childish things;" but no man ever thought of leaving the faith of childhood with its rattle and its toys. Faith is, in fact, the soul and life of friendship. What is a friend, but one whom I can trust, one who, I believe, will mingle his tears with mine, and whose support I reckon on when my back is at the wall? Without faith in each other's friendship, kindness, and honesty, this world would be turned into a Bedouin desert; men would become Ishmaelites;—my hand against every man, and every man's hand against me. Faith is the marriage tie; the guardian angel of conjugal felicity; the jeweled zone that binds society together; the power, mightier than steam, or wind, or water, that moves all the wheels of commerce. Unless man could trust his fellow-man, business would come to a dead stand; the whole machinery of the world would stop; our busy streets would bear crops of grass; and, though winds blew and tides flowed as before, rotting ships would fall to pieces in our silent and deserted harbors.

Leaving the busy city for rural scenes, or setting your foot on board ship, and pushing out upon the heaving ocean, you find faith ploughing the fields of both—faith in the laws of nature, in the ordinances of Providence. When the air has still a frosty breath, and, although cleared of winter snow, the earth is cold and—looks dead as a corpse disrobed of its shroud— it shows neither flower nor leaf, nor sign of life, the husbandman, notwithstanding, yokes his team and drives the ploughshare through its breasts. With confidence in his step, liberality in his hand, and hope in his eye, he scatters the seed far and wide on the bosom of the ground. He is a believer; a believer in Providence—in the laws and procession of the seasons. He has faith; not saving faith indeed, but still true faith. He believes that out of these frosty skies gentle zephyrs shall blow, and soft showers shall fall, and summer beams shall shine; and, looking along the vista of time, he sees golden corn waving thick upon these empty fields, and hears in this silent scene the joy of light hearts ringing in the laugh and song of the reapers. His ploughing and his sowing are acts of genuine faith; and, as he strides across the field with his sowing sheet around him, he is an example of one, who, with his eye, as well as his foot, on earth, " Walks by faith, not by sight."

Then again, sailing as much as sowing is an act of faith. In this rough and weather-beaten mariner, on board whose ship we are dashing through the thick gloom of a starless night, and over the waves of a pathless ocean, I see faith standing at the helm. That man has faith in the needle; and believing that the heart of an angel is not more true to God than this needle to the north, he presses forward over the watery waste in a voyage, that may with perfect truth be called a voyage of faith. Would to God we had as strong a faith in our Bible! Would to God that our trembling hearts pointed as true to Jesus, as his needle in all weathers, and on all seas, to the distant pole! What we want divine grace to do, is not so much to give us faith, as to give to the principle or faculty of faith, which we have by nature, a right, holy, heavenward direction; to convert it into faith in things eternal. The faith that sees an unseen world—a faith just as strong in the revelations of the Bible as in the ordinary laws of nature, this is what we need. Let it be sought in earnest, persevering prayer. It is "the gift of God." Saving faith has God for its author, the Spirit for its agent, Christ for its object, grace for its root, holiness for its fruit, and heaven for its reward. Accepting the righteousness of Christ, it makes us just; and seeing every sin pardoned, all guilt removed, God smiling, and heaven opening to receive us, it is the spring of a peace of mind which is worth more than the wealth of worlds, which passeth all understanding. May God help us to the confession and the prayer, "Lord I believe, help thou mine unbelief."

We have already stated that while salvation was the one thing needful, there were two things needful for salvation. Having considered the first of these, namely, the remission of sin and justification of the sinner, we now enter on the second, namely, the renovation of the soul as enunciated in the words, "A new heart also will I give you, and a new spirit will I put within you, and I will take away the stony heart out of your flesh, and I will give you a heart of flesh." And we remark—

I. This is a great change. Not that all men think so. Once on a time, for instance, we wandered into a church in this city. The preacher read these words for his text, "Except a man be born again, he can not see the kingdom of God." And just as at the fords of Jordan, they knew a man's country by the way he sounded Shibboleth, so you will never fail to know a man's creed by the way in which he handles such a passage as that. The preacher read his text; and then, as it were, sat down by the cradle, where his charge was sleeping, to rock them over into a deeper slumber. The text, forsooth, was an oriental figure! a hyperbole! pointing to an outward change. No more was needed. In the strong and highly figura-tive language which eastern nations indulge in, it described the change undergone by the man who abandons a wild and wicked life for habits of decency, honesty, and temperance. Far be it from me to speak lightly of temperance societies, or of any scheme, in-deed, that aims at the dignity and elevation of man; yet, according to the preacher, our Lord's language meant nothing more than the change which these in-stitutions are of themselves able to accomplish—a change of habits without any gracious change of heart. Did a drunkard become sober? he was born again; a libertine pure? or thief honest? or liar true? he was born again! In short, such was the style and character of the discourse, that if a poor, hungry soul had gone there for bread, he could have got nothing—carried away nothing—but a stone; and instead of a fish, we saw the serpent's coil, and heard her hiss. The preacher taught that these words were applicable only to the scum and off-scourings of the city—the dregs of society—those poor, depraved, degraded creatures, who, weighed down by a load of poverty and ignorance and guilt, have sunk to the bottom, and to our shame are left to lie there in distressing and dreadful pollu tion. So far as any congregation of decent, well-dressed, sober, honest, reputable professors of religion were concerned, that truth had no bearing on them; our Lord—although he assuredly found in Nicodemus one of this class—did not speak of them; they, happy mortals! had no need to be born again.

You cannot fancy any two things more opposed to each other than that doctrine and ours. We believe that the purest, gentlest, loveliest, most amiable creature that blesses fond parents, and adorns earth's happiest home—one of nature's fairest flowers—stands as much in need of a new birth as the vilest outcast who walks these streets—the lost one, whose name is never mentioned but by broken hearts and in wrestling prayers to God. The best of mankind are so bad that all have need to be born again ; so bad, that the change promised in the text, and insisted on by our Saviour, can not be a surface or superficial matter.— any mere defilement of the skin which nitre and soap may remove. Words have no meaning unless this change is a radical reform—a change great in its character, and lasting in its consequences—a change, which, affecting not the habits only, but the heart, both reaches downward into the deepest recesses of the soul, and stretches forward into the ages of eternity.

Now, I am afraid that some—dreaming, as they slumber, that they have been born again, and so are safe, because their conduct is changed, and because, so far as their mere habits are concerned, they are better than once they were—have gone to sleep before this work is even begun. Beware of rash conclusions of such momentous importance. Have we not seen passions, like the fire upon the hearth, burn out and die for want of fuel? Have we not seen the course of vice, like a worn out machine, stop from the decays of nature—from the mere wear and tear of its materials. Virtue is cheap; vice is costly; and, proving a heavy tax upon the purse, destructive of health, and damaging to character, we have seen self-interest turn a man from the indulgence of his strongest vices. Old age cools hot blood. Successive bereavements will in a way break the heart, and some deep disappointment may wean those, who have the keenest appetite for its pleasures, from the gayeties and vanities of the world. And, as in Roman Catholic countries, many a cowled monk, and many a veiled nun, enters convent or monastery more from feelings of disappointment than devotion; so, when hopes are blasted, and pride is mortified, and ambition has missed her mark, you may get sick of the world. Alas! all who bid adieu to the ball-room and theater, and giddy round of fashion, do not leave the circle of their enchantments for the closet, for the sanctuary, for fields of Christian benevolence. As by sleight of hand and necromantic trick, Egypt's magicians produced a set of mimic miracles, that were clever counterfeits of those which God wrought by the hand of Moses, may not other causes than true love of holiness or godly hatred of sin work such an outward, as bears some considerable likeness to a saving change? In matters of religion, beware of confounding an *almost* with an *altogether* Christian. So far as it goes, any change for the better is good. We hail it with hope. It is good so far as it goes, and good so long as it lasts; but Oh, let us not fall into the fatal mistake of confounding an outward reformation with that divine, inward, eternal transformation which is wrought by the Spirit, and promised in the words, " A new heart also will I give you."

Leaving the nature of this change to be afterwards considered, let me attempt meanwhile to show that this is a great change. In illustration of the truth, look, I pray you, to the symbols under which it is presented in the Word of God.

It is a birth.

When an infant leaves the womb—that darksome dwelling, where it has passed the first stage of its existence,—although the same creature, it may be said to be a new creature, and to enter on a new being. How great the change from that living sepulcher, where it lay entombed, nor saw, nor heard, nor breathed, nor loved, nor feared, nor took any more interest than the dead in all that was happening around it! Alive, yet how like death its state has been. Having eyes, it saw not, and ears it heard not, and feet it walked not, and hands it handled not, and affections it felt not. Its state was a strange and mysterious mingling of the characters of life and death When the windows of its senses are thrown open, and streams of knowledge come rushing in on its young and wondering soul, and its eyes follow the light, and with its restless hands it is acquainting itself with matter, and sounds are entering its ears, amid whose mingled din it soon learns to distinguish the sweet tones of one tender voice—its mother's, and it loves, and is loved, and lies nestling in dreamy slumbers on her bosom, or sweetly smiles in her smiling face—how great the change! Now, just because the change wrought on the soul in conversion is also great, and introduces its subject into a new and delightful existence, it borrows a name from that change. That is

the first, this is the second birth; aye, and infinitely
the better of the two. Better! because in that a son
of man is born but for the grave, whereas in this a
son of God is born for glory. Better! because the
march of these little feet is along a rough path be-
tween a cradle and a coffin; whereas, the way of
grace, however full of trials, toil, and battle, is from
the pangs of birth onward and upward to a crown in
heaven. Happy for you if you are heaven-born and
heaven-bound. It may be that a stormy life lies be-
fore you; but let storms rage and tempests roar—
however rude the gale or high the rolling billows—a
heaven-born passenger in a heaven-bound bark, you
cannot miss the haven. "There remaineth a rest to
the people of God."

This change is a resurrection. A resurrection is a
great change. Go to the churchyard. Go where death
shall one day carry you, whether you will or not.
"Come," said the angels, "see the place where the
Lord lay." Come, let us see the place where we our-
selves shall lie, and look at man as we ourselves shall
be. Take him in any of his stages of decay. Look
at this compressed line of mold, that by its color
marks itself out as different from the neighboring
clay; it is black earth, and retains no apparent ves-
tige of organization. What resemblance does it bear
to a man? None. Yet gather it together and give
it to the chemist; he analyzes it, and pronounces this
unctuous dust to have been once a human creature.
It may have been a beauty, who with alarm saw the
roses fading on her cheek, and age tracing wrinkles
on her ivory brow, and mixing in gray hairs with her
raven locks. It may have been a beggar, who, tired
of his cold and hungry pilgrimage, laid his head gladly

in the lap of mother earth, and ended his weary wan-
derings here. It may have been a king, who was
dragged from amid his guards to the tomb, and sul-
lenly yielded to the sway of a monarch mightier than
himself. Or, look here at these yellow relics of mor-
tality which the grave-digger—familiar with his trade
·—treats with such irreverent contempt. Look at these
preachers of humility—at this moldering skull, the
deserted palace of a soul, within which high intellect
once sat enthroned—at those fleshless cheeks, once
blooming with smiles and roses—at that skeleton hand,
which may once have grasped the helm of public
affairs, or swayed the passions of capricious multi-
tudes, or held up the cross from sacred pulpits to the
eyes of dying men—at those moldering limbs, which
piety may have bent to God—and at these hollow
sockets—now the nest of slimy worms—where glances
of love have melted, and looks of fire have flashed.

· Turning away your head with horror and humilia-
tion, to think that you shall lie where they are—and be
as they are—you say, Alas! what a change is there!
Ah! but Faith steps forward, plants a triumphant
foot on the black grave's edge, and silencing my
fears, dispelling my gloom, and reconciling me to that
lowly bed, she lifts her cheerful voice, and exclaims,
True! but what a change shall be there! Looking
through her eyes, I see the spell broken. 1 see that
dust once more animate. And when the blast of the
trumpet—penetrating the caves of the rocks, and felt
down in the depths of ocean—pierces the ear of death
in this dark, and cold, and lonely bed, where I have
lowered a coffin, and left the dear form and sweet face
of some loved one, mortality shall rise in form immor-
tal, more beautiful than love ever fancied, or poet

sang. How great the change, when these moldering bones, which children look at with fear, and grown men with solemn sadness, shall rise instinct with life! Think of this handful of brown dust springing up into a form like that on which Adam gazed with mute astonishment, when for the first time he caught the image of himself mirrored in a glassy pool of Paradise; or better still, in a form such as, when awakening from his slumber, he saw with wondering, admiring eyes, in the lovely woman that lay by his side on their bed of love and flowers. And now, because the change which conversion works on the soul is also inexpressibly great, it borrows a name from that mighty change; that, a resurrection of the body from the grave, this, a resurrection of the soul from sin. In this "we pass from death to life"—in this we are "created anew in Jesus Christ." "We rise with Him," says the Apostle, "to newness of life."

The greatness of the change is set forth in the symbolical representation of it in the next chapter. Seized by the hand of the Spirit, Ezekiel is borne aloft, carried away through the air, and set down in a lonely valley among the hills of a distant land. This valley seems to have been, at some former period, the scene of a great battle. There hosts had sustained the charge of hosts, and crowns were perhaps staked and won. The peace of these solitudes had been rudely broken by the shrieks of the wounded, the wild shouts of the victors, the clash of arms, and the savage roar of battle. It was silent now. The tide that swept over it had left it strewed with wrecks; the dead had moldered unburied where they fell; the skull rattled in the cloven helmet; the sword of the warrior lay rusting beside his skeleton, and the handle was still in the

11

relaxed grasp of the bony fingers. On these unburied corpses the "birds of the air had summered," and "the wild beasts of the field had wintered." The rain had washed, and the sun had bleached them;—they were white and dry. In these grim and ghasty skeletons a doleful picture of death lay stretched out before the prophet; and while he surveyed the scene, there was neither sign nor sound of life, but, it may be, the croak of the raven, or the howl of the famished wolf, or the echo of his own solitary footfall. Such was the scene Ezekiel was contemplating when a voice made him start. It came from the skies, charged with this strange question, "Son of man, can these bones live?"

We stay not to relate all that happened and was done. It serves our purpose to say, that after the prophet had preached to the bones, he prayed to Him who—to dead bones, dead bodies, dead hearts, dead souls, dead families, and dead churches—is "the Resurrection and the Life." Ezekiel's was the prayer of faith—and it had its answer. How encouraging to us, when on our knees, that answer! We feel as if Aaron and Hur sat at our side, and held up our weary arms. Ezekiel, after preaching, prayed; and there came from heaven a living and life-giving breath. It blows down the valley; and as it kisses the icy lips of the dead, and stirs their hair, and fans their faces, man after man springs to his feet, till the field which Ezekiel found covered with ghastly skeletons is crowded with a mighty army—all armed for battle and war—the marshaled host of God.

That was a great change, and not less great the work of grace in conversion. While the prophet is gazing with astonished eye on this martial array, where, amid trumpet echoes, spears are gleaming, and plumes are dancing, as, bold in aspect and stout for war, the serried ranks march on, mark what the Lord said:—"Son of man, these bones are the whole house of Israel; behold they say, Our bones are dried, and our hope is lost." Now, is not this the very judgment—the very sentence—which the sinner often pronounces on his own case when his eyes are first opened, and he sees himself lost and undone? What is the house of Israel here but a type of God's chosen people? In Israel we see our state by nature; a state of death; a state in which we are "dead in trespasses and sins." On this account Satan would have us yield to despair. He says that for such sinners there is no help—no hope. It is he who speaks in the complaint, "Our bones are dried, and our hope is lost." Yes, it is he, the father of lies, the enemy of souls. Yield not even to a doubt, for here "he that doubteth is damned;" but mark God's gracious answer to that unbelieving, dark, desponding complaint— "Thus saith the Lord God; behold, O my people, I will open your graves, and I will put my spirit within you, and ye shall live."

Hereafter, we will enter particularly into the nature of this great change; meanwhile, let me ask, Have you any experience of it? I neither ask when, nor where, nor how you felt its first impressions. On these subjects the experience of saints is very different. Some can tell the time of it—giving day and date, the hour, the providence, the place, the text, the preacher, and all the circumstances associated with their con version. They can show the arrow, which, shot from some bow drawn at a venture, pierced the joints of their armor, and quivered in their heart. They can show the pebble from the brook, that, slung, it may be, by a youthful hand, but directed of God, was buried in the forehead of their giant sin. They can show the word that penetrated their soul, and—in some truths of Scripture—the salve that healed the sore, the balm that stanched the blood, and the bandage that Christ's own kind hand wrapped on the bleeding wound. Able to trace the steps and whole progress of their conversion—its most minute and interesting details—they can say with David, "Come and hear, all ye that fear God, and I will declare what he hath done for my soul."

It is not so, however, with all, or, perhaps, with most. Some, so to speak, are still-born; they were unconscious of their change; they did not know when or how it happened; for a while at least, they gave hardly a sign of life. With many the dawn of grace is, in more respects than one, like the dawn of day. We turn our face to the east, and our back to the setting stars, to note the very moment of the birth of morning; yet how hard it is to tell when and where the first faint, cold, steel-gray gleam appears. It is so with many in regard to their spiritual dawn,—with the breaking of an eternal day,—with their first emotions of desire, and of alarm, as with that faint and feeble streak, which brightened, and widened, and spread, till it blazed into a brilliant sky.

The great matter, about which to be anxious, is not the time, nor place, nor mode of the change, but the fact itself. Has this change taken place in you? Are you other than once you were? Rather than be what once you were, would you prefer not being at all? Would you prefer annihilation to your old corruption? Some, alas! change to the worse, giving themselves up to _ins, which once they would have blushed to mention. Dead to all sense of shame, breaking loose from the innocence of their childhood, casting off the comely habits and pious practices of a paternal home, they plunge into excess of riot; and, borne on by the impetus they have acquired in the descent, like one running down hill who can not stop although he would, when they reach the mouth of the pit they are borne over into perdition. They change, but, like "Seducers," they " wax worse and worse." The night grows darker and darker; the edge of conscience duller and duller; the process of petrifaction goes on in their heart, till it acquires the hardness of stone; and, wallowing in the mire of the lowest sensuality, they can make a boast of sins—sins, in regard to which, on the day when they left their father's roof, with his blessing on their head, and a mother's warm tears on their cheek, they would have said with feelings of indignant abhorrence—"Is thy servant a dog that he should do such a thing." What a melancholy change!

In blessed and beautiful contrast to a metamorphosis so sad, has the change in you taken an opposite direction? Can you say, I am not what once I was,— but better, godlier, holier! Happy are you! Happy, although, afraid of presumption, and in the blushing modesty of a spiritual childhood, you can venture no further than one who was urged to say whether she had been converted? How modest, yet how satisfactory her reply! That, she answered, I cannot—that I dare not say; but there is a change somewhere; either I am changed, or the world is changed. If you can say so, it is well. Such an answer leaves no room for painful doubts. Our little child—watching with curious eye the apparent motion of objects—calls out in ecstasy, and bids us see how hedge and house are flying past our carriage. It is not these that move, nor is it the fixed and firm shore, with its trees and fields, and boats at anchor, and harbors and headlands, that is gliding by the cabin windows. That is an illusion of the eye. The motion is not in them but us. And if the world is growing less in your eye, it shows that you are retreating from it, rising above it, and ascending in the arms of grace to higher regions; and if the fashion of this world, to our eye, seems passing away, it is because we ourselves are passing—passing and pressing on in the way to heaven. Sin never changes. And if what was once lovely looks loathsome now—if what was once desired is detested now, if what was once sought we now shun and shrink from, it is not because sin is changed, but—blessed be God, and praise be to his grace—we are changed. Our eyes are opened; the scales have dropt from them; and the solution of the problem may be found in the blind man's answer—"Whereas I was blind, now I see."

The Heart of Stone.

A new heart also will I give you, and a new spirit will I put within you; and I will take away the stony heart out of your flesh.— Ezekiel xxxvi. 26.

THERE is a mine of sound sense in the adage of an old divine, "seriousness is the greatest wisdom, temperance the most efficient physic, and a good conscience the very best estate." Early habits of self-restraint, total abstinence from all excess, diligence in business, attention to our duties, and that tranquility of mind which piety breeds, and which those enjoy who are at peace with God,—these, we confidently affirm, would do more to abate disease than all our physicians, much more to feed the hungry, and clothe the naked, than our Poor Laws and charitable institutions, and very much more than any Acts of Parliament to promote the comforts of the people, and preserve the liberties of the commonwealth. The older we grow, and the more our observation enlarges, the deeper grows our conviction, that "godliness is profitable unto all things, having promise of the life that now is, and of that which is to come."

One of the most remarkable instances of the truth, which it was ever our good fortune to see, presented itself in the immediate vicinity of this church. A weary day had passed in visiting a degraded neighborhood. The scenes were sad, sickening, repulsive. Famine, fever, want, squalid nakedness, moral and physical impurities, drunkenness, death, and the devil were all reigning there. Those only who have known the sickness and sinking of heart which the miseries of such scenes produce, especially when aggravated by a close and foul atmosphere, can imagine the gratification and surprise with which, on opening a door, we stepped into a comfortable apartment. Its white washed walls were hung round with prints; the furni ure shone like a looking-glass; and a bright fire was dancing merrily over a clean hearth-stone. It was an oasis in the desert. And we well remember, ere ques· tion was asked or answered, of saying to ourselves, "Surely the fear of God is in this place; this must be the house of a church-going family." It proved to be so. A blind man dwelt there. It was a home where squalid poverty might have been excused. And from it we carried away with us a lively sense of the temporal advantages of piety; and felt inclined to chalk these words on the blind man's door, as a lesson to his neighbors—"The fear of the Lord, that is wis dom; and to depart from evil is understanding."

Suppose—and we suppose nothing impossible, nor in coming days improbable, for the promise waits fulfillment, "a nation shall be born in a day"—suppose, then, that in the plentitude of divine grace, God should bend an eye of pity on the wretched inhabitants of our immediate neighborhood, and pour down his Spirit on them in showers from heaven. At present, with a few bright exceptions, they are the votaries and victims of dissipation—I say votaries and victims, because vice is such a damning thing, that he who begins by ministering at her altar always ends by becoming the sacrifice. Around us thousands live who never enter a house of God. Their children, unless they are fortunate enough to die early, are reared in ignorance, vice, and crime; and by habits of intemperance, many of them have reduced themselves to pinching hunger, ill-relieved by the uncertain supplies of charity, and the most squalid wretchedness. Now, suppose that God were pleased to send life to these " dry bones,"— that from lip to lip, and house to house, the cry were passing, " Oh, sirs, what shall I do to be saved?"— that the last shilling that vice had left, were spent for the purchase of a Bible; that, like water by men parched in the desert, and dying of thirst, God's word were bought, borrowed, or begged, and that, rising to the summons of the Sabbath bell, these streets, where only a solitary worshiper may now be seen, were filled with the unaccustomed spectacle of a ragged crowd pouring into the houses of God;—how soon would their common aspect change? A few weeks, and we should hardly recognize them.

Save these picturesque and old-fashioned tenements, the blue heavens above, that rocky citadel with its frowning batteries, yonder noble arm of the sea, and the same green fields, rich valleys and romantic crags, of the everlasting hills around us, all old things else would have passed away. Prisons, that now complain of crowded cells, would be found too large; and many churches, cold now with empty pews, would be found too small. The smoldering fever would, like an un-fed fire, go out for want of fuel; and rank church-yards would grow green at Christmas, for lack of their too-frequent burials. The brutal features of dissipa tion would give place to an expression of intelligence and humanity; roses would blow on childhood's pal-lid cheek, and mother's smiles would chase the sadness from many a poor, sallow, infant face. Then, under the patronage of religion, and the sign of the Bible, the craft of the honest mechanic, and the trade of the useful merchant would flourish, while the panderer to vice would fall into unpitied bankruptcy, and the voice of a virtuous people would tell him to shut shop and begone. Furniture would crowd these empty rooms; the rags, through whose loopholes poverty stared out upon a pitying world, would change into decent attire. Piety, descending like an angel from the skies, would come to these dwellings with a prophet's blessing; beneath her celestial feet happiness would spring up like summer flowers; plenty would pour her horn into the lap of poverty; there would be meal in every household barrel, and oil in every widow's cruse. Underneath the benign and blessed influences of religion, this wilderness would be glad; our city Ishmaelites would change into Israelites, and these moral deserts would rejoice and blossom like the rose. "Even so, come, Lord Jesus; come quickly."

The truth is, the world's great want is the want of religion. Perhaps men want more equal laws, more liberal institutions, and through their happy influence, better and more stable governments. The greatest want of nations is, however, that without which liberty has no solid pedestal to stand on—a genuine, mass-pervading piety. To drop all reference to foreign countries, I am sure that he who attempts to cure our own social maladies, independently of this best and most sanatory element, may be a philanthropist, but is not a philosopher. We had almost said he is a fool. He is an idle schemer, who would fain make bricks without straw, and heal the waters of Jericho without the prophet's salt. His theories are as baseless and unsolid as if they conceived of man as a creature without a soul--of the solar system as without its central sun—of the universe without its God. But while religion is thus the mortar that binds society together,—while the poor man may remember to his comfort, that if he leave his family no inheritance but his prayers and the priceless legacy of a godly example, he leaves them rich indeed,—while an education of domestic piety is better than all Greek and Roman lore,—and while godliness is the most stable basis on which to erect an earthly fortune,—I pray you to observe that the change promised in the text does not necessarily imply any temporal advantage—any improvement either in our bodily condition or worldly circumstances. We live in a world of mysteries. We sometimes see religion languishing neglected on a bed of sickness; and piety, in other cases than that of Lazarus, may be found clad in rags and covered with sores, sitting a beggar at the rich man's gate. The change is on the man within. The change is on the tenant, not the tenement; on the heart, not the body; on our circumstances, not so much in this life as in the life to come. If by faith in Christ you come to God, I can not promise for him that he will pour health into your veins or money into your purse. But he will endow you with infinitely better gifts. Hear what he promises in the text—"A new heart also will I give you, and a new spirit will I put within you ; and I will take away the stony heart out of your flesh, and I will give you an heart of flesh."

Having already illustrated the greatness of this change, I now proceed to examine its nature; and remark—

I. The old heart is taken away, and a new one put in its place.

The head was justly considered by the ancients to be the residence of the intellectual faculties, where the soul sat enthroned, as in a palace—presiding over all. On the other hand, they regarded the affections as having dwelling in the heart—that other great organ of our system. Within the breast, love and hatred, grief and joy, aversion and desire, generosity, jealousy, pity, revenge, were supposed to dwell; and thus (to dismiss the metaphor), that substitution of one heart for another which is promised in the text, just implies an entire change in the character and current of our affections. Now, a change may be simply a reform, or, extending farther, it may pass into a revolution. The spiritual change, which we call conversion, is not a mere reform. It is a revolution—a mighty revolution, if aught was ever worthy of that name—a revolution greater than the tomes of profane history, or any old monuments of stone or of brass record. It changes the heart, the habits, the eternal destiny of an immortal being. On the banner, borne in triumph at the head of this movement, I read the words that doom old things to ruin, "Overturn, Overturn, Overturn." For the old mischievous laws which it repeals, it introduces a new code of statutes ; it changes the reigning dynasty, wrenches the scepter from a usurper's hand, and, banishing him forth of the kingdom, in restoring the throne to God, restores it to its rightful monarch.

The Gospel is indisputably revolutionary ;—there can be no doubt of the fact. The old charge brought against its preachers is true. "These that have turned the world upside down, are come hither also."

The world requires to be turned upside down. Like a boat capsized in a squall, and floating keel uppermost in the sea, with men drowning around it, the world has been turned upside down already; and to be set right, it must just be turned upside down again. If the order which God established has been reversed by sin—if in our hearts and habits time has assumed the place of eternity—the body of the soul—earth of heaven, and self of God;—if that is first which should be last, and that last which should be first,—if that is uppermost which should be undermost, and that undermost which should be uppermost, then happy the homes and the hearts of which, in reference to the entrance of God's Word, Spirit, and converting grace, it can be said, "These that have turned the world upside down, are come hither also."

Where, it may be asked, lies the inevitable necessity for a change so pervadingly elementary, so radical, so revolutionary? such an inward and total change? We must seek for that necessity in the records of a distant past. It lies in an old event—in the Fall. By reason of that great crime and sad calamity, the condition of our hearts has become naturally so bad—in reference at least to spiritual objects and interests—as not to admit of repair. We understand how this may be true of a house. The tenement may have fallen into such utter decay, so many cracks may gape in its bulged and tottering walls, the timbers may be so moth-eaten, the foundations so shaken, post, pillar, and lintel so moldered away, that nothing remains but to pull it down level with the ground, and on its old site to erect a new and stately edifice. Or—to vary the illustration—a watch, which has slipped through careless fingers, and crashed on the pavement,

may be so shattered as to have its works damaged be-
yond repair. It passes the skill of the most accom-
plished mechanic to mend them. He must clean out
the shell, take away the old works, and substitute new
machinery. In that case, although wheels, axles,
levers, move within the old casements, the watch, in
fact, is new; even so, when converted, although there
is no loss of personal identity suffered, he who gets
a new heart becomes, in a sense, a new man: to use
the Apostle's words, " He is, in Christ, a new creature."

It is no doubt true that there are many, and some
very serious injuries which admit of repair. A steady,
honest, enterprising merchant may repair a bankrupt
fortune; a sagacious statesman may solder a broken
crown; a physician may patch up a worn-out constitu-
tion; even some Mary Magdalene, returning to the
paths of virtue, may repair that most fragile of all
things—a woman's character; and, with time and
God's grace given me, I will undertake to heal a bro-
ken heart. In the divine government we see the
most remarkable provision made for the reparation of
those injuries to which his creatures are exposed.
The bark grows on the peeled surface of an old elm
or oak, so as in time to obliterate the letters that
friendship or fond love has carved. From the lips of
the gaping wound a liquid flesh is poured, which, re-
ceiving nerves and blood-vessels into its substance,
solidifies, and at length fills up the breach. From its
shattered surfaces, the broken limb discharges a fluid
bone—a living cement—which, growing solid, restores
the continuity of the shaft, and gives the sufferer a
leg or arm, strong as before. In some of the lower
animals, indeed, this power of reparation is equal to
the task, not only of repairing a broken, but of even

restoring a lost member. With such renovating powers has God endowed certain creatures, that, if by accident or otherwise, the writhing worm, for example, is divided, the headless portion not only survives such a formidable lesion, but, strange to see! produces and puts on a new head; and offers us an example of animal life, which, besides being fortified against the most formidable injuries, is actually multiplied by division—"How marvelous are thy works, Lord God Almighty!"

There are many striking and very interesting analogies between grace and nature. But there is no analogy between these cases and the case before us. So far as man's natural and inherent powers are concerned, his heart sustained an irreparable injury by the Fall. Sin is a disease which our constitution has no power to throw off; and which no human skill can remove. The preacher is here assisted by none of that "healing power of nature" which is the physician's best ally. Not only so, but God himself—with whom in a sense all things are possible, and to whom nothing is too hard—does not attempt its repair. In the work of conversion, it is not an old heart which is to be mended, but a new one which is to be given. In any attempt to patch up the old garment, the new cloth is lost, and the rent gapes but wider. On the old, frail, musty bottle, heaven wastes not her costly wine. The truth is, man does not admit of being repaired; and the more we become acquainted with our hearts, the more ready shall we be to describe their desperate and deplorable condition in the words of Holy Scripture—"The heart is deceitful above all things, and desperately wicked." The first thing, therefore, which you, who are seeking the kingdom of God and his righteousness, have need to seek, is what God promises in the text, and David pleads for in this prayer—"Create in me a clean heart, O God, and renew a right spirit within me."

Let me press this truth upon your thoughtful atten-tion. May God impress it upon your hearts! A lively and profound sense of it is of the highest im-portance. To feel our need of a new heart, and to feel that this old one will not mend nor make better, is, in fact, the first step in salvation; and the deeper our impression of the reality of the truth, the more diligently shall we labor, and the more earnestly shall we pray to be renewed day by day. It is a convic-tion that will secure our cordial assent to the mem-orable saying, with which one of England's greatest men, her bravest and noblest spirits, closed an illus-trious career on the scaffold of an ungrateful country. When Sir Walter Raleigh had laid his head upon the block, he was asked by the executioner whether it lay right. Whereupon, with the calmness of a hero, and the faith of a Christian he returned an answer—the power of which we all shall feel, when our own head is tossing and turning on death's uneasy pillow—"It matters little, my friend, how the head lies, provided the heart is right."

Now, as the view of the old heart, given in my text, is eminently calculated, with the divine blessing, to show us how much we need a new one, let us con sider—

II. The view which our text gives of the natural heart.

It is a heart of stone. "I will take the stony heart out of your flesh." We shall best understand the meaning of this figure, in its application to the heart, by considering, in a popular point of view, some of the characteristic properties of a stone.

A stone is cold. Coldness is characteristic of a stone. The lapidary, using his tongue to test the temperature, can, by that simple means, tell whether the seeming jewel is paste, or a real gem; and when our eye has been deceived by the skill of the painter, the sense of touch has informed us, that what seemed marble was only wood. It is a common saying, "As cold as a stone." But what stone so cold as that in man's breast? Cold is the bed of the houseless, who lies stretched on the wintry pavement, and cold the cell within whose dank stone walls the shivering prisoner is immured; but colder far by nature is this heart of ours to God and Christ. We are born lovers of pleasure rather than lovers of God. God is not an object of our love, nor do we make any return to Jesus for his warm and fond affection. Blessed Lord! he had many a cold lodging on this ungrateful earth; his couch was oft the open field, where his locks were wet with the dews of night; drenched with the spray of the sea, and the lashing rain, his weary frame found sleep on the hard benches of a fisher's boat; yet on these he lay not on so cold a bed as he would find in the dark, dreary chambers of an unrenewed heart. Sin has quenched a fire that once burned bright and holy there, and has left nothing now on that chill hearth, but embers and ashes—cold as death. "The carnal mind is *enmity* against God; is not subject to the law of God, neither indeed can be."

A stone is hard. Fire melts wax, but not stone; water softens clay, but not stone; a hammer bends the stubborn iron, but not stone. Stone resists these

influences; and, emblem of a heart crushed, but not
sanctified by affliction, it may be shattered into frag-
ments, or ground to powder, yet its atoms are as hard
as ever. It is with the dust of diamonds that the
diamond is cut. We have stood on a sea rock, when
every billow, swung on by the tempest, broke against
it with the roar of artillery, and shot up a shower of
snowy spray; we have looked to the crag, on whose
bald brows the storm was bursting, and wondered
how these could have braved for so many thousand
years the war and wear of elements; and yet there is
more cause to be surprised at what a man's heart will
stand. He sits in the church under a series of affect-
ing sermons,—or a succession of affecting providences
like great sea waves breaking over him; and he is
unshaken, at least unaltered, and to all but Divine
grace unalterable. He *can* be saved; but he can only
be saved, because there is nothing impossible to God.
Sitting there, so hard, so cold, he reminds us of a
mountain crag, cut by nature's fantastic hand into the
features of a man, which looks out with cold and
stony eye upon the gathering tempest, prepared, as it
has already weathered a thousand storms, to weather
a thousand more.

The man who remains unmoved under a ministry
of mercy, who is insensible to at once the most appall-
ing and appealing lessons of providence, who fears no
more than a rock the thunders and lightnings that
play round his brow, and feels no more than a rock
the influences that fall like summer sunbeams from
the face and cross of Jesus, is manifestly beyond all
human power. I would despair of his salvation, but
for the omnipotence and benevolence of God; and,
because I know that he, who of the stones of the street

could raise up children to Abraham, can turn that heart of stone into a heart of flesh. What need here of the Spirit of God! Oh! there is an obstinacy, an obduracy, a strength of resistance, an impenetrability to impression in the unconverted, before which man, however anxious to save, is utterly powerless. In dealing with such a case, we seem to hear the voice of God addressing us in his words to Job—" Canst thou draw out leviathan with a hook? or his tongue with a cord which thou lettest down? Canst thou put a hook into his nose, or bore his jaw through with a thorn? Wilt thou take him for a servant? Wilt thou play with him as a bird? or wilt thou bind him for thy maidens? His scales are his pride; joined one to another they stick together that they cannot be sundered. His eyes are like the eyelids of the morning. Out of his mouth go burning lamps, and sparks of fire leap out. The sword of him that layeth at him can not hold; the spear, the dart, nor the habergeon. He esteemeth iron as straw, and brass as rotten wood. Darts are counted as stubble; he laugheth at the shaking of a spear. He maketh the deep to boil like a pot; he maketh the sea like a pot of ointment; he maketh a path to shine after him; one would think the deep to be hoary. His heart is as firm as a stone, yea, as hard as a piece of the nether mill-stone."

A stone is dead. It has no vitality, no feeling, no power of motion. It lies where it is laid. The tomb-stone above and the dead man below undergo no change, other than that both, by a slower or speedier decay, are moldering into dust. In that hall of nobles the marble forms of departed greatness look down unmoved upon scenes where once they themselves played a distinguished part, and are, alike unmoved, whether their statesmanship be reviled or praised. In this statue—however skillful the sculptor's imitation—there is no life; no speech breaks from these mute lips; the limbs seem instinct with power, yet they never leave their pedestal; no fire flashes in the dull, gray eyes, nor passions burn within the stony breast. The stone is deaf, and dumb, and dead. In grief's wild and frantic outbursts affection may address the the form of one deeply loved, and for ever lamented. Speak to it, it returns no answer; weep to it, it sheds no tears; image of a lost and loved one, it feels not the grief that itself can move. Now, how many sit in the house of God as unmoved? Careless as mere spectators who have no concern in what takes place before them, they take no interest in any thing that was done on Calvary! Is it not sad to think that more tears are shed in playhouses than in churches; and that by those who call themselves Christians, the new novel is sought more eagerly, and devoured more greedily than the New Testament? What a deplorable account of the human heart! One would think it is of stones, and yet it is of living men, too like, alas! to many of ourselves—these words are spoken —"Having eyes, they see not; having ears, they hear not; neither do they understand."

We have described a stone as cold, hard, dead. Is this, some may ask, a fair and just picture of the human heart? The question is a fair one, and deserves a frank answer. I should hinder a cause I desire to help, and do injustice to divine truth, were I to answer that question by simply affirming, that the picture is a true portrait of the natural heart in all its sentiments and emotions. Human nature is bad enough without exaggerating its evils. There is no need to exaggerate them. In one sense, they do not admit of exaggeration. And, if we dared, instead of exaggerating, we should be happy to excuse them, and to our mother nature, render the kind and filial office of casting a cloak upon her shame.

We know as well as others do, and would ever remember, that although man be dead to gracious affections, until sin has had "its perfect work," he is not dead to many tender and lovely emotions of nature. Many beauties are lingering about this ruin—the engaging, but melancholy vestiges of its former glory. We freely admit, that, so far as regards father and mother, wife and children, brother and sister, and the beloved friends of our social circles, an unrenewed heart may be the warm nest of kindliest affections. There can be no doubt, I think, that the Christian will prove the best father, the best husband, the best wife, the best master, the best servant, the best citizen, the truest, trustiest friend. Nay, for their pith and truth, notwithstanding their homeliness, I will venture to quote the words of Rowland Hill, who said, "I would give nothing for the Christianity of a man whose very dog and cat were not the better of his religion." Still, it is no treason against the Gospel to believe that one, yet unhappily a stranger to the grace of God, may be endowed with many most pleasant and lovely virtues.

Away among the rough moors, by the banks of tumbling river, or the skirts of green wood, or on sloping acclivity, or steep hill-side, we have gathered, remote from gardens and the care of men, bunches of wild flowers, which, although very perishing, were exquisitely beautiful, and steeped in fragrant odors; and such as these are some men and women, who have never yet been transplanted from a state of nature into a state of grace. There is no sin in loving them. In the young ruler who declined to take up his cross and follow Christ, was not there so much that was amiable, gentle, lovely, that Jesus' own heart was drawn to him? It is said that he "loved him;" and the emotions of a Saviour's bosom cannot be wrong in mine. Nor is his a rare phenomenon—a solitary case. We have seen men who made no great profession of religion, who certainly were not pious, but who were yet so kind, tender, affectionate, generous, large-hearted, and open-handed, that it was impossible not to love them. Nature never asked our permission. Whether we would or not, we felt drawn to them, as Jesus was to the amiable youth who refused to follow him. And as we have rooted up from the moor some wild flower to blow and shed its fragrance in a sweeter than its native home, have we not longed to do the same with these fine specimens of the natural man? Transplanted by grace into the garden of the Lord, baptized with the dews of heaven, converted to the faith, they would be flowers fit to form a wreath for the brow that men wreathed with thorns. I am compelled to acknowledge that I have known some, whom even charity could not reckon among true Christians, who, yet in point of natural virtues, put Christians to shame. In some beautiful traits they were more like Jesus than not a few of his real disciples.

Let there be no mistake, then; when I speak of the heart as a stone, I am looking at it as *it* looks on God, a Saviour, salvation, and eternity. However distressing it is (and it is most distressing) to think that persons otherwise most lovely and of most loving hearts are so cold and callous to the claims of Jesus, yet, so far as divine love to sinners, and so far as the kindnesses of saving mercy are concerned, I am convinced that among the rocks which beat back the roaring sea —up in the crags where dews, and rain, and bright sunbeams fall—down in earth's darkest and deepest mines, there lies bedded no stone colder, harder, less impressible, more impenetrable, than an unrenewed heart. Does unbelief suggest the question, Why, then, preach to the unconverted? as well preach to stones? as well knock with thy hand upon a door which is locked on a coffin and a corpse? In a sense, true; and altogether true, but for the promise—"Lo I am with you alway, even unto the end of the world." That promise is the soul of hope and the life of preaching. It forbids despair. And should coward ministers, yielding to despair, hold their tongues, and pulpits all be silent, Christ still were preached. Strange evangelists would start up in these streets to break this awful, unbelieving silence. Asked by an envious priesthood to silence the hosannas of the multitude, Jesus turned on them and said, "I tell you, that if these should hold their peace, the stones would immediately cry out." Thus assured, not only of our children, not only of our people, not only of the dead womb of Sarah, but of the very stones of the street, that "God can raise up children to Abraham," despair we cannot feel, and dumb we cannot be. He who shall raise the dead in church-yards can waken the dead in churches. Therefore we expect conversions, and in hope offer Christ to the chief of sinners, beseeching you, "Be ye reconciled to God."

The New Heart.

A new heart also will I give you, and a new spirit will I put within you; and I will take away the stony heart out of your flesh, and I will give you an heart of flesh.—Ezekiel xxxvi. 26.

As in a machine where the parts all fit each other, and, bathed in oil, move without din or discord, the most perfect harmony reigns throughout the kingdom of grace. Jesus Christ is the " wisdom," as well as the " power" of God ; nor in this kingdom is any thing found corresponding to the anomalies and incon‧ gruities of the world lying without. There we some‧ times see a high station disgraced by a man of low habits ; while others are doomed to an inferior condi‧ tion, who would shine like gilded ornaments on the very pinnacles of society. That beautiful congruity in Christ's kingdom is secured by those who are the objects of saving mercy being so renewed and sancti‧ fied that their nature is in harmony with their position, and the man within corresponds to all without.

Observe how this property of *new* runs through the whole economy of grace. When Mercy first rose upon this world, an attribute of Divinity appeared which was new to the eyes of men and angels. Again, the Saviour was born of a virgin ; and He who came forth from a womb where no child had been previously conceived, was sepulchred in a tomb where no man had been previously interred. The Infant had a **new** birth-place, the Crucified had a new burial-place.

Again, Jesus is the mediator of a new covenant, the author of a new testament, the founder of a new faith. Again, the redeemed receive a new name; they sing a new song; their home is not to be in the Old, but in the New Jerusalem, where they shall dwell on a new earth, and walk in glory beneath a new heaven. Now it were surely strange, when all things else are new, if they themselves were not to partake of this general renovation. Nor strange only, for such a change is indispensable. A new name without a new nature were an imposture. It were not more an un-truth to call a lion a lamb, or the rapacious vulture by the name of the gentle dove, than to give the title of sons of God to the venomous seed of the Serpent.

Then, again, unless man received a new nature, how could he sing the new song? The raven, perched on the rock, where she whets her bloody beak, and impatiently watches the dying struggles of some un-happy lamb, cannot tune her croaking voice to the rich, mellow music of a thrush; and, since it is out of the abundance of the heart that the mouth speak-eth, how could a sinner take up the strain and sing the song of saints? Besides, unless a man were a new creature, he were out of place in the new creation. In circumstances neither adapted to his nature, nor fitted to minister to his happiness, a sinner in heaven would find himself as much out of his element as a finny inhabitant of the deep, or a sightless burrower in the soil, beside an eagle, soaring in the sky, or sur-veying her wide domain from the mountain crag.

In the works of God we see nothing more beautiful than the divine skill with which he suits his creatures to their condition. He gives wings to birds, fins to fishes, sails to the thistle-seed, a lamp to light the glow-

12

worm, great roots to moor the cedar, and to the aspiring
ivy her thousand hands to climb the wall. Nor is the
wisdom so conspicuous in nature, less remarkable and
adorable in the kingdom of grace. He forms a holy
people for a holy heaven—fits heaven for them, and
 hem for heaven. And calling up his Son to prepare
the mansions for their tenants, and sending down his
Spirit to prepare the tenants for their mansions, he
thus establishes a perfect harmony between the new
creature and the new creation.

You cannot have two hearts beating in the same
bosom, else you would be, not a man, but a monster.
Therefore, the very first thing to be done, in order to
make things new, is just to take that which is old out
of the way. And the taking away of the old heart is,
after all, but a preparatory process. It is a means, but
not the end. For—strange as it may at first sound—
he is not religious who is without sin. A dead man is
without sin; and he is sinless, who lies buried in dream-
less slumber, so long as his eyes are sealed. Now, God
requires more than a negative religion. Piety, like
fire, light, electricity, magnetism, is an active, not a
passive element; it has a positive, not merely a nega-
tive existence. For how is pure and undefiled religion
defined? "Pure religion and undefiled is to visit the
fatherless and widows in their affliction." And on
whom does Jesus pronounce his beatitude? "If ye
know these things, happy are ye if ye *do* them." And
what is the sum of practical piety—the most portable
form in which you can put an answer to Saul's ques-
tion, "Lord, what wouldst thou have me to do?"
What but this, "Depart from evil, and do good."
Therefore, while God promises to take the stony heart
out of our flesh, he promises more. In taking away

one heart, he engages to supply us with another; and
to this further change and onward stage in the process
of redemption, I now proceed to turn your attention :
and, by way of general observation, I remark--

I. Our affections are engaged in religion.

An oak—not as it stands choked up in the crowded
wood, with room neither to spread nor breathe, but as
it stands in the open field—swelling out below where
it anchors its roots in the ground, and swelling out
above where it stretches its arms into the air, presents
us with the most perfect form of firmness, self-support,
stout and sturdy independence. So perfectly formed,
indeed, is the monarch of the forest to stand alone,
and fight its own battles with the elements, that the
architect of the Bell Rock Lighthouse is said to have
borrowed his idea of its form from God in nature, and
that, copying the work of a Divine Architect, he took
the trunk of the oak as the model of a building which
was to stand the blast of the storm, and the swell of
winter seas.

In striking contrast with this tree, there are plants
—some of them of the richest perfume and fairest
beauty—such as the passion-flower, the ivy, the cle-
matis, and the woodbine, which can not stand alone.
They have neither pith nor fiber to maintain them-
selves erect.

Yet these are not doomed to the base fate of being
trodden in the dust by the hoof of every passing beast,
and have their beauty soiled in the mire. Types of
one whom God has called by his grace, and beautified
with salvation, who is strong in weakness, and rises
to the highest honors of heaven, these plants may
overtop the tallest oak, and, holding on by the ever-

lasting rocks, they have laughed at the storm which laid his proud head in the dust. This strength they have, and these honors they win, by help of the tendrils, the arms, those instruments of attachment with which God has kindly furnished them. These plants are formed to attach themselves to other objects; it is their nature to do so. If they get hold of one noble and lofty, they rise to the height of its nobility; if of a mean one—some rotten stake or shattered wall—they embrace the ruin, and, like a true friend, share its fate; and we have seen, when they had no other object on which to fix themselves, how—like a selfish man, who is the object of his own affections, and has a heart no bigger than his coffin, just large enough to hold himself—they would embrace themselves, and lie basely on the ground locked in forced embarrassment in their own arms.

It is with man as with these. What their tendrils are to them, our affections are to us. Ambition aims at independence; and men fancy, that when they have accumulated such or such a fortune, obtained such or such a place, arrived at such or such an age, they shall be independent. Independent! what folly! man was never made to be self-supporting, and self-satisfying. Even when his home was Eden, and he enjoyed the full favors of a benignant God, the Lord said—"It is not good for man to be alone."

We are constituted with affections, of which we can no more divest ourselves than of our skin. Be the object which we love noble or base, good or bad, generous or selfish, holy or sinful, belonging to earth or to heaven, some object we must love. It were as easy for a man to live without breathing, as to live without loving. It is not more natural for fire to burn, or light to shine, than for man to love. And the commandment, "Love not the world, neither the things that are in the world," had been utterly impracticable, and impossible, save in conjunction with the other commandment, "Thou shalt love the Lord thy God with all thy heart, and soul, and mind." It is with man's soul as with this plant which is creeping on the earth; to upbraid it for its baseness, to reproach it for the mean objects around which its tendrils are entwined, will never make it stand erect; you can not raise it unless you present some lofty object to which it may cling. It is with our hearts as with vessels; you can not empty them of one element without admitting or substituting another in its place. And just as I can empty a vessel filled with air or with oil by pouring water into it, because water is the heavier fluid, or as I can empty a vessel of water by pouring quicksilver into it, because the specific gravity of mercury is greatly in excess of that of water, so the only way by which you can empty my heart of the world, and the love of the world, is by filling it with the love of God. This is the divine process and science of the Gospel. The Gospel is accommodated to our nature; its light is adapted to our darkness; its mercy to our misery; its pardon to our guilt; its sanctification to our impurity; its comforts to our griefs; and in substituting the love of Christ for the love of sin, in giving us an object to love, it meets our constitution, and satisfies the strongest cravings of our nature. It engages our affections, and, in taking away an old heart, supplies its place with a new one and a better.

II. Consider now the new heart—"A new heart also will I give you."

We have said enough in a preceding discourse to show that we are not to look for evidence of the new heart in the natural affections. Religion does not bestow these. We are born with them. We have some of them in common with the brutes that perish; and they may be found flourishing in all their beauty in those who are strangers to the love of God. To them, as to all things else, indeed, which are his gifts, sin is antagonistic and injurious. Let sin ripen, so as to have "its perfect work," and it acts like a cancer on man's best affections. It first indurates, then deadens, and at length destroys. Sinners are essentially selfish; and—as we see exemplified every day—the more men grow in sin, they grow the more heartless, and hesitate less to sacrifice the tenderest feelings and best interests of others to their own base and brutal gratifications. There is a picture in the book of Romans, painted by the hand of a master, which is more appalling and affecting than any which Roman artists have hung on the walls of Rome. Here it is, a full-length portrait of sinners drawn by the hand of Paul, in these vivid and terrible colors:—"God gave them over to a reprobate mind, to do those things which are not convenient, being filled with all unrighteousness, fornication, wickedness, covetousness, maliciousness; full of envy, murder, debate, deceit, malignity; whisperers, backbiters, haters of God, despiteful, proud, boasters; inventors of evil things, disobedient to parents, without understanding, covenant breakers, without natural affection, implacable, unmerciful." What a dark and dreadful picture of humanity! Behold the monster into which sin, when fully developed, turns the sweetest child. What an abominable thing is sin! Like God, may we hate it with a perfect hatred!

Observe, that although the state of the natural affections does not furnish any certain evidence of conversion, it is the glory of piety that these are strengthened, elevated, sanctified by the change. The lover of God will be the kindest, best, wisest lover of his fellow-creatures. The heart that has room in it for God, grows so large, that it finds room for all God's train, for all that he loves, and for all that he has made; so that the church, with all its denominations of true Christians, the world, with all its perishing sinners, nay—all the worlds which he has created, find orbit-room to move, as in an expansive universe, within the capacious enlargement of a believer's heart. For while the love of sin acts as an astringent—contracting the dimensions of the natural heart, shutting and shriveling it up—the love of God expands and enlarges its capacity. Piety quickens the pulse of love, warms and strengthens our heart, and sends forth fuller streams of natural affection toward all that have a claim on us, just as a strong and healthy heart sends tides of blood along the elastic arteries to every extremity of the body.

This new heart, however, mainly consists in a change of the affections as they regard spiritual objects. Without again traveling over ground which we have already surveyed, just look at the heart and feelings of an unconverted man. His mind being carnal, is enmity or hatred against God. This may be latent—not at first sight apparent, nor suspected—but how soon does it appear when put to the proof? Fairly tried, it comes out like those unseen elements which chemical tests reveal. Let God, for instance, by his providences or laws, thwart the wishes or cross the propensities of our unrenewed nature—let there be a collision between His will and ours—and the latent enmity flashes out like latent fire when the cold black flint is struck with steel.

The Apostle pronounces men to be by nature lovers of pleasure more than lovers of God; and is it not a fact that the services of religion are so contrary to all our natural tastes, that we are prone to say of them, as of that day which brings down heaven to earth— "It is a weariness; when will it be over?" The affections of the natural man are like the branches of what are called weeping trees—they droop to the earth, and sweep the ground; harmless or deleterious, they are all directed earthward. This world is his god; his heaven is on earth; the paradise he seeks is here; his ten commandments are the opinions of men; his sins are his pleasures; his prayers are a task; his sabbaths are his longest, weariest days; and, although no sheeted ghosts rise at midnight and walk the church-yard to scare him, he has, in thoughts of God, of judgment, of eternity, specters that haunt him, and to escape from which he will fly into the arms of sin.

Now, if you have received a new heart, this state is past, or is passing. Your affections are not dried or frozen up; they are as warm, or rather warmer than ever—still flowing, only flowing toward different objects, and in a different channel. In obedience to a divine impulse, their course is not only in a different, but in a contrary direction; for the grace of God works such a complete change of feeling, that what was once hated you now love, and what was once loved you now loathe; you fly from what once you courted, and pursue what you once shunned.

For example. Did you not once, like Adam in the garden, hide yourself from God? Like Jacob, when about to encounter an angry brother, did you not once tremble at the prospect of meeting God? How did you fret under the yoke of his law? In those who bore his image, how did you revile, and shun, and hate him? You could not banish him from the universe, but how did you try to banish the thought of him from *your* thoughts, and so put him and keep him out of your mind, that it might be that black, cold, empty, dark, dead, atheistic spot of this creation, where God should not be? Believers! Oh what a blessed revolution has grace wrought? Praise ye the Lord. Although our attainments come far short of David's, and the love of our bosoms may burn with a dimmer and feebler flame, and we should therefore perhaps pitch the expression of our feelings on a lower key, let the Psalmist express for us the language of a renewed heart—"Oh how love I thy law! it is my meditation all the day. Thy testimonies are better to me than thousands of gold and silver. Like as the hart panteth after the water brooks, so panteth my soul after thee, O God. My soul thirsteth for God, for the living God. When shall I come and appear before God. One thing have I desired of the Lord, that will I seek after, that I may dwell in the house of the Lord all the days of my life. I love the Lord because he hath heard my prayer and the voice of my supplication. Bless the Lord, ye his angels, that excel in strength. Bless the Lord, all ye his hosts. Bless the Lord, all his works. Bless the Lord, O my soul. Let every thing that hath breath praise the Lord. Praise ye the Lord."

III. In conversion God gives a new spirit.

Conversion does not bestow new faculties. It does not turn a weak man into a philosopher. Yet, along with our affections, the temper, the will, the judgment partake of this great and holy change. Thus, while the heart ceases to be dead, the head, illuminated by a light within, ceases to be dark; the understanding is enlightened; the will is renewed; and our whole temper is sweetened and sanctified by the Spirit of God. To consider these in their order, I remark—

By this change the understanding and judgment are enlightened. Sin is the greatest folly, and the sinner the greatest fool in the world. There is no such madness in the most fitful lunacy. Think of a man risking eternity and his everlasting happiness on the uncertain chance of surviving another year. Think of a man purchasing a momentary pleasure at the cost of endless pain. Think of a dying man living as if he were never to die. Is there a convert to God who looks back upon his unconverted state, and does not say with David, "Lord, I was as a beast before thee."

Now conversion not only restores God to the heart, but reason also to her throne. Time and eternity are now seen in their just proportions—in their right relative dimensions; the one in its littleness, and the other in its greatness. When the light of heaven rises on the soul, what grand discoveries does she make—of the exceeding evil of sin, of the holiness of the divine law, of the infinite purity of divine justice, of the grace and greatness of divine love. On Sinai's summit and on Calvary's cross, what new, sublime, affecting scenes open on her astonished eyes! She now, as by one convulsive bound, leaps to the conclusion that salvation is the one thing needful, and that if a man will give all he hath for the life that now is, much more should he part with all for the life to come. The Saviour and Satan, the soul and body, holiness and sin, have competing claims. Between these reason now holds the balance even, and man finds, in the visit of converting grace, what the demoniac found in Jesus' advent. The man whose dwelling was among the tombs, whom no chains could bind, is seated at the feet of Jesus, "clothed, and in *his right mind.*"

By this change the will is renewed. Bad men are worse, and good men are better than they appear. In conversion the will is so changed and sanctified, that although a pious man is in some respects less, in other respects he is more holy than the world gives him credit for. The attainments of a believer are always beneath his aims; his desires are nobler than his deeds; his wishes are holier than his works. Give other men their will—full swing to their passions—and they would be worse than they are; give that to him, and he would be better than he is. And if you have experienced the gracious change, it will be your daily grief that you are not what you not only know you should be, but what you wish to be. To be complaining with Paul, "When I would do good, evil is present with me; that which I would I do not, and what I would not, that I do," is one of the best evidences of a gracious, saving change.

Children of God! let not your souls be cast down. This struggle between the new will and the old man—painful and prolonged although it be—proves beyond all doubt the advent of the Holy Spirit. Until the Saviour appeared there was no sword drawn, nor ɒlood shed in Bethlehem, nor murderous decree issued against its innocents—they slept safely in their mothers' bosoms, Herod enjoyed his security and pleas ure, and Rachel rose not from her grave to weep for her children because they were not. Christ's coming rouses all the devil in the soul. The fruits of holy peace are reaped with swords on the fields of war; and this struggle within your breast proves that grace, even in its infancy a cradled Saviour, is engaged in strangling the old Serpent. When the shadow of calamity falls on many homes, and the tidings of victory come with sad news to many a family, and the brave are lying thick in the deadly breach, men comfort us by saying, that there are things worse than war. That is emphatically true of this holy war. Rejoice that the peace of death is gone.

By conversion the temper and disposition are changed and sanctified. Christians are occasionally to be found with a tone of mind and a temper as little calculated to recommend their faith as to promote their happiness. I believe that there are cases in which this is due to a deranged condition of the nervous system, or the presence of disease in some other vital organ. These unhappy persons are more deserving of our pity than our censure. This is not only the judgment of Christian charity, but of sound philosophy, and is a conclusion to which we are conducted in studying the union between mind and body, and the manner in which they act and re-act upon each other. So long as grace dwells in a " vile body," which is the seat of frequent disorder and many diseases—these infirmities of temper admit no more, perhaps, of being entirely removed, than a defect of speech, or any physical deformity. The good temper for which some take credit, may be

the result of good health and a well developed frame
—a physical more than a moral virtue; and an ill
temper, springing from bad health, or an imperfect
organization, may be a physical rather than a moral
defect—giving its victim a claim on our charity and
forbearance. But, admitting this apology for the un-
happy tone and temper of some pious men, the true
Christian will bitterly bewail his defect, and, regret-
ting his infirmity more than others do a deformity, he
will carefully guard and earnestly pray against it.
Considering it as a thorn in his flesh, a messenger of
Satan sent to buffet him, it will often send him to his
knees in prayer to God, that the grace which conquers
nature may be made "sufficient for him."

Those, however, who have no such plea to urge in
palliation of a suspicious, sour, discontented, irritable
temperament, have good ground to suspect their Chris-
tianity. Grace sweetens where it sanctifies. In the
name of God and Christianity, what has Christ to do
with Belial? What has grace to do with that ava-
ricious, envious, malignant, implacable disposition,
which is utterly opposed to the genius of the Gospel
and the Spirit that was in Jesus Christ? Am I told
that his disciples sought fire from heaven to consume
their enemies? Am I told that, with the intolerance
of bigotry, and a narrowness of mind still too common,
they thought to silence those whom they regarded as
rivals? Am I told that, set on fire of an earthly am-
bition, they blazed out into unseemly quarrels with
each other? Am I told that, even on the solemn eve
of a Saviour's sufferings, when their tears should have
quenched all unhallowed fires, they strove for the
highest place in the kingdom? Am I told how
harshly they silenced the cries, and rebuked the im

portunity of suffering, and how haughtily these proud
fishermen bore themselves to the mothers and babes
of Israel? True; but this temper passed away. Their
Master cast out the unclean spirit. Pentecost baptized
them with another nature. With the peace of Jesus
they received his gentle, generous, gracious, loving,
forbearing, forgiving temper. These Elishas entered
on their work clothed in the mantle of their ascended
Master. Had it been otherwise—had they not been
made of love, as well as messengers of love—had the
love they preached not breathed in every tone, and
beamed in every look—had they not illustrated in
their practice the genius of the Gospel, their mission
had been a signal failure; they had never opened the
hearts of men; they had never made their way in a
resistant world—never conquered it. Just as it is not
with stubborn but pliant iron that locks are picked,
the hearts of sinners are to be opened only by those
who bring a Christ-like gentleness to the work: and
who are ready, with Paul's large, loving, kind, and
generous disposition, to be all things to all men, if so
be that they may win some. Never had the disciples
gone forth "conquering and to conquer," had they
brought their old bigoted, quarrelsome, unsanctified
temper to the mission. They might have died for
Christianity, but she had died with them; and, bound
to their stake, and expiring in their ashes, she had
been entombed in the sepulcher of her first and last
apostles.

I pray you to cultivate the temper that was in Jesus
Christ. Is he like a follower of the Lamb who is
raging like a roaring lion? Is he like a pardoned crim-
inal who sits moping with a cloud upon his brow?
Is he like an heir of heaven, like a man destined to a

crown, who is vexed and fretted with some petty loss?
Is he like one in whose bosom the Dove of heaven is
nestling, who is full of all manner of bile and bitter-
ness? Oh, let the same mind be in you that was in
Jesus. A kind, catholic, gentle, loving temper is one
of the most winning features of religion; and by its
silent and softening influence you will do more real
service to Christianity than by the loudest professions,
or the exhibition of a cold and skeleton orthodoxy.
Let it appear in you, that it is with the believer under
the influences of the Spirit as with fruit ripened be-
neath the genial influences of heaven's dews and
sunbeams. At first hard, it grows soft; at first sour,
it becomes sweet; at first green, it assumes in time a
rich and mellow color; at first adhering tenaciously
to the tree, when it becomes ripe, it is ready to drop
at the slightest touch. So with the man who is ripen-
ing for heaven. His affections and temper grow sweet,
soft, mellow, loose from earth and earthly things. He
comes away readily to the hand of death, and leaves
the world without a wrench.

IV. In conversion God gives a heart of flesh. " I
will give you a heart of flesh."

Near by a stone—a mass of rock that had fallen
from the overhanging crag—which had some wild
flowers growing in its fissures, and on its top the fox-
glove, with its spike of beautiful but deadly flowers,
we once came upon an adder as it lay in ribbon coil,
basking on the sunny ground. At our approach the
reptile stirred, uncoiled itself, and raising its venom-
ous head, with eyes like burning coals, it shook its
cloven tongue, and, hissing, gave signs of battle. At
tacked, it retreated; and, making for that gray stone,

wormed itself into a hole in its side. Its nest and
home were there. And in looking on that shattered
rock—fallen from its primeval elevation—with its
flowery but fatal charms, the home and nest of the
adder, where nothing grew but poisoned beauty, and
nothing dwelt but a poisoned brood, it seemed to us
an emblem of that heart which the text describes as
a stone, which experience proves is a habitation of
devils, and which the prophet pronounces to be despe-
rately wicked. I have already explained why the
heart is described as a stone. It is cold as a stone;
hard as a stone; dead and insensible as a stone. Now,
as by the term "flesh" we understand qualities the very
opposite of these, I therefore remark that—

In conversion a man gets a warm heart.

Let us restrict ourselves to a single example. When
faith receives the Saviour, how does the heart warm
to Jesus Christ! There is music in his name. "His
name is as an ointment poured forth." All the old
indifference to his cause, his people, and the interests
of his kingdom, has passed away; and now these have
the warmest place in a believer's bosom, and are the
objects of its strongest and tenderest affections. The
only place, alas! that religion has in the hearts of
many is a burial-place; but the believer can say with
Paul, "Christ *liveth* in me." Nor is his heart like the
cottage of Bethany, favored only with occasional
visits. Jesus abides there in the double character of
guest and master—its most loving and best loved in-
mate; and there is a difference as great between that
heart as it is, and that heart as it was, as between the
warm bosom where the Infant slept or smiled in Mary's

arms and the dark, cold sepulcher where weeping fol-
lowers laid and left the Crucified.

Is there such a heart in you? Do you appreciate
Christ's matchless excellences? Having cast away
every sin to embrace him, do you set him above your
chiefest joy? Would you leave father, mother, wife,
children, to follow him, with bleeding feet, over life's
roughest path? Rather than part with him, would you
part with a thousand worlds? Were he now on earth,
would you leave a throne to stoop and tie his latchet?
If I might so speak, would you be proud to carry his
shoes? Then, indeed, you have got the new, warm
heart of flesh. The new love of Christ, and the old
love of the world, may still meet in opposing currents;
but in the war and strife of these antagonistic princi-
ples, the celestial shall overpower the terrestrial, as, at
the river's mouth, I have seen the ocean tide, when it
came rolling in with a thousand billows at its back,
fill all the channel, carry all before its conquering
swell, dam up the fresh water of the land, and drive
it back with resistless power.

In conversion a man gets a soft heart.

As "flesh," it is soft and sensitive. It is flesh, and
can be wounded or healed. It is flesh, and feels alike
the kiss of kindness and the rod of correction. It is
flesh; and no longer a stone, hard, obdurate, impene-
trable to the genial influences of heaven. A hard
block of ice, it has yielded to the beams of the sun,
and been melted into flowing water. How are you
moved now, stirred now, quickened now, sanctified
now, by truths once felt no more than dews falling out
of starry heavens, in soft silence. upon rugged rock.

The heart of grace is endowed with a delicate sensi
bility, and vibrates to the slightest touch of a Saviour's
fingers.   How does the truth of God affect it now!
A stone no longer, it melts under the heavenly fire—
a stone no longer, it bends beneath the hammer of the
word ; no longer like the rugged rock, on which rains
and sunbeams were wasted, it receives the impression
of God's power, and retains the footprints of his pres-
ence.   Like the flowers that close their eyes at night,
but waken at the voice of morning, like the earth that
gapes in summer drought, the new heart opens to re-
ceive the bounties of grace and the gifts of heaven.
Have you experienced such a change ?   In proof and
evidence of its reality, is David's language yours—" I
have stretched out my hands unto thee.   My soul
thirsteth after thee as a thirsty land ?"

In conversion a man gets a living heart.
The perfection of this life is death—it is to be dead
to sin, but alive to righteousness, alive to Christ, alive
to every thing which touches his honor, and crown,
and kingdom.   With Christ living in his heart, the
believer feels that now he is not himself—not his
own ; and, as another's, the grand object of his life is
to live to Christ.   He reckons him an object worth
living for, had he a thousand lives to live ; worth
dying for, had he a thousand deaths to die.   He says
with Paul, " I am crucified with Christ, nevertheless
I live."   In the highest sense alive, he is dead—dead
to things he was once alive to ; and he wishes that he
were more dead to them—thoroughly dead.   He
wishes that he could look on the seductions of the
world, and sin's voluptuous charms, with the cold,

unmoved stare of death, and that these had no more power to kindle a desire in him, than in the icy bosom of a corpse. "Understandest thou what thou readest?"

It is a mark of grace, that the believer, in his progress heavenward, grows more and more alive to the claims of Jesus. If you "know the love of Christ," his is the latest name you will desire to utter ; his is the latest thought you will desire to form ; upon Him you will fix your last look on earth ; upon Him your first in heaven. When memory is oblivious of all other objects,—when all that attracted the natural eye is wrapped in the mists of death,—when the tongue is cleaving to the roof of our mouth, and speech is gone, and sight is gone, and hearing gone, and the right hand, lying powerless by our side, has lost its cunning, Jesus! then may we remember Thee! If the shadows of death are to be thrown in deepest darkness on the valley, when we are passing along it to glory, may it be ours to die like that saint, beside whose bed wife and children once stood, weeping over the wreck of faded faculties, and a blank, departed memory. One had asked him, "Father, do you remember me?" and received no answer; and another, and another, but still no answer. And then, all making way for the venerable companion of a long and loving pilgrimage—the tender partner of many a past joy and sorrow—his wife, draws near. She bends over him, and as her tears fall thick upon his face, she cries, "Do you not remember me?" A stare—but it is vacant. There is no soul in that filmy eye ; and the seal of death lies upon these lips. The sun is down, and life's brief twilight is darkening fast into a starless night.

At this moment one, calm enough to remember how the love of Christ's spouse is "strong as death"—a love that "many waters cannot quench"—stooped to his ear, and said, "Do you remember Jesus Christ?" The word was no sooner uttered than it seemed to recall the spirit, hovering for a moment, ere it took wing to heaven. Touched as by an electric influence, the heart beat once more to the name of Jesus; the features, fixed in death, relax; the countenance, dark in death, flushes up like the last gleam of day; and, with a smile in which the soul passed away to glory, he replied, "Remember Jesus Christ! dear Jesus Christ! he is all my salvation, and all my desire."

IV. *By conversion man is ennobled.*

Infidelity regards man as little better than an animated statue, living clay, a superior animal. She sees no jewel of immortality flashing in this earthly casket. According to her, our future being is a brilliant but baseless dream of the present; death, an everlasting sleep; and that dark, low, loathsome grave our eternal sepulcher.

Vice, again, looks on man as an animal formed for the indulgence of brutal appetites. She sees no divinity in his intellect, nor pure feelings, nor lofty aspirations worthy of cultivation for the coming state. Her foul finger never points him to the skies. She leaves powers and feelings which might have been trained to heaven to trail upon the ground; to be soiled and trodden in the mire, or to entwine themselves around the basest objects. In virtuous shame, in modesty, purity, integrity, gentleness, natural affection, she blights with her poisonous breath whatever vestiges of beauty have survived the Fall; and when she has done her perfect work, she leaves man a wreck, a wretch, an object of loathing, not only to God and angels, but—lowest and deepest of all degradation—an object of contempt and loathing to himself.

While infidelity regards man as a mere animal, to be dissolved at death into ashes and air, and vice changes man into a brute or devil, Mammon enslaves him. She makes him a serf, and condemns him to be a gold-digger for life in the mines. She puts her collar on his neck, and locks it; and bending his head to the soil, and bathing his brow in sweat, she says, Toil, Toil, Toil; as if this creature, originally made in the image of God, this dethroned and exiled monarch, to save whom the Son of God descended from the skies, and bled on Calvary, were a living machine, constructed of sinew, bone, and muscle, and made for no higher end than to work to live, and live to work.

Contrast with these the benign aspect in which the Gospel looks on man. Religion descends from heaven to break our chains. She alone raises me from degradation, and bids me lift my drooping head, and look up to heaven. Yes; it is that very Gospel which by some is supposed to present such dark, degrading, gloomy views of man and his destiny, which lifts me from the dust and the dung-hill to set me among princes—on a level with angels—in a sense above them. To say nothing of the divine nobility grace imparts to a soul which is stamped anew with the likeness and image of God, how sacred and venerable does even this body appear in the eye of piety! No longer a form of animated dust; no longer the subject of passions shared in common with the brutes;

no longer the drudge and slave of Mammon, the once "vile body" rises into a temple of the Holy Ghost. Vile in one sense it may be; yet what, although it be covered with sores? what, although it be clothed in rags? what, although, in unseemly decrepitude, it want its fair proportions? that poor, pale, sickly, shattered form is the casket of a precious jewel. This mean and crumbling tabernacle lodges a guest nobler than palaces may boast of; angels hover around its walls; the Spirit of God dwells within it. What an incentive to holiness, to purity of life and conduct, lies in the fact that the body of a saint is the temple of God!—a truer, nobler temple than that which Solomon dedicated by his prayers, and Jesus consecrated by his presence. In Popish cathedral, where the light streamed through painted window, and the organ pealed along lofty aisles, and candles gleamed on golden cups and silver crosses, and incense floated in fragrant clouds, we have seen the blinded worshiper uncover his head, drop reverently on his knees, and raise his awe-struck eye on the imposing spectacle; we have seen him kiss the marble floor, and knew that sooner would he be smitten dead upon that floor than be guilty of defiling it. How does this devotee rebuke us! We wonder at his superstition; how may he wonder at our profanity! Can we look on th· lowly veneration he expresses for an edifice which has been erected by some dead man's genius, which holds but some image of a deified Virgin, or bones of a canonized saint, and which—proudly as it raises its cathedral towers—time shall one day cast to the ground, and bury in the dust; can we, I say, look on that, and, if sensible to rebuke, not feel reproved by the spectacle? In how much more respect, in how much holier veneration should we hold this body? The shrine of immortality, and a temple dedicated to the Son of God, it is consecrated by the presence of the Spirit—a living temple, over whose porch the eye of piety reads what the finger of inspiration has written —"If any man defile the temple of God, him shall God destroy; for the temple of God is holy, which temple ye are."

"THERE are three that bear record in heaven: the Father, the Son, and the Holy Ghost." They form the mystery of one Godhead, and act in harmony. As might be expected, the divine record represents these three Persons as all connected with, and co-operating in creation. With the honors of a work, usually ascribed to the Father, Paul crowns the Son. Mark what he says of the Son—"By *him* were all things created, that are in heaven, and that are in earth, whether they be thrones or dominions, or principalities or powers;" and speaking elsewhere of God, he says—"He, who at sundry times, and in divers manners spake to our fathers by the prophets, hath in these last days spoken unto us by his Son, whom he hath appointed heir of all things, by whom also he made the worlds." Now, as to the third person, or Holy Spirit, we discover indications of his existence even in the Mosaic record of creation. He appears in the earliest epochs of time, and amid those sublime and magnificent spectacles with which the Bible opens.

The curtain rises upon the first act of creating power, and, through the enveloping shroud of darkness, we see the earth—a shapeless mass, crude and chaotic. It is a world in embryo. "The earth was without form and void." Yet at this early period, when there was neither golden cloud nor blue sky, nor green land, nor silver sea; when no waves broke upon the shore, and there were no shores for waves to break on; when no mountains rose to greet the morning sun, and there was no sun to shine on them; when no wing of bird was cleaving the silent air, nor fin of fish the waters; when—like the rude and various materials from which an architect intends to rear the fabric he has designed—the elements of fire, air, earth, and water, lay mingled in strange confusion, through the darkness that lies on the face of the deep, we discover some mighty presence. He is moving and at work. It is the Spirit of God. He presides at the birth of time. He is evoking order from confusion, forming the world in the womb of eternity and preparing a theater for scenes and events of surpassing grandeur. Concerning that early period of creation, Moses has recorded this important fact— 'The Spirit of God moved on the face of the waters." In this glorious creation, therefore—in this beautiful world, and the starry skies that rose over it—we behold the mighty monuments of his presence and power. He sprung the arch of this crystal dome, and studded it over with these gems of light. Listen to the magnificent hymn of the Patriarch— "He stretcheth out the north over the empty place, and hangeth the earth upon nothing. He holdeth back the face of his throne, and spreadeth his cloud upon it; he hath compassed the waters with bounds, and divideth the sea with his power. By his *Spirit* he hath garnished the heavens." In the temple of nature, therefore, as in that of grace, we adore a Godhead—the Three in One; and see Father, Son, and Holy Ghost, the presiding and co-equal authors of a first creation.

But let us come to man. The pillar is finished, and

wants nothing but its capital; the house, built and furnished, now waits its tenant. He is about to be formed who is to be not merely a work, nor a servant, but a son of God; a mirror in which Divinity may complacently contemplate itself; a being who is to exhibit what, amid their bright and beautiful forms, neither sun, nor sea, nor earth could boast of—an image of God. The crown of creation is to be topped with its brightest gem. This province of the divine empire is to be provided with a king, who, wielding a delegated scepter, shall exercise dominion "over the fish of the sea, the fowls of the air, the cattle, and the creeping things." It is a great occasion. And, as was worthy of it, the three persons of the Godhead appear. God fashions the plastic clay into the form of man, and molds those features which, given by his hand, have descended to us;—bending over the prostrate and inanimate statue, he breathes into its hollow nostrils the element of life; rushing in, this mysterious power sets its organs into play, and, as the heart begins to beat, and the current of the blood to flow, man opens his eyes in life and on the world; but, ere this crowning act—ere, by this greatest act he closes the drama of creation—addressing the Son on this hand and the Spirit upon that, the Father saith, "Let us make man in *our* image."

In many respects, the new creation corresponds with that old one—the Paradise Regained with the Paradise Lost. Man is the subject of both; his good and the divine glory are the ends of both; devils are the enemies, and angels are the allies of both; the Father, Son, and Holy Ghost are the authors of both. Now while the first chapter of Genesis—raising a portion of the vail which hangs upon the mysteries of creation—shows us the Holy Spirit as an active agent in that work, my text introduces the same divine person, as discharging functions as important in the more exalted and enduring work of a new creation. The Father decrees redemption; the Son procures it; the Holy Spirit applies it. For that purpose this promise is both given and fulfilled—"I will put my Spirit within you." In illustration of the doctrine, 1 remark—

I. The Holy Spirit is the great agent in conversion and sanctification.

Man cannot be saved unless elected, nor elected without the Father; nor saved unless redeemed, nor redeemed without the Son; nor saved unless converted, nor converted without the Spirit. Do you ask why? Is there not a fountain opened to the house of David, and to the inhabitants of Jerusalem, for sin and for uncleanness? Is it not true that whosoever seeks salvation there, may wash and shall be clean? Most true. Jesus has filled that fountain with blood, and, once bathed there, the foulest become white as snow. Blessed truth! that fountain is free to all; free as air, free as light, free as the waves of ocean, where man, who parcels out God's earth, and forbids other foot than his own to tread on it, claims no exclusive property—where the beggar may go in to bathe abreast of a king.

What need I more, then? you may ask. We require much more. Our necessities are those of the cripple—of that man who, for thirty years, sat uncured by Bethesda's pool, nor took his anxious eye off the water as he waited for its first stir and ruffle. The healing of that pool was regulated by a law, and it was this. Like an electric battery, which to one and the first touch discharges all its fluid, this pool cured but one at a time, and he got its benefit who first stepped in after the angel's descent. Whatever his disease might be, he was cured. Was he dumb? he sung. Was he lame? he leaped. Was he a cripple? he shouldered his crutch, and walked. And why had this man sat out these weary years unhealed? Had the vision tarried, and was it the rare advent of the angel to this pool which suggested the figure, " Like angels' visits, few and far between?" Had these waters not been agitated at all for that long period of thirty years? Often. Many a time this cripple had seen the sudden spring, and heard the loud plunge, as some neighbor flashed into the water; and as the cured left the scene, many a time had he followed them with envious eyes. Many a time had he witnessed proofs of the healing power—the lame man bounding away like a deer, the song of the dumb ringing out his joy, and pallid sickness standing on the brim of the glassy pool, and—as she contemplated herself in its mirror--smiling to see the light of her beaming eyes, and fresh roses blooming upon her wasted cheek. Poor man! why was he not cured as well as others? He was impotent, powerless; he could not go down unassisted; and—one of the friendless poor, as he told Jesus—" he had no one to help him in." Even so, although seated by the fountain, where sins are lost and sinners washed, we need some one, so to speak, to help us in. In the words of Paul, we are " without strength;" and it is to help us to seek, to believe in, to love—in one word, to embrace the Saviour—that God puts his Spirit within us. For this end he fulfills the promise

" My grace shall be sufficient for thee, and my strength made perfect in weakness."

In a preceding discourse, we compared the change wrought in conversion to the removal of old, shattered machinery, and the supplying of its place with a new mechanism. But what is mere machinery? Just what the new heart were without the Spirit of God Besides the machinery, we must have a moving power. Of what use would be the machinery which is to be moved, without a force adequate to move it? Without a main-spring within the clock, however complete all its wheels, pinions, pivots, and axles, these hands would stand on the face of time, nor advance one step over the numbered hours. So were it with the renewed soul without the Spirit of God to set its powers in motion, bring them into play, and impart to them a true and heavenward character. For this purpose God fulfills the promise, " I will put my Spirit within you."

In order to illustrate this, and with God's blessing fix it in your heart, let me avail myself of the element which gives a name to the Spirit, and which our Saviour selects as his emblem—" The wind bloweth where it listeth, and thou hearest the sound thereof, but canst not tell whence it cometh, nor whither it goeth, so is every one that is born of the Spirit."

Here is a noble ship: what further does she need to move her? Her masts are all in; and her canvas is all shaken out; yet no ripple runs by her side, nor foam flashes from her bows, and she has no motion but what she receives from the alternate swell and sinking of the wave. Her machinery is complete. The forests have masted her; in many a broad yard of canvas a hundred looms have given her wings; her anchor has been weighed to the rude sea chant; the needle trembles on her deck; with his eye on that friend—unlike worldly friends—as true in storm as in calm, the helmsman stands impatient by the wheel; and when, as men bound to a distant shore, the crew have said farewell to wives and children, why lies she there over the self-same ground—rising with the flowing, and falling with the ebbing tide? The cause is plain. They want a wind to raise that drooping pennon, and fill these empty sails. They look to heaven—and so they may—the skies only can help them here. At length their prayer is heard; the pennon flutters at the mast head; spirits of the air sing aloft upon the yards; the sails swell; the wind whistles through the rattling cordage; and now, like a steed, touched by the rider's spur, she starts, bounds forward, plunges through the waves, and—heaven's wind her moving power—she is off, and away, amid blessings and prayers, to the land she is bound and chartered for. Even so, although heaven-born, heaven-called, heaven-bound, endowed with a new heart, new mind, new will, we stand in the same need of celestial influences—of the grace and Spirit of God. That heart, mind, and will, are the machinery, he is the moving power; these the instruments, and he the agent.

This heavenly gift neither circumscribes nor supersedes our own exertions. These gracious influences descend not to set us idle, any more than the breeze blows to send the sailor to his hammock and rock him over in the arms of sleep. On the contrary, long away, and wearying to be home, his eye often turned homeward across the water's waste, he shakes out every yard of canvas on the bending mast, and works the harder to gain the full advantage of propitious winds. It should be so with us. May it be so with us! The more full the gifts and divine breathings of the Spirit, the busier let us be—busier in the use of prayer, of sacraments, of the Bible, and of all those ordinances through which the Spirit works, and impels souls onward and homeward in a heavenly course.

Were God, provoked by our indifference, to withdraw or withhold his Spirit, would it not be with the best of us as in a dead calm at sea? No progress would be, or could be made; or rather, with the run of the tide against us—the tendencies of a depraved nature and a wicked world working the other way—instead of gaining ground, we should lose the ground already gained, and drift astern. The Bible says, "Remember Lot's wife." Here we say, Remember David. With what full sail he is bearing on to heaven! how far ahead he has shot of his countrymen and contemporaries! But he enters into temptation; yields to it; falls into sin; the Spirit is withdrawn, and, although finally saved, how nearly is he lost! What a fearful backsliding! what an awful warning! and, yet—an example most encouraging to a penitent backslider—see how God fulfills the promise, "I will heal thy backsliding and love thee freely."

Let me now urge on you the advantage and duty of improving to the utmost every season of heavenly visitation. There are seasons more favorable and full of grace than others. In this there is nothing surprising, but much that is in harmony with the common dispensations of Providence. Does not the success of the farmer, seaman, merchant, of men in many other circumstances, chiefly depend on their seizing opportunities, which come and go like showers—which flow and ebb like the tides of ocean? The sea is not always full. Twice a day she deserts her shores, and leaves the vessels high and dry upon the beach; so that they who would sail must wait and watch, and take the tide; and larger ships can only get afloat, or, if afloat, get across the bar and into harbor, when, through a favorable conjunction of celestial influences, the sea swells in stream or spring tides beyond her common bounds. The seaman has his spring tides; the husbandman has his spring time, and those showers, and soft winds, and sunny hours, on the prompt and diligent improvement of which the state of his barn and barn yards depends.

"Let it be," said the Lord to David and his men of war, when—lying in ambush, and expecting divine assistance—they waited for the signal of battle, "let it be, when thou hearest the sound of going on the tops of the mulberry trees, that thou shalt bestir thyself." Such a signal, like the feet of the angelic host marching over the tops of the trees, heaven may vouchsafe to us in some holy desire, emotion, thought, which, if yielded to and improved, may lead to heaven; but neglected, rejected, or repelled, may leave us to perish in hell. In these, which occasionally come to the most careless sinner, you hear the Spirit moving —in them you hear the Spirit calling. Improve them.

If improved, who can tell but it may be with you as with one well known to us. She was a fair enough professor, yet had been living a careless, godless, Christless life. She awoke one morning, and, most strange and unaccountable! her waking feeling was a strong desire to pray. She wondered. It was early dawn, and what more natural than that she should say, there is time enough—meanwhile "a little more sleep, a little more slumber, a little more folding of the hands to sleep?" As she was sinking back again into unconsciousness, suddenly, with the brightness and power of lightning, a thought flashed into her mind, filling her with alarm—this desire may have come from God; this may be the hour of my destiny —this, the tide of salvation, which, if neglected, may never return. She rose, and flung herself on her knees. The chamber was changed into a Peniel, and when the morning sun looked in at her window, he found her wrestling with God in prayer; and, like one from a sepulcher, she came forth that day at the call of Jesus to follow him henceforth, and in her future life to walk this world with God.

II. God's Spirit is not only given to his people, but dwells in them. "I will put my Spirit within you."

The communication between spirits, otherwise than through the medium of matter, and our bodily organs, is so great a mystery, that we are not prepared to say how far unconverted men may or may not be "possessed of the devil." Of many a wretched slave of vice, on whom tears, and prayers, and expostulations, and rewards, and punishments, have all been tried, and tried in vain, it may be said without exaggeration, "He is grievously tormented of a devil." There are incidents and expressions also in the Word of God, which invest the subject of demoniacal possession with a painful and very alarming interest. On one occasion Peter endeavors to dissuade his Master from the cross, and stands between him and the salvation of the lost, whereupon, as if he saw the devil looking through a disciple's eyes, and heard his speech in a disciple's tongue, Jesus turned on Peter, saying—" Get thee behind me, Satan." Again, when Judas received the sop, it is said that "Satan entered into him," and immediately—as the ship turns to the helm, when a new hand steps on board, and taking it changes her course —he left the supper table, to do his Master's business. Again, Paul speaks of a "fellowship with devils," a "cup of devils," and a "devil's table." Who knows but that those terrible spectacles of possession, where the bodies of unhappy men were seized, inhabited, tormented by unclean spirits, may have been visible emblems of the unclean and unconverted heart? When God left man at the Fall, and abandoned that heart which had once been his holy and happy home, it became a vacant, empty house for Satan to occupy; and, like bands of robbers, who haunt some ruined castle, where power and grandeur and rank once resided, many devils may be secretly lurking in the dark chambers of this desolate and dismantled palace.

We have sometimes thought that we saw the fittest emblem of man's fallen state, in the ruins of an old church. Now deserted, desecrated, defiled, what a change is there! Save in the ivy, that like pity clings to the crumbling wall—sustaining and vailing its decay—and in some sweet wild flower rooted in window sill, or gaping rent, beauty and life are gone. Yet there, once on a time, many a beautiful babe was baptized to God; there holy words were spoken; holy vows were taken, and holy communions held. There are eyes in glory that turn with interest to that lonely spot—God and man often met within these roofless walls; "This and that man was born there." But now the only sounds are the sighing of the wind.

or the roar of the storm—the hoot of the owl, or the hiss of the serpent; nor life is found there now, but in the brood of the night bird, which has its nest among the ruins above, or in the worms that fatten upon the dead in their cold graves below. "The glory is departed." And once a shrine of God, but now a deserted sanctuary, may we not write "Ichabod" on the heart? The ruin resounds with the echoes which the ear of fancy hears muttering among the desolate heaps of Babylon—"Fallen, fallen, fallen!"

Whatever habitation the prince of darkness may have within unconverted men—and however, also, holding for a time some footing even in God's people, he may raise up within them those thoughts of blasphemy, and desires of sin, which come as unbidden as they are unwelcome—the saints of God enjoy a blessed possession. Not the angels, but the Spirit of God inhabits them. Heaven has descended into their bosoms, and their bodies are become a holy temple. God now in very truth not only dwells "with man," but *in* man. "I will put my Spirit within you." He is enshrined within them; and as the soul dwells in the body, God dwells in the soul. "Know ye not," says an apostle, "that ye are the temple of God, and that the Spirit of God dwelleth in you?" Thus—although in a subordinate sense—the members resemble their crowned and exalted head; their bodies, like his own, are a temple, and the heart of the believer is the happy, honored shrine of him whom the heaven of heavens cannot contain.

Speaking of the man that loves him, our Lord said, "We will come unto him." This promise is one which he fulfills in the daily communications of his word and Spirit. Earth has no lovers who meet so often as Jesus and his bride. The lowliest and poorest Christian God honors with daily visits. He comes at the time of prayer; he occupies the mercy-seat at the stated hour of worship; and into the closet where the good man goes, he goes along with him. He is closeted there with God; and comes forth like a warrior from his tent, inspired with courage, and armed for the battle of life. Happy man! he sleeps at night in God's arms; happy man! in every trial he weeps on God's bosom! happy man! although his fare be but a crust of bread and cup of water, he dines every day at heaven's royal table.

Contented, not coveting the luxuries which wealth commands, he has bread to eat and company to keep the world knows not of; and, although he be the poorest of God's poor ones, there are none of the great ones of this earth, who, with their privileged and prized access to court, move in such high society. Could you see the angels who wing their flight to this straw-thatched cottage—the telegraph of prayer, that, with extended lines stretched up to the throne, is ever working—the messages that go up, and the answers that come down—Jesus himself descending to bow his kingly head at that lowly door, with "Peace to this house" on his lips, gifts in his hand, love beaming in his eye and burning in his bosom, you would not wonder how the poor pious man can suffer so many hardships, and yet live so contented. Pitying the poverty of riches, the meanness of rank, the littleness of greatness—envying no man his high acquaintances, coveting no man's large estates—all he needs is to wear his honors meekly; with a rank higher than kings possess or kings can bestow, with a patent of nobility that never can be forfeited, all he needs is to be "clothed with humility;" while he opens his heart and invites his Lord to come in, all he needs is to do that with the modesty of the man who said, "I am not worthy that thou shouldst enter beneath my roof."

Here, however—as also in those words of Christ, to which I have referred—God not only promises to visit his people, but by his Spirit to abide with them. "I will put my Spirit within you." "Happy is that people whose God is the Lord." For who or what else abides? Not our parents or pastors; the arms that embraced us are moldering in the grave, and on the lips that taught us knowledge the dust of death lies thick. Our health may not abide; there is a griefless, graveless land, where "the inhabitant never says that he is sick;" but faith lifts her eye to heaven, and seeks it yonder—not here. Our wealth may not abide; and so one who, better than many, remembered its uncertainty, when remonstrated with for giving lavishly to the cause of Christ, replied, "Riches take to themselves wings and flee away; and I think it best to clip them." Our children may not abide; the earth sounds hollow to the foot—it is so full of graves. Ah! how few gardens are there where death has not left his foot prints, when he came to steal away some of our sweetest flowers. Few are the trees standing on this earth, from which he has not lopped off some goodly boughs. In this world, have I not seen one and another stand bleak and branchless; and Oh, how blessed for the father who has laid the last survivor in the dust, and returns from that saddest funeral to find God waiting for him in his desolate home!

When the believer is alone,—God in his Holy Spirit abiding with him,—he is not alone. How happy, yet how strange a man he is! Those paradoxes by which Paul describes him—"Unknown, and yet well known; dying, and behold we live; sorrowful, yet always rejoicing; poor, yet making many rich; having nothing, and yet possessing all things"— admit of important additions. Kill him, and he lives; bury him, and he rises; exalt him, and he is humbled; humble him, and he is exalted; curse him, and he prays for you; hate him, and he loves you; an orphan, he clings to a living father; a widow, she sleeps on the bosom of a living husband. "A father of the fatherless, and a judge of the widow is God in his holy habitation." Piety sits on a husband or father's grave, confident in that living relationship, and calm beneath the protection of him who says— "You shall not afflict any widow or fatherless child. If thou afflict them in any wise, and they cry unto me, I will surely hear their cry. And my wrath shall wax hot, and I will kill you with the sword; and your wives shall be widows, and your children shall be fatherless." Let a believer never count himself desolate. Let others never call him so. If thy heart is right, it matters not how mean thy house may be; God shall abide with thee there on earth, till thou leavest this earth to abide with him in heaven.

The New Life.

[wh.   cause you to walk in my statutes, and keep my judg
ents, and do them.—EZEKIEL xxxvi. 27.

THE Divine Being has established certain laws—
some of a physical, others of a moral nature. And it
is as impossible to violate with impunity a moral as a
physical law; although the consequences in the former
case may be more remote, and the suffering may not
follow so closely on the heels of the sin. Solomon
asks, " Can a man take fire into his bosom, and not be
burned?" "Can he touch pitch, and not be defiled?"
You at once answer no. He who walks into the fire
shall certainly be burned; he who falls into the water
shall certainly be drowned; and if any man were mad
enough to pitch himself over a lofty bartizan, he
lights not on the ground like a winged bird or angel
—he shall certainly be crushed to pieces. Not only
so, but a passive as well as active violation of nature's
laws is followed by suffering. He who resists her de-
mand for sleep—he who turns a deaf ear to the calls
of hunger—he who denies his body the rest and re-
freshment that nature needs, must die. Now, no less
certainly shall he suffer who neglects or violates those
moral laws which have been established by the decree
of God.

It may seem a strange, and even foolish thing to
assert, but it is not the less true, that it is safer to
touch fire than sin, and safer in a sense to drink off a

cup of poison, than quaff the cup of devils. A man
stands a better chance of escape who violates a physi
cal than a moral law. This is difficult to be believed.
And why? Just because, in the breach of moral laws,
judgment does not, as in the breach of physical laws,
follow speedily on the transgression, nor succeed it
as the peal thunders on the flash. Yet it is not more
strange than true; and true, for this plain, satisfactory,
and unanswerable reason, that he who made the laws
which govern the physical world, may modify, may
change, may even altogether repeal them. He has
already done so. Iron is heavier than water; yet did
not the iron axe swim like a cork at the prophet's
bidding? Did not the unstable element of sea stand
up in walls of solid crystal, till the host passed over?
Did naked foot, when bathed in morning dew, ever
feel the green grass cooler than those three Hebrews,
when, on the floor of the burning furnace, they trod at
once beneath their feet a tyrant's power and the red
hot coals of fire? Fire may not burn, and water may
not drown. He who gave their laws to these elements
may alter them as he sees meet; but that moral law,
which is a transcript of his own mind and will, is, and
must be unchangeable as himself. Be sure, therefore,
that you can not sin with impunity. Be sure that
your sin will find you out. Be sure that what you
sow you shall reap. Be sure, that although the cloud
is long of gathering, it shall one day explode. Be
sure that sin and sorrow are linked together by an
adamantine chain—a chain durable and eternal as that
which binds the creature to the throne of God. When,
therefore, Satan, the flesh, or the world solicit, re-
member, that if your weakness yields, you are more
certain of suffering, than you would be of burning the

finger which you thrust into the fire. Sin is the fire that a man can not take into his bosom, and not be burned.

Do you ask, by way of objection, do not God's people escape suffering—commit sin, and yet escape the penalty? True. But their exemption from future punishment forms no exception to this rule. In their case, indeed, the debtor escapes, but then the creditor is paid. The sufferings from which they are exempted were endured by their substitute, and in a suffering Saviour their sins were punished. "He bore our griefs, and carried our sorrows. The chastisement of our peace was upon him, and with his stripes we are healed."

Entertaining these views, we ought not to be suspected of losing sight of the dignity and claims of the moral law in our faith in a crucified Saviour. That holy law was not buried in Jesus' sepulcher nor left behind with the grave-clothes in the tomb. We no longer hope, indeed, to be saved by the law yet we hold with the Apostle—hold as strongly as any can do—that "the law is holy, and the commandment holy, just, and good," and that these moral laws which were enshrined in the ark of Moses, and most awfully illustrated on the cross of Christ, have lost none of their authority. They remain to this day as imperative as those which regulate the tides, direct the procession of seasons, or steer the planets through the realms of space. Obedience to the law has indeed ceased to be the condition of salvation; it is well it is so. Otherwise, who should have been saved? "If thou, Lord, shouldst mark iniquities, O Lord, who shall stand?" "Enter not into judgment with thy servant, for in thy sight shall no man living be justified." The law is not now the gate of life; yet although it has ceased to be the gate, it has not ceased, and never shall cease, to be the rule of life. We preach, indeed, a free and full salvation; and we glory in the theme. We say that the greatest law-breaker may be saved; the foulest sinner washed white as snow; the basest of the base, the vilest of the vile, exalted to a throne in heaven; and that as no obedience rendered to the law since the fall of Adam can open heaven to fallen man, so since the death of Christ no disobedience can shut its gates against him. We say with Paul, "It is a faithful saying, and worthy of all acceptation, that Jesus Christ came into the world to save sinners, of whom I am chief." Blessed be God, the law, so stern-like in a sinner's eyes, no longer carries the keys of heaven. Purchased by his blood, they are in the custody of him who is very pitiful and of great mercy, and who --never turning a deaf ear to the cry of human distress—cheers the expiring hours of guilt, and said even to a thief, "To-day thou shalt be with me in paradise."

"Do we then make void the law through faith?" as Paul asks. Some have done so. Wild and wicked fanatics have risen to trouble the church, and bring a gospel of grace into contempt. They have asserted that it has set them free from the obligation of these holy commandments, and granted to believers a plenary indulgence to commit all manner of iniquity. From such licentious and immoral doctrines, from doctrines not less calculated to dissolve society than to dishonor the church of Christ, child of God! shrink with holy abhorrence; this your language,

" My soul, come not thou into their secret ; unto their assembly, mine honor, be not thou united."

I know that Paul says, " We are delivered from the law, that being dead wherein we were held ;" but are we delivered that we may sin ? Assuredly not. On the contrary, we are delivered that we may serve God ; serve him better, serve him holier ; serve him, as Paul also says, " in the newness of the spirit, and not in the oldness of the letter." Addressing us not with the voice of Sinai's thunders, but in the melting and mightier tones of a Redeemer's love, the Gospel lays this injunction upon all, " Be careful to maintain good works." These, although not always the believer's attainment, will always be his aim. Committing to his heart, and enshrining there those tables which Moses, in honor of their excellence, deposited in the tabernacle's holiest shrine, he will say, " O how I love thy law, O Lord;" and he will pray that God would fulfill to him this gracious promise of the text—" I will cause them to walk in my statutes, and they shall keep my judgments and do them."

In now addressing ourselves to the subject of that new life, which the believer lives in obedience to the law of God, I remark—

I. It is a willing obedience.

Many movements take place in the universe independent of any will but that of God. The sap ascends the tree, the planets revolve round the sun, the stars rise and set in the heavens, the tides flow and ebb upon our shores, and nature walks in God's statutes, keeping his judgments, and doing them, moved to obedience by no will but his. So soon, however, as, leaving inanimate matter below, we ascend into those regions where mind, or even instinct and matter are united, we discover a beautiful and benevolent law, by virtue of which God at once secures the happiness and pro· vides for the welfare of his creatures. He so orders it that their will is in perfect harmony with their work; their inclinations with their interests; and their in- stincts with the functions which they are called on to perform. The bee constructs its cell, the bird weaves her nest, the eagle among the crags above teaches her brood to fly, and in cairn or cave below, the fox suckles her young; and these are all labors of love— labors to which they bring a willing heart. Thus their happiness lies in their work. And to ascend even into heaven, this is no doubt the secret of its felicity; for as the law of gravity extends itself to the most distant stars, so that that which rounds a tear-drop gives its shape to every sun, I have no doubt that this law of divine power and benignity reaches the highest and holiest existences. The will and work of angels are in perfect harmony; therefore an angel's duty is an angel's delight.

Observe, also, how, when God changes the condi- tion of his creatures, he accommodates their will to the change. Take, for example, that insect to which I have elsewhere alluded. It comes from the egg a creeping worm; it is bred in corruption; it crawls on the ground; its aliment is the coarsest fare. In time it undergoes its wonderful metamorphosis. The wrig- gling caterpillar becomes a winged and painted butter- fly; and at this change, with its old skin it casts off its old habits and instincts. Now, it has a will as well as wings to fly. And with its bed the bosom of a flower, its food the honied nectar, its home the sunny air, and new instincts animating its frame, its will plays in harmony with its work. The change within corresponds to the change without. It spurns the ground; and, as you may gather from its merry, mazy dance, the creature is happy, and delights in the new duties which it is called to perform. Even so it is in that change which grace works in sinners. The nature of the redeemed is so accommodated to the state of redemption, their wishes are so fitted to their wants, their hopes to their prospects, their aspirations to their honors, and their will to their work, that they would be less content to return to polluted pleasures than this beautiful creature to be stripped of its silken wings, and condemned to pass its days amid the old, foul garbage, its former food. With such a will and nature as they now possess, their old life would be misery—would be hell. Would not the reclaimed prodigal, rather than leave his father's table, bosom, and love, for the company of harlots and the husks of swine troughs, embrace death and go to his grave? Even so God's people would rather not be at all, than be what once they were. Hence, on the one hand, their unhappiness in sin; and, on the other, their enjoyment in God's service; hence David's longing for the place of ordinances; hence the beauty of a Sabbath scene, and the music of Sabbath bells, and the answer of their hearts to the welcome sound, "I was glad when they said unto me, Let us go unto the house of the Lord."

Are you unconverted? Let this teach you what most you need. To men who are strangers to the happiness to be found in piety, and have their will set contrary to the law of God, religion seems, and can not but seem, a very sad, demure, miserable thing. Oh! it appears a weary thing to be singing psalms!

—they would sing songs rather; a dull book the
Bible—a most uninteresting task to be poring over
these pages—they would prefer a novel or a newspa-
per. Rather than sit at the communion table, they
would be guests where the board groans with luxuries,
bowls flow with wine, peals of laughter follow the
bright flashes of wit, and thoughtless joy dances away
the hours. Earth's short Sabbaths seem long and are
weary; and it is a mystery which they can not fathom,
how, when they go to heaven (and who is not hoping
to get there?), they are to pass an endless Sabbath of
psalms, and songs, and such listless services.

No wonder, if this is your state, that piety has no
charms for you. Without the clean heart and the
right spirit, your attempts to obey the law must be as
unpleasant as they are unprofitable. It is hard to row
against the tide, hard to swim against the stream, but
harder still, under no impulse but the lash of a guilty
conscience, and the terrors of a coming judgment, to
attempt conformity to the will of God. And, admit-
ting your conformity to be much greater than it is,
what possible value can it have in the eyes of God?
If even we would rather do the work ourselves, or
want the work altogether, than have it done for us by
a sullen, sulky servant—what pleasure can God have
in your slavish service? I would not be served by a
slave; nor will Jesus Christ. His arguments are not
whips—his reasons are not blows—his servants do
not walk and work in fetters. He is the beloved sov
ereign of a people who are free, devoted to his inter-
ests, and ready to die for his crown. He measures the
value of services not so much by the work done, as by
the willingness to do it. They serve that wait. Then,
as the Apostle says, 'Let there be first a willing

mind, and it is accepted according to that a man hath, and not according to that he hath not."

In short, the union between the Saviour and the soul, like the marriage of Isaac and Rebecca, stands on a cordial assent. "Peradventure," said Eleazer to his master, "peradventure the woman will not be willing to follow me." "Then," said Abraham, "if the woman be not willing to follow thee, thou shalt be clear from this my oath." On this condition, Eleazer sets off to woo and win a wife for Isaac. He arrives at Nachor; he is introduced to Laban, and the scene in that house at Nachor excites in us these two wishes.

First, Would to God that those who hold a higher commission, and are stewards of the mysteries of the Gospel, were as intent on their office, as this steward on his. Laban presses his hospitality upon him; the savory meat appeals to his hunger; he has had a long journey, and it is reasonable surely that he take some rest, get the dust of the road washed from his feet, and refresh exhausted nature before he enters upon business! No—Pattern of fidelity! He says—"I will not eat until I have told mine errand." And would to God, also, that he who dealt with Rebecca's heart, would persuade sinners to accept a better offer—backed by tokens of better love—and give us, as ambassadors for Christ in his love suit, that maiden's ready answer. Isaac had sent a far way for her. She saw his messenger; he stood before her, covered with the dust, and embrowned with the sun of the desert. She saw Isaac's love in these sparkling gems—the golden tokens of his affection. Her heart was won. Fair and lovely pattern of faith! Whom she had not seen she loved; she walked by faith, not by sight;

and paying a last visit to a mother's grave, forgetting "her father's house and her own people," the companions of her youth, and the sweet home of her early days, she turned round to her brother, and to his question—"Wilt thou go with this man?" with maiden modesty, but masculine firmness, she replied, "I *will* go."

II. This is a progressive obedience.

To "walk," is expressive of progress in grace. Walking is an act, and one not acquired in a day; for the power to walk is not ours, in the same sense, as the power to breathe. We are born with the one power, but born without the other. Like every other habit, walking becomes so easy by use, that we are unconscious of any effort; yet step into the nursery, and you see that this art, acquired by labor, is the reward of continuous, conquering perseverance. In fact, our erect attitude and progressive motion over the ground—simple as they seem—are achieved by means of most delicate and dexterous balancing. The marble statue does not stand erect without foreign support; and you have no sooner raised a dead man, and set him up on his feet, than he falls at yours, a heap of loathsome mortality.

In beauty and splendor, the figure of my text may yield to other images, expressive of a believer's progress—such as that of a seed dropped into the soil, where, striking down a delicate fiber, and sending up a green and tender shoot, it first rises into a seedling, which the finger of an infant could crush, but which grows, after a hundred summers have come and gone, into a robust and lofty tree, that, with its roots moored in the rock, lifts a proud head on high, and defies the storm. Or, such as that furnished by the birth and growth of day, from the first faint streak of dawn— when the face of morn blushes, as it were, to look on the crimes of earth—to the moment when the sun rises to bathe mountains, plain, and sea, in a golden flood of light. In so far, however, as the setting forth of one prominent and important feature of a believer's progress is concerned, the figure of my text yields the palm to none—nay, is perhaps superior to any. Other images convey the idea of progress, but this, of pro- gress accomplished by unwearied exertion—progress, the triumph of an intelligent mind, and the reward of a determined will. To explain this special point, let me borrow an illustration from our Lord, when he took a little child, and, presenting the blushing boy to the wondering assembly, said, Masters of Israel, doctors of the temple, priests of the altar, chiefs of the Sanhedrim, behold this pattern; " whosoever would enter the kingdom of heaven must be as this little child."

In this image God's people find comfort and encourage ment.

Does the infant who is learning to walk abandon the attempt, or yield to despair, because its first efforts are so feeble, and so often fail of success? If not, why then should we despond, because, in attempting to walk in God's ways, we often stumble, and not sel dom fall? We—many of us, at least—are but babes in Christ; and he no more gives up hope of his peo- ple because they fall, than the fond mother her hope and confidence that this infant, who is now creeping across the floor, shall one day stand erect in the beauty of its form, balanced on firm feet, and with free and perfect command of all its limbs. And why, then,

14

should we despond? Every man was once a babe. Samson himself—the mighty Nazarite who burst asunder new-spun ropes like flax touched with fire—who, with more than a giant's strength, wrenched the gates of Gaza from the city's port, and, heaving them on his back, climbed the steep acclivity—was once a feeble, wailing infant, who could barely carry his own head erect, and hesitated to venture from a mother's knee. The believer takes a law of God, and tries to walk in it—he tries to resist a temptation to which he has often yielded—he fixes his eye on Jesus, and, fired with a holy ambition, attempts to imitate him. He fails. Repeated attempts and repeated failures cast him into despondency. He lies where he fell. He gives himself up to dark and distressing doubts. Satan takes advantage of his failure, and insinuates that he has never been converted—that his religious impressions are a delusion—that his fair profession has been a vile hypocrisy. In such distressing circumstances, our children become our teachers. God ordains strength out of the mouth of babes, and the lesson of the nursery is invaluable. Learning in that school that walking is a progressive and not a sudden attainment, I get heart to say with David, "Why art thou cast down, my soul, and why art thou disquieted within me?" That to my soul, and this to the devil, who stands brandishing his sword over me, when I am lying with my back to the ground, but my eyes on heaven, "Rejoice not against me, O mine enemy, though I fall, I shall arise."

This image stimulates to exertion, as well as comforts under failure.

In attempting to walk, the child falls; there is blood upon its brow, and tears in its eye. Does it lie there

just to weep? By no means Looking through these
tears, and stretching out its little arms—if not by
speech, yet by signs that go to a mother's heart—for
it can pray before it speaks—it implores her help
Nor in vain. She flies to raise it; and when she has
stanched the bleeding wound, and kissed away the
tears, and soothed it in her gentle bosom, and it has
there sobbed out its grief, what then? Recovering
from the alarm, and soon forgetting its wounds, it
seeks the floor again. Perhaps it has been taught
some caution—perhaps it has learned to cling more to
a mother's hand—perhaps it ventures less rashly from
her side; yet, moved by an indomitable will, see how
it returns to the attempt, tries it again and again, until,
after some blows, and many falls, it earns the reward
of its perseverance. Now, with bright health on its
cheek, with grace in every motion, and beauty in all
its attitudes, laughing in its joy, and luxuriating in the
exercise of its new-born powers, it runs "without
wearying, and walks without fainting."

We teach our children; let us here be their scholars,
and take a lesson from the nursery. Why, then, do
we make so little progress in grace? Why at this
time of day, when some of us are bowed, wrinkled,
and grey, are we so unable to walk in God's statutes
—to keep his judgments and do them? It is not be-
cause our education has been neglected. It is not be-
cause any child has a mother so fond, so kind, so
quick to help, so able to raise the fallen and guide the
tottering step, as He who suffered for us more than
mother's birth's pangs, and feels for us more than a
mother's love. What child in earth's happiest home
enjoys a believer's advantages? "Happy art thou, O
Israel? who is like unto thee, O people saved by the

Lord? The eternal God is thy refuge, and beneath the everlasting arms." Why, then, is the progress of the Church so slow, compared with the progress of the nursery? Why has child after child in our families learned to walk, while the best of us are but creeping, tottering, stumbling, on our way to heaven?

There are mysteries in grace; but there is no mystery here. The reason is plain. Every hour of the day the infant is on its knees or feet; it falls, but it is to rise; it fails, but it is to begin again; its very happiness and business lie in the acquisition of this power and the smile which lights up its beautiful face, and its proud-like air when it can stand alone, or cross the floor to throw itself laughing into a mother's arms, show that its heart and happiness are in this work We say to God's people, "go, and," by God's grace, "do likewise." Take more pains and give more prayer to learn this holy art. Let the perseverance of the nursery be imitated by the church. Let our knees be as much employed in prayer, and our powers and hours in attempting a holy life, as those of infancy in learning to walk. Oh, if we would give the same "diligence to make our calling and election sure"—the same diligence to "work out our salvation," I am certain that we should be holier—much holier than we are. Our life would present a happy illustration of these sublime and resplendent emblems—" Ye are the light of the world:" "The path of the just is as the shining light, that shineth more and more unto the perfect day:" "They shall mount up with wings as eagles; they shall run and not be weary, they shall walk and not faint.'

III. This willing and progressive obedience is the sign and seal of salvation.

Am I a child of God? How am I to know that I am? These are anxious questions with the believer; and yet they are questions that admit of a very simple answer. We have not, nor can we expect to have, such a testimony to our sonship as the Saviour received when he went up from Jordan, and the form as of a dove descended out of heaven on his head, still wet with the waters of baptism. By the descent of the dove, and the voice of the thunder, his Father said—"This is my beloved Son, in whom I am well pleased." And yet God's people enjoy that very same testimony. The descent of the Spirit is still the evidence of son ship;—its sign, however, is not a dove perched upon their heads, but the dove nestled within their hearts. By his Spirit God creates them " anew in Jesus Christ unto good works;" and by these—by the fruits of a holy life, by the joys of a Holy Ghost, by the advanc- ing stages of a holy progress—his Spirit witnesses with their spirits that they are sons of God. A witness this, as certain, and therefore as satisfactory, as the voice of the skies, or the verdict of final judgment.

The fruit is now, as it shall be hereafter, the test of the tree. There is no such thing as faith without works. Without these, your profession is a lie, your faith is dead, your hope is a delusion. It is a delusion and a snare, like the phosphoric light, the product of putre- faction which, to the terror of superstitious peasants, and the destruction of unwary travelers, gleams and burns at night, above the pool in whose dark depths life has been lost, and a body, evolving gases capa- ble of spontaneous combustion, is going to decay. Now as the fruit is the test of the tree, obedience is the test of love; hear our Lord—"He that hath my commandments, and keepeth them, he it is that loveth me." Do not mistake us. We do not mean to say that any man keeps these commandments perfectly. Alas! the history of the church, and each man's own personal history, prove to our shame and sorrow, that God's people may, and do fall into sin; and, but for the restraining and constraining grace of God, would fall into the deepest, grossest sin. Let the conviction teach us to walk softly, humbly, circumspectly! Oh, never leave God's side, nor let go the hand of grace. Cling to Christ's arm, as if the storm of Galilee were beating about your head, and every footstep were planted upon a swelling wave.

I do not say that saints will not fall into sin, but I do say that, even when they are so unhappy, there will be an unmistakable difference between them and the ungodly. Judas sinned, and went and hanged himself; Peter sinned, and went out and wept. The sins of saints are the occasion of saintly sorrows. God shall see them at the fountain weeping and washing away their guilt in the blood of Jesus; and to Jesus himself they will go, to make on their knees the con fession of Peter—Lord, I know that I have sinned, I know that I am a great sinner; yet "thou knowest all things; thou knowest that I love thee."

There is one test—nor any more sure in the labo ratory of the chemist—by which to distinguish the godly from the ungodly, when both have fallen even into the very same sin. It is worth knowing, and never fails. It is very simple, and yet a most sure criterion. A child may comprehend it, and any one may apply it. I pray you to apply it, not to your neighbors' cases but to your own—nor reject it because it is humble, and plain, and simple, and vulgar, if you will It is the test by which you may know a sheep from a swine, when both have fallen into the same slough, and are, in fact, so bemired, that neither by coat nor color can the one be distinguished from the other. How then distinguish them? Nothing more easy! The unclean animal, in circumstances agreeable to its nature, wallows in the mire; but the sheep—type of the godly---bleats, and strives, and struggles to get out.

The New Life

I will . . . . . cause you to walk in my statutes, and keep my judgments, and do them.—EZEKIEL xxxvi. 27.

THE predestination which I believe in, is that of Paul—"Whom he did foreknow, he also did predestinate to be conformed to the image of his Son." To redeem us from the power, as well as punishment of iniquity, Jesus died. For this his precious blood was shed—for this the Spirit has descended. We are "called with a holy calling;"—called to pluck the love of sin from our hearts, to dethrone every idol that usurps the place of God; and having nailed to the cross the old man, with his affections and lusts, we we are called to be like Jesus. His meat and drink was to do his Father's will. He was "holy, harmless, undefiled, separate from sinners." By this lofty end of a good's man's life, by the regard which you cherish to Christ, by the welfare of your soul, by the interest of other men's souls, you are called to beware of every thing which might blemish your profession, obscure the luster of your graces, and hinder you from walking in God's statutes, and keeping his judgments, and doing them. So far, therefore, as circumstances permit you, "depart from evil," and in the choice of your company and companions, follow the example of David, and remember the warning of his son, "I am a companion to all them that fear thee;"—"a companion of fools shall be destroyed." Shun the place of infection, and—more than if they had plague or fever—the company of the infected. Avoid and abjure every scene, pleasure, pursuit, which experience has taught you tends to sin, dulls the fine set edge of conscience, nfits for religious duties or religious enjoyments, ends you prayerless to bed, or dull and drowsy to prayer. As the seaman does with surf-beaten reef or iron-bound shore, give these a wide berth; and passing on, hold away in your course straight for heaven.

Never fear to suffer; but Oh! fear to sin. Stand in awe of God, and in fear of temptation. "Watch and pray, that ye enter not into temptation." It is not safe to bring gunpowder within reach even of a spark. Nor safe, however dexterous your driving, to shave with your wheels the edge of a beetling precipice. Nor safe in the best-built bark that ever rode the waves, to sail on the rim of a roaring whirlpool. The seed of the woman has, indeed, bruised the head of the serpent; yet beware! the reptile is not dead. It .s dangerous to handle an adder, or approach its poison fangs, if the creature is alive, even although its head be crushed.

Let me also warn you that such a holy life as the text enjoins, is impossible to all but those who are on their guard against the beginnings of evil. Take alarm at an evil thought, wish, desire. These are the germs of sin—the floating seeds which drop into the heart, and finding in our natural corruption a fat and favorable soil, spring up into actual transgressions. These, like the rattle of the snake, the hiss of the serpent, reveal the presence and near neighborhood of danger. The experience of all good men proves that sin is most easily crushed in the bud, and that it is

14*

safer to flee from temptation than to fight it. Fight
like a man when you can not avoid the battle, but
rather flee than fight. Be afraid of it, avoid it, abhor
it; let your answer, as you tear yourself from the
encircling arms of the enchantress, and seek safety in
flight, be that of Joseph's—"Shall I do this great
evil, and sin against God?"

True, religion, however, consists not in a passive but
active piety. We are to *walk* in God's statutes, keep
his judgments, and *do* them. Our pattern is not the
man who wears a monkish cowl, and tells his beads,
and keeps his vigils, and goes through the dull routine
of prayers and fastings within the walls of a monas-
tery; nor she who, having assumed the black vail and
renounced the world, seeks safety from its contamina-
tion, or solace from its sorrows, within the cell and
cloisters of a convent. The pattern of a Christian is
that divine man, who—while he passed a brief period
of probation in the lonely desert, and often spent
whole nights on the mountain in solitary communion
with his God—walked the fields of Galilee, frequented
the fishing villages on the shores of Tiberias, and was
often to be met with in Judah's towns, and on Jeru-
salem's busy streets. Our exemplar is he, who, wher-
ever he went, "went about doing good," earning for
himself this noble opprobrium, "the friend of publi-
cans and sinners."

Observe, that activity of Christian life is implied in
the very terms of the text. Grant that we may
thereby be exposed to hardships and temptations,
from which a quiet and retiring piety might exempt
us. Still, a life of active service will be best for
others, and in the end also for ourselves. A candle
set beneath a bushel is, no doubt, safe from wind and

water; but of what use is it? On whose work does
it shine? Whose path does it illumine? I would
rather burn and waste on some lofty headland to
guide the bark through night and storm to its desired
haven. No light shineth for itself, and "no man
liveth for himself." Besides, the very trials to which
piety is exposed on the stormy heights of duty, will
impart to it a robust and healthy character. The
strongest trees grow not beneath the glass of a green-
house, or in the protection of sheltered and shaded
valleys. The stoutest timber stands on Norwegian
rocks, where tempests rage, and long, hard winters
reign. And is it not with the Christian as with the
animal life also? Exercise gives health, and strength
is the reward of activity. The muscles are seen fully
developed in the brawny arm that plies the ringing
hammer. Health blooms ruddiest on the cheek, and
strength is most powerfully developed in the limbs of
him, who—not nailed to a sedentary occupation, nor
breathing the close atmosphere of heated chambers—
but fearless of cold, a stranger to downy pillows and
luxurious repose, rises with the day, sees the early
worm rise in the dank meadow, and hears the morn-
ing lark high over head, and passing his hours in ath-
letic exercises, increases his strength by spending it.
Even so, the most vigorous and healthy piety is that
which is the busiest, which has difficulties to battle
with, which has its hands full of good works, which
has—I may say—neither time nor room for evil, but
aiming at great things, both for God and man,
promptly, summarily dismisses temptation, with Ne-
hemiah's answer—"I have a great work to do, there-
fore I cannot come down."

This world—with so many living and dying in it

without God and hope, with the whole heathen world
still unconverted, with thousands and tens of thou-
sands at home sunk in the deepest ignorance, and
slaves of the vilest sins, with members of our families
or of friendly circles far from God, and between whom
and us—terrible thought!—death would make an
eternal separation—has much need that we were up
and doing, and throwing ourselves into the cause of
active Christianity. Our opportunities of good are
many and multiform. A Christian man should feel
like some strong swimmer, who has hundreds around
him sinking, drowning, shrieking for help; the diffi-
culty is to make selection, and on whose unhappy
head first to lay a saving hand. Amid such scenes
and calls, Oh, it is lamentable to think how much of
our time has been frivolously and uselessly spent.
"The time past of our lives has been more than suffi-
cient to have wrought the will of the flesh;" to have
enjoyed our own ease, made money, and secured for
ourselves the comforts of life. To nobler ends be its
remaining sands devoted! Take Christ for your copy.
Run in God's statutes without wearying, and walk in
them without fainting; and let the day on which some
good has not been done to ourselves or others—some
glory won for God, some progress made in the divine
life—be a day mourned over, wept for, and this writ-
ten down against it in the calendar of our life—"I
have lost a day." Our Christianity is a name, a
shadow, unless we resemble him who, being incarnate
God, was incarnate goodness, and of whom, although
he stood alone in that hall—without one kind or
brave voice raised to speak for him—there were hun-
dreds and thousands to bear this testimony, that he
went about doing good," and was the friend both of

sufferers and sinners. It is thus that we are to fulfill
the duties of the Christian life, and exhibit a living
picture of one in whom this promise is fulfilled—" I
will cause you to walk in my statutes, and to keep my
judgments and do them." In closing my observations
on this part of our subject, I remark—

I One of the most powerful means to accomplish
the duty of the text is to cultivate the love of Christ.

They who would live like Jesus must look to Jesus.
What effect will follow? Look at the sun—and now
to the eyes which have been bathed in his dazzling
beams, how do other objects appear? Why, all are
changed. They have grown dim, if not dark and in-
visible. Candles, that burned bright, have no flame;
flowers, that looked beautiful, have no color; the very
diamond has lost its sparkling. And could we see
Jesus Christ in the full effulgence of his Saviour
glory, all sinful and even all common created objects,
would appear to undergo some such change.

We see but through a glass darkly. The dimness
of sin impairs our vision, but were we to see Jesus,
as we shall see him in heaven, I think it would happen
to us as once it happened to a celebrated philosopher.
Pursuing his discoveries on the subject of light—with
a zeal not too often consecrated to science, but too
seldom consecrated to religion—he ventured on a bold
experiment. Without protection of smoked or colored
glass, he fixed his gaze steadily, for some time, on
the sun—exposing his naked eyes to the burning
beams of its fiery disc. Satisfied, he turned his head
away; but, strange to see!—such was the impression
made on the organ of sight—wherever he turned, the
sun was there; if he looked down, it was beneath his

feet; it shone in the top of the sky in the mirkest midnight; it blazed on the page of every book he read; he saw it when he shut his eyes, he saw it when he opened them. It was the last object which he saw when he passed off into sleep; it was the first to meet his waking eyes. Happy were it for us if we got some such sight of Christ, and this glory of that sun of righteousness were so impressed upon the eye of faith that we could never forget him, and, ever seeing him, ever loved him. With Christ ever present to our mind's eye, then we should be able more fully to adopt the words of Paul, and say, "the love of Christ constraineth us, because we thus judge, that if one died for all, then we are all dead, and that he died for all, that they which live should not henceforth live unto themselves, but unto him who died for them, and rose again."

Experience has proved that of all instruments, the mightiest for conversion is the love of Jesus. It was only "Christ and him crucified," that Paul was to know and preach; and in every age of the church and region of the world has not that proved the rod to smite rocky hearts? Let me illustrate the fact by referring to oft-quoted experience of some Moravians who had gone to carry the glad tidings of salvation to the cold clime and rude savages of Greenland. For what reason I know not, but it is a fact that they commenced and continued for months to preach to these savages of their sins. They told them of the wrath of God; they sounded Sinai's thunders; they blew its loudest trumpet in their ears; they appealed to their conscience, to their fears, to their self love and self interest. They told them of a heaven above, with a sun that never set, and of a dark and dreary hell below, where nor sun, nor hope ever rose; of fire that burned and a worm that gnawed incessantly. Thus they preached. But their preaching was all in vain. The aspect of their hearers had its counterpart in the wintry landscape of these northern regions; characterized by perpetual night—the intensest cold—death-like silence; a sunless sky; and a sea bound fast in chains of ice. These good men changed their plan. They chose another theme. Exchanging the law for the love of God, they preached of Calvary, and expatiated on the love which brought Jesus to a cross, and opened his blessed arms to embrace the world. The effect was almost as immediate as remarkable. When summer came and the snows melted on their hills, and, with sounds, like the salvos of cannon that announce a victory, the ice broke on these frozen seas; and beneath the beams of a sun, which blazed at midday, nor set at midnight, the earth —like a corpse come to life—disrobed itself out of its snowy shroud; and the sea, rejoicing in freedom from its icy bonds, with tides that ebbed and flowed, once more answered to the influences of heaven, and rising to the wind, praised God night and day with the voices of its roaring breakers, this glorious change was but a picture of the melting, moving, transforming, regenerating power felt by the soul of the poor, wondering savage, as he looked with weeping eye on the love of Christ and the bloody cross of Calvary.

As the love of Christ to us is the mightiest power to awaken faith, so in the love of our hearts to Christ will be found the mightiest power to secure obedience, and insure our walking in God's statutes, and keeping his judgments, and doing them. Therefore, we urge you to cultivate it; for—

Love is the most powerful of all motives.

Samson's great strength lay in his hair. Shorn of that, he was like other men. The Christian's great strength lies in his love; and when Christ invites us to sacrifices and sufferings which the world would pronounce intolerable, love is ready to explain and justify the language of his invitation—"Come unto me, all ye that labor, and are heavy laden, and I will give you rest. Take my yoke upon you, for it is easy, and my burden, for it is light." On the back of love the burden loses more than half its weight, and the work that is done in love loses more than half its tedium and difficulty. It is as with a stone, that in the air, and on the dry ground, we strain at, but can not stir. Flood the field where it lies; bury the block beneath the rising water. Now when its head is submerged, bend to the work. Put your strength to it. Ah! it moves—it rises from its bed—it rolls on before your arm. So, when the tide of love goes swelling over our duties and difficulties, a child can do a man's work, and a man can do a giant's. With love in the heart, "out of the mouths of babes and sucklings God ordaineth strength." Strength! What strength? Death pulls down the youngest and the strongest; but love is stronger than death. She welcomes sacrifices, and glories in tribulation. Duty has no burden, and death has no terror for her.

Look at that bird, which, with wings outstretched, sits dead on the scorched and blackened tree. She might have flown away in safety. The smoke below alarmed her. Dashing through and through it on frightened wing, she screamed, as, climbing from branch to branch, the fire rose to her nest and brood. She dashes right into the danger; and, perched on the brim of the nest—a tender mother,—she fans her young ones with her wings. Now the flames lick it with their fiery tongues—she leaves her perch. False to her offspring? No. A true mother. She abandons it—not to soar away to heaven—but, as on dewy nights and in happier hours, to seat herself above her young to die with them; and, with expanded wings, protecting them to the last—to be found dead with a dead brood beneath her. I look on that—or I look on this other mother, who stands with her child on the side of the sinking wreck, to catch the last chance of a passing boat. She catches it—not to leap in herself; but, lifting her boy in her arms, and printing a mother's last kiss upon his rosy lips, she drops him in, and remains behind herself to drown and die. Or I look at that maid in old border story, who, having caught a glance of the arrow that, shot by a rival's hand, came from the bushes on the other bank, flung herself before her lover, and received the fatal shot in her own true and faithful heart. I look at these things, and, seeing that love is strong as death, I urge you to cultivate the love of Jesus, and go in its divine strength to the field of duty, and the altar of sacrifice.

I do not say that you will find it easy to walk in God's statutes, to keep Christ's commandments, and do them. To pluck sin from a bleeding heart—to put our right hand on the block and cut it off—to pull a right eye from its socket, and put our foot upon it—for a proud man to learn humility—for a lover of the world not to love it—for one who has strong native corruption to nail it to the cross, and keep it nailed there till it die—when the path of duty is strewed with flints and thorns, to walk over them with bleeding feet—is, and must be painful. There is no use of

concealing t, of denying it. No. But all the more
need there is that you inflame your love by looking to
Christ. Go often, and, with the shepherds, gaze on
the heavenly babe laid on a pallet of straw in the
corner of a manger. With the disciples, accompany
him to Gethsemane, and sit beneath her hoary olives
to listen in the stilly night to the moans and groans
of the Son in the hands of his Father. Or join the
weeping women, and, with the other Marys and his
fainting mother, take up your station near the awful
cross, and meditate on these things till you can say
with David, " While I was musing, the fire burned."

Love is a motive to duty as pleasant as it is powerful.
Love weaves chains that are tougher than iron, and
yet softer than silk. She unites the strength of a
giant to the gentleness of a little child; and, with a
power of change all her own, under her benign and
omnipotent influence, duties that were once intolera-
ble drudgeries become a pure delight. The mother,
for instance, away from scenes of gayety, without
which to others and once also to herself the cup of
life was flat and tasteless, is awakened to new enjoy-
ments. She never wearies watching by her infant's
cradle; nor does she grudge the nights of broken rest,
the toils, the cares, the troubles that creature costs her,
although these have blanched her cheek and paled the
luster of her eye. To cares that others would feel
irksome, she cheerfully devotes herself, even before
the babe can lisp her name, or reward her kindness
with a look of recognition and its grateful, winning
smile. Nor does the father weary of the toil that
wins his children's bread. The thought of these
strengthens the arms of daily labor, fires the patriot's

zeal, kindles a soldier's courage, cheers the seaman on his lonely watch, and reconciles thousands of our honest poor to a life of incessant struggle—carrying them through toils and hardships, otherwise intolerable, with a cheerful, contented, happy, singing spirit.

You would think it a most weary and dreary thing to lead the life which that mother passes. You think so, because you do not feel her love. And it is just because they are strangers to the love of Jesus—because they have never known him, nor loved him, that many can not comprehend such things as—how a pious life can be a pleasant one—how any man can think that the finest music is the sound of Sabbath bells—that God's is the best house—and the Lord's the best table—how a man of exalted grace would rather sit down with a pious peasant at the Lord's supper, than at a banquet where he was the guest of kings—and how King David should have thought a day spent in the sanctuary better than a thousand passed amid the stirring scenes of a camp, or the glory and luxuries of a palace. They can not understand how, unless they were fools or fanatics, the disciples should leave the judgment-seat with bleeding stripes, and rejoice that they were counted worthy to suffer for Christ; how Paul and Silas should have sung as cheerfully in a dungeon as ever lark that shook the night dew from its wings, and rose to greet the morning sun; and how the only fear of that brave old man, John Welch, in yonder rocky prison of the Bass, was lest, that when others were winning the crown of martyrdom, he should miss it, nor be counted worthy of that bloody honor. But they, in some measure at least, understand these things, whose pulse beats true to the law of God, and whose heart burns with the love of Christ. To the feet of love the ways of that law are like the fresh and flowery sward, "ways of pleasantness and paths of peace." Love changes bond-age into liberty, and, delighting in that law which was once to us what his chain is to the dog, what his task is to the slave, and against which our corrupt passions once foamed and fretted like angry seas on their iron shores, she takes up the harp of David, and thus sings its praises;—"The law of the Lord is per-fect, converting the soul; the statutes of the Lord are right, rejoicing the heart; the judgments of the Lord are true, and righteous altogether; more to be desired are they than gold, yea, than much fine gold; sweeter also than honey and the droppings of the honeycomb." "Oh! how I love thy law, O Lord; it is my medita-tion all the day."

II. A powerful motive to the duties of the text lies in the fact, that by our obedience to these statutes the verdict of judgment shall be settled.

We are saved by grace, but shall be tried by works. We are to be judged by the "deeds done in the body whether they were good or bad." "Every one of us," says Paul, "shall give account of himself to God." Oh! how should these solemn truths hedge, wall up our path to a close and holy walk in his stat-utes! The great realities of eternity are projected in outline on the field of time, and this world lies under the long, solemn shadow of coming events. Imagine them come—the day of judgment come! For what-ever purpose met, there is something most impressive in the spectacle of a great multitude; that vast sea of faces—that mighty aggregate of human beings with living hearts, immortal souls, eternal destinies—all in a few years to be dead and gone; and the joys and sorrows, the fears and hopes, that now animate and agitate them, cold and buried in the dust. But how unspeakably more solemn a world come from their graves to judgment! and amid circumstances of terrible and transcendent sublimity—thunders that rend the skies—the perpetual hills passing away—burning mountains hurled into boiling seas—the sun dying— the starry heavens rolling up like a scroll—and all eyes fixed on the " great, white throne," which rises in lonely majesty high above the countless crowd.

It shall be a solemn thing to meet the dead again, and see those—father and mother, children, our brethren—who are now moldering in the dust. How solemn it was to part with them—to stand by the dying bed, and look on as they passed away, till we heard life's departing sigh, and saw the last convulsion quiver on the lip of one that was our own. But the meeting of those who, although lying side by side, have been long parted—who, although their coffins and dust commingle, have held no communion in these silent graves, will be a more solemn thing; and an awful thing, if we should meet, as many shall meet —how dreadful the thought!—with mutual accusations and bitter recriminations; awful, overwhelming, unless we meet with mutual congratulations, to spend eternity together in a better than our old, earthly home—in the mansions where friends meet to part no more.

Still the solemnity rises. If it shall be a solemn thing to find ourselves face to face with the dead, how much more solemn to stand face to face with the great Judge both of the quick and dead. We have read—we have often thought of Jesus Christ, till we felt as if we saw him. We have followed him in

fancy's vision through the checkered scenes of his
earthly history—along his rough and bloody path,
from the night that angels sung his advent, to the day
when they returned to escort the conqueror home.
We have seen his form stretched out—for want of a
better bed—upon the dewy field, or wrapped up in
coarse boat-cloak as he lay buried in slumber amid
the storm on Galilee. We have seen the eyes of pity
he bent on the weeping Magdalene—the expression
of reproachful love he cast on a recreant disciple—
that dying look, so full of fond affection, which he
turned on a fainting mother. We have seen him
standing calm and collected before a prejudiced and
time-serving judge, patient and self-possessed beneath
the bloody scourge, mute and meek before the frenzied
multitude; and as we watched the successive events
of the cross, we have seen the joy—typified by the
passing away of this eclipse—that gleamed in his
dying eyes as he raised them to heaven and cried, "It
is finished." We have often in fancy seen him. When
our dust revives, and the grave that is now awaiting
us shall give up its dead, with these very eyes we
shall see him—by the light of a world in flames we
shall see him, a God-enthroned for judgment.

The day grows yet more solemn; its solemnity
reaches its highest point, and culminates in the mo-
mentous issues of judgment. It is God's day of set-
tlement with a world that has had a long credit. It is
the winding up of this earth's bankrupt estate, and
each man's individual interests. It is the closing of
an open account that has been running on ever since
the Fall. It is the day when the balance is struck,
and our fate is heaven or hell; and what invests my
text with solemn and sublime importance is this, that

by the manner in which we have walked in these
statutes, and kept these judgments, and done them,
shall our destiny be determined. The most common
action of life, its every day, every hour, is invested
with a solemn grandeur, when we think how they ex-
tend their issues into eternity. Our hands are now
sowing seed for that great harvest. We shall meet
again all we are doing and have done. The graves
shall give up their dead, and from the tombs of ob-
livion the past shall give up all that it holds in keeping,
to be witness for or witness against us. Oh, think of
that, and in yonder hall of the Inquisition, see what
its effect on us should be. Within those blood-stained
walls, for whose atrocious cruelties Rome has yet to
answer, one is under examination. He has been as-
sured that nothing he reveals shall be written for the
purpose of being used against him. While making
frank and ingenuous confession he suddenly stops.
He is dumb—a mute. They ply him with questions,
flatter him, threaten him; he answers not a word.
Danger makes the senses quick. His ear has caught a
sound; he listens; it ties his tongue. An arras hangs
beside him, and behind it he hears a pen running
along the pages. The truth flashes on him. Behind
that screen a scribe sits committing to the fatal page
every word he says, and he shall meet it all again on
the day of trial. Ah! how solemn to think that there
is such a pen going in heaven, and entering on the
books of judgment all we say, or wish, all we think,
we do. Would to God we heard it—every where, and
always heard it! What a check! and what a stimulus!
Are we about to sin, how strong a curb; if slow to
duty, how sharp a spur. What a motive to pray for
the blood that blots out a guilty past, and for such

grace, as, in time to come, shall enable us to walk in
God's statutes, to keep his judgments, and to do them.

Do any flatter themselves that, as to *their* sins and
transgressions, God hath not seen, or doth not regard,
or hath forgotten? Most fatal delusion! "I have
seen all that Laban hath done unto thee," said the
Lord to Jacob in a dream. "Surely I have seen
yesterday the blood of Naboth," are his words to
Elijah, when he sends away his ambassador with a
commission to throw down the gauntlet at a king's
feet, and to proclaim war between heaven and the
bloody house of Ahab. Naboth has been foully mur-
dered, but lies quiet in his bloody shroud. The crime
is concealed. Cunning and cruelty have triumphed;
and no living man now stands between Ahab and the
vineyard. His evil genius approaches his bed. "Arise,"
says his wife, "Naboth is dead, arise and take possess-
ion." The king rises, rides down in royal state to
Jezreel, and luxuriates among the clustered grapes of
his ill-got possession. Suddenly a man clothed in
rough garment, unsummoned, unwelcomed, appears
upon the scene, and intrudes himself on royalty. It
is Elijah. With steady step and stern look, he marches
up to Ahab, and, fixing his eyes on the quailing
coward, asks, "Hast thou killed and also taken pos-
session? In the place where dogs licked the blood of
Naboth, they shall lick thy blood, even thine." Tread
upon a worm and it will turn on you. To be a king,
and yet be bearded before his court by this rude, un-
mannerly intruder, to have the damning deed—which
had been contrived with such cunning, and executed
with such success—dragged out from its concealment
by this bold hand into the light of day, to be
branded before his courtiers, and proclaimed through-

out all the country as Naboth's murderer, stirs—if not
the courage—at least the wrath of Ahab. With guilt
on his scowling brow, and malignant anger burning
in his eyes, he turns on the prophet, saying, "Hast
thou found me, O mine enemy?" "I have found thee,"
was the calm, terrible, intrepid answer..

Impenitent and unbelieving sinner! flatter not thy-
self that God hath not seen, or doth not regard; fancy
not that thy crimes are buried in a grave deeper than
Naboth's, and that, as the dust of death lies on the
lips of the partners or witnesses of thy guilt, therefore
you may be at ease, since the dead tell no tales. The
day is coming when every unpardoned sin shall find
out its father;—when what has been done in darkness
shall be revealed in daylight, and the word whispered
in the ear shall be published upon the house-top. We
shall be tried by our obedience to these statutes and
judgments. We have often disobeyed them, and if,
on that dread day, we would not have these sins to
meet us as Elijah met the king—if we would meet not
our sins but our Saviour, Oh let us have recourse now
to the blood that blotteth them out. Without a par
don, Jesus shall have no answer to us but one, the
terrible reply of Jehu, "What hast thou to do with
peace?"

Peace!—Yes, there shall be peace—"Being justified
by faith, we have peace with God, through our Lord
Jesus Christ;" and the secret of our peace shall lie in
that which held up the head of a royal favorite, while
undergoing trial before his country for a very heinous
crime. Men wondered at his strange serenity, and
how he could bear himself so calmly. He passed on
to the bar without a cloud upon his brow, or an ex-
pression of anxiety in his eye, as he looked around

15

him on judges, accusers, the crowd of anxious specta·
tors. The trial began. His case grew darker and
darker—not so his aspect. Witness after witness bore
crushing evidence against him, yet the keen eyes of
his enemies could detect no quiver on his lip, or shade
upon his brow. Long after hope had expired in the
breast of anxious friends, and they looked on him as
a doomed man, there he was, looking round serenely
on that terrible array. His pulse beat calm, nor started
suddenly, but went on with a stately march; while
peace sat enthroned upon his placid brow. When at
length, amid the silence of the hushed assembly, the
verdict of "Guilty" is pronounced, he rises. Erect
in attitude, in demeanor calm, he stands up, not to
receive the sentence—which was already trembling on
the judge's lip—but to reveal the secret of this strange
peace and self-possession. He thrusts his hand into
his bosom, and lays on the table a pardon—a full, free
pardon for his crimes, sealed with the royal signet.

Would to God we all were as well prepared! Then
fare ye well, earth, sun, moon, and stars; fare ye well,
wife and children, brothers and sisters, sweet friends,
and all dear to us here below. Welcome death, wel
come judgment, welcome eternity; welcome God and
Christ, angels and saints made perfect, welcome heaven
In the grace that leads to a holy walk, in some mea·
sure of godly obedience to these statutes, in the faith
that worketh by love, purifieth the heart, and over-
cometh the world, have you the evidence that you
are forgiven? In these, do you carry in your bosom
God's pardon, ready to be produced when you are
summoned to trial? Look forward without fear to
the great account. These shall be witnesses that you
have received the righteousness which makes the

sinner just. Best of all shrouds, may you be wrapped in the " clean linen " of Jesus' righteousness! With that robe around you may you rise from the grave! —this your plea—" Almighty God! of my own works I have nothing to say but this, What is bad in them is mine; what is good in them is thine. Behold this pardon—look on this robe, and know now whether it be thy Son's coat or no."

Nature, Necessity, and Power of Prayer.

I will yet for this be inquired of by the house of Israel, to do it for them.—EZEKIEL xxxvi. 37.

IN pursuing his voyage to the shores of the new world the seaman steers southward. His object is to catch the trade wind. It blows so steadily from east to west, that having once caught it in his sails he has often nothing else to do. With his ship's head set before that wind, he is borne steadily along beneath a brilliant sun, and gently wafted over a summer sea. His voyage is one extended, happy holiday. The thrilling cry of land comes at length from the out-look on the topmast, and he drops his anchor in some quiet bay of those lovely islands, where the waves wash coral strands, and the breezes that blow seaward from their spicy forests, come loaded with delicious perfumes.

It is not thus man reaches the shores of heaven. That landing may be a picture of his arrival—the voyage is not. In yonder vessel, which enters the harbor with masts sprung, sails in rags, bulwarks gone, bearing all the marks of having battled with many a storm and ridden many a crested wave, and on her deck a crew of weather-beaten and worn men, happy and glad to reach the land again—behold the plight in which the believer arrives at heaven It is hard work to get there? No doubt of it. Paul, the man, in labors more abundant, in stripes above

measure, in prisons more frequent, in deaths of—
Paul, the martyr, thrice beaten with rods, once
stoned, thrice shipwrecked, in journeyings often, in
perils of waters, in perils of robbers, in perils by his
countrymen, by the heathen, in the city, in the wilder-
ness, on the sea—Paul, the patient sufferer for Christ,
of a life of weariness, and painfulness, and watchings,
hunger, thirst, fastings, cold, nakedness—Paul even
stood alarmed, lest he himself should be a castaway.
"The righteous scarcely are saved." The busiest in
praying, watching, working, fighting, are no more than
saved. O then, "if the righteous scarcely are saved,
where shall the ungodly and the wicked appear?"

My text summons you to prayer. But does any
man think, that, by repeating a daily prayer—learned
long ago perhaps at his mother's knee, reading some
verses of Scripture, abstaining from grosser sins, at-
tending church on Sabbath, and the Lord's table on
communion days, he is by this smooth and easy way
to reach the kingdom, and receive its crown? What
says our Lord, "The kingdom of heaven suffereth
violence, and the violent take it by force;" it is the
prize of men who are valiant in faith and strong in
prayer—men like those who, at bugle's sound or flare
of rocket, rush from the trenches, and springing into
the deadly breach—leaping into the very mouth of
death—fight their way on and up till their flag of
victory waves above the smoke of battle.

Or, take Paul's figure of the energies and activities
of the Christian life. Look at these two men, strip-
ped to the skin, who stand face to face, confronting
each other in the public arena. They have been in
training for weeks and months. Strangers to the
pleasures of ease and sweets of luxury, they have

been on foot every day by the dawn. Abstaining from all indulgences which might enervate their frame, in hard bed, hard food, hard work, they have endured every trial which could develop their muscular powers, and add to their strength. And now these athletes are met to contend for the prize; foot touches foot, eyes watch eyes, and their spare but sinewy and iron forms are disrobed, that nothing may impede the lightning rapidity of their movements, or lessen the power of the stroke. The signal is given. Blows fall thick as hail; and now the candidates are rolling on the ground; now they emerge from a cloud of dust to continue the fight, till one—planting a tremendous stroke on the head of his antagonist—stands alone in the arena, and amid applauses that rend the sky and waken up the distant echoes, holds the field. At this moment Paul steps forward, and, addressing Christians, says, So fight; so win. "They do it to obtain a corruptible crown, but we an incorruptible."

Woe to the man, in these old games, who allowed his competitor to catch him off his guard. Woe to the man who turned to look on father, mother, wife, or mistress. Woe to the man who lifted his eyes but for a moment from the glaring eyeball of his antagonist; that moment a ringing blow fells him to the earth—he bites the dust.

Not less does our safety depend on constant prayer and watchfulness. "Be instant in prayer." "Pray without ceasing." "Watch and pray." Ah! you will never have to offer Satan an advantage twice. Should he catch you asleep, as David caught Saul—when he put aside the spear of Abashai that gleamed in the moonlight above the unconscious sleeper, and whispered, "Destroy him not"—Satan will not be satisfied with carrying off spear and water-cruse, or skirt of robe; he will not be content to prove how he had you in his power, and that, like a noble enemy who declines to take advantage of a sleeping man, he had generously left you your peace and piety. Constant prayer, unceasing watchfulness, are what your interests imperatively demand. These the Christian life requires, and these the crown of redemption rewards. Observe how in my text God hangs all the blessings of salvation upon prayer. He says—as it were—I have had pity upon sinners; I have provided pardon for the guilty, justification through the righteousness, and life through the death of my Son; I have promised to take away the heart of stone and replace it with one of flesh; I have promised my Spirit to sanctify, sufficient grace, a certain heaven— all these blood-bought, gracious, happy, holy blessings shall be yours, freely yours; yet not yours, unless they are sought in prayer. "I will yet for this be enquired of by the house of Israel, to do it for them."

In directing your attention to prayer, let me notice—

I. Nature itself teaches us to pray.

Like our intuitive belief in the existence of the soul, or in man's responsibility, there seems to be lodged in every man's breast, what I may call an instinct to pray, and an intuitive belief in the efficacy of prayer. Prayer must be natural, because it is universal. Never yet did traveler find a nation upon earth but prayed in some form or other to some demon or god. Races of men have been found without raiment, without houses, without manufactures, without the rudiments of arts, but never without prayers; no more than without speech, human features, or human passions.

Prayer is universal, and seems to be as natural to man as the feelings which prompt an infant to draw the milk of a mother's bosom, and by its cries to claim a mother's protection. Even so man is—as it were instinctively—moved to cast himself into the arms of God, to seek divine help in times of danger, and in times of sorrow to weep on the bosom of a Father who is in heaven.

Nature and necessity have wrung prayers even from an atheist's lips.

There was a celebrated poet, who was an atheist— or at least professed to be so. According to him there was no God. Very strange! A rude heap of bricks shot from a cart upon the ground was never seen to arrange itself into the doors, stairs, chambers, and chimneys of a house. The dust and filings on a brass-founder's table had never been known to form themselves into the wheels and mechanism of a watch. The types loosely flung from the founder's mould never yet fell into the form of a poem, such as Homer, or Dante, or Milton would have constructed. The rudest hut of Bushmen, the Indian's simple canoe— fashioned by fire from a forest tree, the plainest clay urn, in which savage affection had enshrined the ashes of the dead, were never supposed to owe their form to the hands of chance. Yet this man believed (if it is possible to think so,) that nature's magnificent temple was built without an architect, her flowers of glorious beauty were colored without a painter, and her intricate, complicated, but perfect machinery constructed without an intelligent mind. According to him there was no God—the belief in a God was a delusion, prayer a base superstition, and religion but the iron fetters of a rapacious priesthood. So he held

when sailing over the unruffled surface of the Ægean
Sea. But the scene changed; and, with the scene,
his creed. The heavens began to scowl on him; and
the deep uttered an angry voice, and, as if in aston-
ishment at this God-denying man, "lifted up his hands
on high." The storm increased until the ship became
unmanageable. She drifted before the tempest. The
terrible cry, "breakers ahead!" was soon heard;
and how they tremble to see death seated on the hor-
rid reef—waiting for his prey! A few moments more,
and the crash comes. They are whelmed in the
devouring sea? No. They were saved by a singular
providence. Like apprehended evils, which, in a
Christian's experience, prove to be blessings, the
wave, which flung them forward on the horrid reef,
came on in such mountain volume as to bear and float
them over into the safety of deep and ample sea-room.
But ere that happened, a companion of the atheist—
who, seated on the prow, had been taking his last re-
gretful look of heaven and earth, sea and sky—turned
his eyes down upon the deck, and there, among pa-
pists, who told their beads and cried to the virgin, he
saw the atheist prostrated with fear. The tempest had
blown away his fine-spun speculations like so many
cobwebs; and he was on his knees, imploring God
for mercy. In that hour—in that terrible extremity
—Nature rose in her might, asserted her supremacy,
vindicated the claims of religion, smote down infi-
delity by a stroke, and bent the stubborn knees of
atheism in lowliest prayer.

Danger may thus extort prayer; it does not follow
that God will accept it. How can a man expect to
have prayers accepted which are only wrung from him
by the hand of danger or the fear of death? Let us

translate their language? Is it not this? 1 will serve
my lusts as long as I dare. So long as I can say it
safely, I will say—Evil be thou my good; my vices,
be ye my gods; I will turn to religion when I can do
no better. Does Jesus stand at my door? are his
locks wet with the dews of night? are his limbs weary
standing? is his hand weary knocking? Till another
hand is knocking there—the loud, impatient hand of
death—Jesus comes not in. "What have I to do
with thee, thou Son of God?" With thy religion—
"Art thou come to torment me before the time?"
"Go thy way at this time: when I have a convenient
season I will call for thee."

In the name of reason, religion, gratitude, love, is
this the treatment which a Saviour deserves? De-
luded sinner! "Is this thy kindness to thy friend?"
Beware! What if he should mete out to us the meas-
ure we mete to him? Remember the warning—"I
have spoken, and ye have not heard; I have called,
and ye have not answered; when ye speak I will not
hear; when ye call I will not answer. I will laugh
at your calamity, and mock when your fear cometh."

II. Some difficulties connected with this duty.

The decrees of God, say some, render prayer use-
less. Are not all things, they ask, fixed by these de-
crees—irrevocably fixed? By prayer I may, indeed,
prevail on a man to do a thing which he has not pre-
viously resolved not to do, and even although he
should have so resolved—man is changeable; and 1
may show him such good reasons for doing it, as to
change his resolution. But if an immutable God has
foresettled every thing by an eternal and irreversible
decree, what purpose can prayer serve? Who shall

change the unchangeable?   Thus men have argued,
saying--"What profit shall we have if we should
pray unto him?"

It were not difficult to expose the fallacy of this
reasoning.   The objection may be entirely answered.
We might show that the decrees of God embrace the
means as well as the end; and since prayer is a means
of grace, being a means to an end, it must be em-
braced within these very decrees, and can not be ex-
cluded by them.   I content myself, however, with
simply saying, that this objection is not honestly, at
least not intelligently, entertained by any man.   For,
if the objection is good against prayer, it is good
against many things besides.   If it stops action in the
direction of prayer—if it arrests the wheels of prayer
—it ought to stop the wheels of our daily business.
If a good objection against prayer, it is an equally
good objection to ploughing, sowing, taking meat or
medicine, and a thousand other things.   Might not an
unwilling or indolent husbandman, in spring, as well
ask, what is the use of sowing?   Has not God ordained
every thing?   If I am to have a harvest—if he has
decreed a harvest for my farm—then, although no
ploughshare turn up a furrow, nor sower walks its
fields, they shall wave in autumn with golden corn.
Or might not one, who sickens at the sight of nauseous
drugs, as well say, Take these away, I'll drink no more
of them.   Has not God ordained every thing?   Can
a sparrow fall to the ground without the Father?   If
he has decreed that I am to live, come cholera, fever,
pestilence, I shall live; if he has decreed otherwise,
all the medicines of the apothecary, and the skill of
science can not avail to save me, or add one grain to
the sands of my existence.   Did any man in his sober

senses ever reason so? With that simple question we dismiss this objection.

Others, more earnest and honest, reading that "without faith it is impossible to please God, reading —and misunderstanding what they read—"he who doubteth is damned"—say that, from want of faith, their prayers must be useless. Most false reasoning! What says the Apostle?—"I will that men pray every where." "God will have all men to be saved." We take, like little children, the simple word, nor trouble ourselves with the metaphysics of the question.

If you were sufficiently alive to your danger, these difficulties would have no more power to hold you than the meshes of a spider's web. I knew of one who, while wandering along a lonely and rocky shore at the ebb of tide, slipped his foot into a narrow crevice. Fancy his horror on finding that he could not withdraw the imprisoned limb! Dreadful predicament! There he sat, with his back to the shore, and his face to the sea. Above his head sea-weed and shells hung upon the crag—the too sure signs that when yonder turning tide comes in, it shall rise on him inch by inch, till it washes over his head. Did he cry for help? Does any man dream of asking such a question? None heard him. But, Oh, how he shouted to the distant boat! how his heart sank as her yards swung round, and she went off on the other tack! how his cries sounded high above the roar of breakers! how bitterly he envied the white seamew her wing, as, wondering at this intruder on her lone domains, she sailed above his head, and shrieked back his shriek! how, hopeless of help from man, he turned up his face to heaven, and cried loud and long to God! All that God only knows. But as sure as there was a terrific struggle, so sure, while he watched the waters rising inch by inch, these cries never ceased till the wave swelled up, and washing the dying prayer from his lips, broke over his head with a melancholy moan.

There was no help for him. There is help for us, although fixed in sin as fast as that man in the rock. Whether we have true faith, may be a question which is not easily settled; but to pray is a clear and commanded duty. The "help, Oh, help, Lord," never yet rose from an anxious heart, but it was heard, and accepted in heaven. And if Satan bids me hold my peace—as the disciples bade the blind man—I bid him hold his own. I refuse to be silent; I but cry the louder, "Jesus, thou Son of David, have mercy on me." In God's hands, when he in smiting, let me be "dumb, opening not the mouth." In my Father's arms I may lie and do nothing but weep—weep upon his loving bosom; but in the arms of this mortal and malignant enemy, who has seized me, and is carrying me off to prison and pit—a lamb bleating in the lion's jaws—"I will cry unto the Lord, and he will answer me, and send help from above, and deliver me."

III. Prayer must be earnest.

The public become suspicious even of good money when coiners have pushed their base metal into wide circulation. Even so, religion falls into disrepute, and the character of piety suffers in the eyes of the world, when the church swarms with pretenders and false professors. And in like manner, the value of prayer has fallen in the eyes of men in consequence of many prayers which are offered, being rejected by God, because they are not genuine Hence prayer comes to be held in light esteem, and—if I might so speak—the bills drawn on the bank of heaven being dishonored, man says—" Who is the Lord, that I should serve him, or what profit shall I have if I pray unto him?"

Among other gross and venal impieties, the Church of Rome sells prayers. By her prayer-market she converts God's house into a house of merchandise and a den of thieves. Her prayers—although their price, like that of other goods, varies with the locality—may be bought for money, under this general rule of the market, that the praying shall correspond to the paying. The rude Tartar saves his money by a practice that achieves the object just as well, or rather that fails as completely to do any thing but deceive the blind. He cuts a cylinder from a block of wood. Upon its surface he writes a series of prayers; and then he runs an axle through the cylinder, and fitting it up so that it shall keep turning like a mill-wheel in the running stream, he sets it in motion. He goes away on his hunt, to the pursuit of war, business, or pleasure, and reckons that, whether he sleeps or wakes as the wheel goes round, and the prayers in its revolution turn up to the eye of the skies, heaven reads them there, and God accepts the prayers of the dead cylinder for the desires of a living heart.

Prayers without wishes are like birds without wings; while the eagle soars away to heaven, these never leave the ground. It is the heart that prays—not the knees, nor the hands, nor the lips. Have not I seen a dumb man, who stood with his back to the wall, beg as well with his imploring eye and open hand, as one that had a tongue to speak? If you would have your prayers accepted, they must be arrows shot from the heart. None else mount to the throne of God. You may repeat your prayers every day; you may be punctual as a Mohammedan who, at the Mollah's call from the minaret of the mosque, drops on his knees in public assembly or the crowded street. What then? The prayer of the lip, tongue, memory, of the wandering mind, in its dead formality, are, in the sight of God, no better than the venal prayers of Rome, or the revolutions of the Tartar's wheel. "The sacrifice of the hypocrite is an abomination to the Lord."

Would you see true prayer—would you know what prayer really is? step into this Egyptian palace where Benjamin stands bound—his amazed and trembling brothers grouped around the lad? Judah advances. He bows himself before Joseph. His heart is full. His lip trembles. The tear glistens in his manly eye; and now, with tenderness thrilling in every tone, he pours forth this plea of surpassing pathos—"Oh my lord, let thy servant, I pray thee, speak a word in my lord's ears, and let not thine anger burn against thy servant: My lord asked his servants, saying, Have ye a father, or a brother? and we said unto my lord, We have a father, an old man, and a child of his old age, a little one; and his brother is dead; and he alone is left of his mother, and his father loveth him." Thus on he goes; and every sentence goes like a knife into Joseph's heart. And then he closes and crowns his appeal with this most brave and generous proposal, "Now, therefore, I pray thee, let thy servant abide instead of the lad, a bondsman to my lord; for how shall I go to my father, and the lad be not with me, lest I see the evil that shall come on my father?" Joseph's heart, which has been swelling with emotion, is now ready to burst. He can stand it no longer; nor any wonder. That is prayer; and could we bring such earnestness to Jesus, Oh, how would his tender, much more tender heart melt, like wax, before it. Did we approach him with the fervor that glowed and burned in Judah's speech; did we plead for our own souls or those of others, with such tears, in such tones, as Judah's when he pleaded for Benjamin, how would a divine brother discover himself to us.

Now turn from that Egyptian to this Hebrew palace. There also is prayer. Two women stand before King Solomon. In the darkness of the night one has crept, with noiseless step, to her neighbor's bed, and while the mother slept, and the babe slept in her bosom, softly, cautiously, she steals the living child, and leaves her own cold, dead infant in its place. They carry the dispute to Solomon—each claiming the living, and each repudiating the dead. With a skill that earned him his world-wide fame, the wise monarch summons nature as a witness. Horrible to hear, he orders the living child to be divided. The sword is raised—another moment, and each mother gets a quivering half—another moment, and interference comes too late. One stands calm, firm, collected, looking on with a cruel eye. With a bound that carries her to his feet, and a shriek that rings wild and high over all the palace, the other—the true mother—clasps her hands in agony, and cries—"Oh, my lord, give her the living child, in no wise slay it." That is prayer. That cry, that spring, that look of anguish—all these proclaim the mother—how different from the cold, callous, unimpassioned frame in which, alas! the best too often present themselves at the throne of grace, as if, when we are seeking pardon, it were a matter of supreme indifference whether our prayer were or were not answered. Oh! how should we pray that God would help us to pray, and touch our icy lips with a live coal from off his altar.

IV. Prayer is powerful.

An angel, says our great poet, keeping ward and watch on the battlements of heaven, caught sight of Satan as he flew on broad wing from hell to this world of ours. The celestial sentinel shot down like a sunbeam to the earth, and communicated the alarm to the guard at the gates of paradise. Search was made for the enemy, but for a time without success. Ithuriel entered the bower, whose flowery roof "showered roses which the morn repaired," and where our first parents, "lulled by nightingales, embracing, slept." There he saw a toad sitting, squat by the ear of Eve. His suspicions were awakened. In his hand was a spear that had the celestial power of revealing truth, unmasking falsehood, and making all things to stand out in their genuine colors. He touched the reptile with it. That instant the toad—which was breathing horrid dreams into the ear of Eve—changed its shape, and there, confronting him face to face, stood the proud, malignant, haughty form of the Prince of Darkness.

With such a spear as that with which Milton, in this flight of fancy, arms Ithuriel, prayer arms us. Are we in doubt whether a thing is right or wrong? Are we indulging in pleasures, or engaged in pursuits, with which we are not altogether satisfied, and yet are not ready decidedly to condemn, and promptly to abandon? In any matter of Christian morals, are we halting between two opinions? The simplest and shortest way of determining the doubt is to apply the test of prayer. Take the subject to God. Look at your pleasures and your practices in the light of his countenance. Examine the matter on your knees. Can you make it a subject of prayer? Ah! be sure you are not safe in the place to which you can not ask God to accompany you. Be sure that that good (as the world may call it) is bad—that pursuit or enjoyment, however gainful or pleasant, is an evil—upon which you can not implore God's blessing, and for which you dare not go to a throne of grace, and give God thanks.

Is this test of universal application? is every thing, then, to be made a subject of prayer? Certainly. So thought Fowell Buxton, even of those amusements with which, in holiday times, he was wont to brace up mind and body for noble labors in the cause of God and his country. So thought that Corsican patriot, who never went down to battle till he had gone down to his knees, nor ever leveled a rifle that never missed, without praying for the soul he was about to send into eternity. And so speaks Paul, when, linking peace and prayer together, he writes—"Be careful for nothing; but in every thing by prayer and supplication, with thanksgiving, let your requests be made known unto God; and the peace of God, which passeth all understanding, shall keep your heart and minds, through Jesus Christ."

Such is one of the indirect uses, and not unimportant effects of prayer. Its direct power is, in a sense, omnipotent. Prayer moves the hand that moves the world. It secures for the believer the resources of Divinity. What battles has it not fought! what victories has it not won! what burdens has it not carried! what wounds has it not healed! what griefs has it not assuaged! It is the wealth of poverty; the refuge of affliction; the strength of weakness; the light of darkness. It is the oratory that gives power to the pulpit; it is the hand that strikes down Satan, and breaks the fetters of sin; it turns the scales of fate more than the edge of the sword, the craft of statesmen, or the weight of scepters; it has arrested the wing of time, turned aside the very scythe of death, and discharged heaven's frowning and darkest cloud in a shower of blessings.

Prayer changes impotence into omnipotence; for, commanding the resources of Divinity, there is nothing it can not do, and there is nothing it need want. It has just two limits. The first is, that its range is confined to the promises; but, within these, what a bank of wealth, what a mine of mercies, what a store of blessings! The second is, that God will grant or deny our requests as is best for his glory and our good. And who that knows how we are, in a sense, but children, would wish it otherwise? My little child is angry when I pluck a knife from his hands; he doubts his father's love because he does not always kiss, but sometimes corrects him; and, turning away his head from the nauseous drug, he must be coaxed —sometimes compelled to drink the cup which, although bitter to the taste, is the restorative of health. Who that sees the child seek meat when he needs medicine, eagerly clutch at tempting but unripe fruit, prefer play, and go weeping to school, reject simple but healthful fare for some luscious, but noxious luxury, who, I say, does not feel thankful that God reserves the right of refusal, and makes his answers correspond to our wants rather than to our wishes? This limit to prayer may make poverty our lot; may bind us to a sick bed; may leave us to suffer and bleed under the stroke of an impending calamity; but—while we will get as much of earth as we need on earth—for the pardon of sin, for peace of conscience, for purity of heart, for growth in grace, for all that we need to make us meet for heaven, and at length, for insuring heaven itself, prayer secures to us the help and hand of Omnipotence.

By prayer, besides, God's children can reckon on immediate assistance. Prayer flies where the eagle never flew; and rises on wings broader and stronger than an angel's. It travels further and faster than light. Rising from the heart of a believer, it shoots away beyond that starry sky, and, reaching the throne, enters into the ear of God. So soon as the heart begins to work on earth, it moves the hand of God in heaven; and, ere the prayer has left the lips of faith, Jesus has presented it to his Father, and secured its answer. It is a telegraph stretched not between shore and shore—the mother country and her distant colonies, the seat of government and the far-off scene of battle—but its extended lines connect heaven and earth, man and God, the sinner and the Saviour, the humblest home of piety and a throne of grace.

That high invention of human genius, which, by its wires of iron connects distant countries together, and has, in a sense, abolished both time and space— offers but an imperfect image of a power which piety has been working before science was born—nay, ever since the world began. From remote regions the electric telegraph may convey to a father the tidings that his child is ill; but it carries not the physician to his side, nor the drug of potent virtue which could cure his malady. It leaves him to die. It may bring to-night a detail of the fortunes of the war. Along it our army may send a cry for help—for more men and more munitions; but days and weeks must elapse, and many miles of ocean be traveled, ere ever our ships can pour their bayonets on the hostile shore; and then it may be too late; the tide may have ebbed that, taken at the full, had led on to fortune.

But does God never make his people wait? He does. Faith and patience are put upon their trial; there is no answer, nor reply, nor relief. God is silent, and the church is left to cry, "How long, O Lord, how long?" All true. Jesus addresses to his Bride the language he of old used to his mother, "Woman, my hour is not yet come." But let us need present help, and you shall see that he is "a very present help in time of trouble." Let the disciple be sinking amid the waves of Galilee, crying, "I perish"—let the prophet be on his knees in the depths of the sea and the dark belly of the whale—let the widow's last mite, and the barrel's last handful have come—let the confessor be descending into the lions' roaring den—let the queen have her brave hand upon the door, with these words of high resolve upon her lips, "If I perish, I perish"—let the trembling host have the waters of the Red Sea roaring in their front, and the chariots of Egypt pressing on their rear—let God's people have reached such a crisis—let them stand in any such predicament—and his answer anticipates their prayer. The supply is on the road before the want is expressed; the door opens before the hand has struck it; while prayer is traveling up the one line, the answer is speeding down the other. Hear the voice of the Lord, "It shall come to pass; *before* they call I will answer, and while they are *yet* speaking, I will hear."

V. Prayer is confident.

In speaking of Christ Jesus our Lord, Paul says, "In whom we have boldness and access with confidence by the faith of him ;" " Jesus, our High Priest, has en-tered within the vail, and having reconciled us to God, we have boldness to enter into the holiest by the blood of Jesus ;" "Seeing, then, that we have a great High Priest, that is passed into the heavens, Jesus, the Son of God, let us hold fast our profession. For we have not an High Priest which can not be touched with the feelings of our infirmities ; but was in all points tempt-ed like as we are, yet without sin. Let us, therefore, come boldly unto the throne of grace, that we may obtain mercy, and find grace to help in time of need."

It is easy to know the knock of a beggar at one's door. Low, timid, hesitating, it seems to say, I have no claim on the kindness of this house ; I may be told I come too often ; I may be treated as a troublesome and unworthy mendicant ; the door may be flung in my face by some surly servant. How different, on his return from school, the loud knocking, the bounding step, the joyous rush of the child into his father's presence, and, as he climbs his knee, and flings his arms round his neck, the bold face and ready tongue with which he reminds his father of some promised favor ? Now, why are God's people bold ? Glory to God in the highest ! To a Father in God, to an elder brother in Christ, Faith conducts our steps in prayer ; therefore, in an hour of need, Faith, bold of spirit, raises her suppliant hands, and cries up to God, " Oh that thou wouldst rend the heavens, and come down."

I think that I see the sneer curling on the skeptic's lip as he says, How absurd ! What presumption ! as if it were not below the dignity of Divinity to come at king's or peasant's, prince's or pauper's call. Should the lofty purposes of the Eternal be shaped by your petitions ? Creature of a day and of the dust !

what are you, that the universe should be steered—
its helm moved this or that way for your sake? Well,
no doubt the language is bold; yet with God a Father,
our Father, my Father in Christ, I feel I can be bold
and confident in prayer. I know a father's heart.
Have I not seen the quiver of a father's lip, the tear
start into his eye, and felt his heart in the grasp of his
hand, when I expressed some good hope of a fallen
child? Have I not seen a mother, when her infant
was tottering in the path of mettled coursers, with foam
spotting their necks, and fire flying from their feet,
dash like a hawk across the path, and pluck him from
instant death? Have I not seen a mother, who sat at
the coffin-head, pale, dumb, tearless, rigid, terrible in
grief, spring from her chair, seize the coffin which we
were carrying away, and, with shrieks fit to pierce a
heart of stone, struggle to retain her dead?

If we, that are but worms of the earth, will peril
life for our children, and, when they are moldered
into dust, can not think of our dead, nor visit their
cold and lonesome grave, but our breasts are wrung,
and our wounds bleed forth afresh, can we adequately
conceive or measure, far less exaggerate—even with
our fancy at its highest strain, the paternal love of
God? Talk not of what you suppose to be the dignity
of Divinity. Talk not of the calm, lofty, dignified
demeanor which becomes a king, who sees his child
borne off on the stream that sweeps his palace wall.
The king is at once sunk in the father. Divesting
himself of his trappings—casting away scepter, robe
of gold, and jeweled crown, he at once rushes forth
to leap into the boiling flood. Lives there a father
with heart so dead that he would not, at the sight of
a child fallen overboard, and struggling with death,

back every sail, and, whatever might be the mission on which his ship was bound, or whatever the risk he ran, would not put up her helm, and, pale with dread, steer for the waves were his boy was sinking?

Child of God! pray on. God's people are more dear to him than our children can be to us. He regards them with more complacency than all the shining orbs of that starry firmament. They were bought at a price higher than would purchase the dead matter of ten thousand worlds. He cares more for his humblest, weakest child, than for all the crowned heads and great ones of earth, and takes a deeper interest in the daily fortunes of a pious cottage than in the fall and rise of kingdoms.

Child of God! pray on. By prayer thy hand can touch the stars, thy arm stretch up to heaven. Nor let thy holy boldness be dashed by the thought that prayer has no power to bend these skies, and bring down thy God. When I pull on the rope which fastens my frail and little boat to a distant and mighty ship, if my strength cannot draw its vast bulk to me, I draw myself to it—to ride in safety under the protection of its guns; to enjoy in want the fullness of its stores. And it equally serves my purpose, and supplies my needs, that prayer, although it were powerless to move God to me, moves me to God. If He does not descend to earth, I—as it were—ascend to heaven.

Child of God! pray on. Were it indispensable for thy safety that God should rend these heavens, it should be done—a wondering world should see it done. I dare believe *that;* and "I am not mad, most noble Festus." Have not these heavens been already rent? Eighteen hundred years ago, robed in humanity, God himself came down. These blue skies, where larks sing and eagles sail, were cleft with the wings and filled with the songs of his angel train. Among the ancient orbs of that very firmament, a stranger star appeared, traveling the heavens, and blazing on the banner borne before the King, as he descended on this dark and distant world. On Canaan's dewy ground—the lowly bed he had left—the eye of morning shone on the shape and form of the Son of God; and dusty roads, and winter snows, and desert sands, and the shores and very waves of Galilee, were impressed with the footprints of the Creator. By this manger, where the babe lies cradled—beside this cross, upon whose ignominious arms the glory of the universe is hung—by this silent sepulcher, where, wrapped in bloody shroud, the body is stretched out on its bed of spices, while Roman sentinels walk their moonlit round, and Death—a bound captive—sits within, so soon as the sleeper wakes, to be disarmed, uncrowned, and in himself have death put to death—faith can believe all that God has revealed, and hope for all that God has promised. She reads on that manger, on that cross, deeply lettered on that rocky sepulcher, these glorious words—"He that spared not his own Son, but delivered him up for us all, how shall he not with him also freely give us all things?" And there, lifting an eagle eye to heaven, she rises to the boldest flights, and soars aloft on the broad wings of prayer—

> Faith, bold faith, the promise sees,
> And trusts to that alone,
> Laughs at impossibilities,
> And says, it shall be done.

The Blessedness of the Saints.

And ye shall dwell in the land that I gave to your fathers; and ye shall be my people, and I will be your God. I will also save you from all your uncleannesses; and I will call for the corn, and will increase it, and lay no famine upon you. And I will multiply the fruit of the tree, and the increase of the field, that ye shall receive no more reproach of famine among the heathen.—EZEKIEL xxxvi. 28, 29, 30.

A COUNTRY cleared of its inhabitants wears a mournful aspect. It may be that the emigrant has left poverty for plenty. Still it is not a pleasant thing to see nettles growing where the garden bloomed—the smoke-stained gable—the roofless ruin—the empty window, out of which the fox is peering, and where the morning sun was wont to shine upon the Bible and a pious patriarch. There is something chilling about that cold hearth-stone where the fire of a winter evening gleamed on the faces of a happy circle, while the mother plied her busy wheel, and, forgetful of the toils and dangers of the day, the shepherd dandled a laughing infant on his knee. Those are now silent walls that once sounded to the evening psalm, and from which, when Sabbath rested on the hills, a decent family went out, wending their way by the lake-side to that old ruin beside whose crumbling walls the fathers of the exile sleep. The wind, as it sighed among the trees above that roofless home, has seemed in our fancy's ear to sound the prophet's lament, "Weep not for the dead, neither bemoan him, but weep sore for him that goeth away, for he shall return no more, nor see his native country."

Such scenes, the pain of which, indeed, lies more in fancy than in fact, give us an image of the desolation which reigned in the land of Judah during the time of the long captivity. By rule of contrast, they en‧hance also the pleasure with which we turn to look on this glowing picture—a land teeming with inhabit‧ants, the rich plains studded all over with cities, each busy as a bee-hive—the valleys clothed with corn, crowded with reapers, and ringing to their song—every terrace in the close embrace of vines, and flocks bleat‧ing on a hundred hills. Such a scene, in fact, as sur‧veyed from some eminence, awoke the piety and poetry of David‧—"Thou crownest the year with thy goodness, and thy paths drop fatness; they drop upon the pastures of the wilderness, and the little hills rejoice on every side. The pastures are clothed with flocks, the valleys also are covered over with corn; they shout for joy, they also sing."

The fulfillment of my text to God's ancient people would have invested this prophecy with interest, even although its application had been altogether confined to the Jews; and, for this reason—Their God is our God, and every thing which he did for them is a most precious pledge of what he can and will do for us. "He is the dwelling-place of his people in all genera‧tions." Thus while faith turns her eye upon the future—a future often dark enough—she draws cou‧rage and comfort from the past, saying, "I will remem ber the years of the right hand of the Most High." But, in fact, we have more to do with this prophecy than the Jews had. Under those blessings which God poured into their cup—those temporal mercies which filled their mouths with meat, and their hearts with gladness—lie the better mercies of Messiah's kingdom.

This shines plainly forth through the mystic language of the prophet. The conversion of the Gentiles is, for instance, distinctly announced in the 36th verse, " Then the heathen, that are left round about you, shall know that I the Lord build the ruined places, and plant that which was desolate. I the Lord have spoken it, and will do it." In the succeeding chapter, again, the resurrection of the body and the renovation of the soul are set forth under the vision of dry bones. In the same place also have we not a kingdom shown forth more enduring far, than any which ever had its seat in Palestine? " And David, my servant, shall be king over them, and they all shall have one shepherd; they shall also walk in my judgments, and observe my statutes, and do them; and they shall dwell in the land which I have given to Jacob, my servant, wherein your fathers have dwelt; and they shall dwell therein, even they, and their children, and their children's children, for ever; and my servant David shall be their prince for ever." It appears to us that this language can not, without violence, be applied to the old Jewish land and people; and that the Roman ploughshare has buried such a fancy under the ruins of Jerusalem. With the blood of man's best brother on their heads, the Jews, like Cain, are vagabonds. They have no dwelling in the land which God gave to Jacob; for eighteen hundred years they have been wandering the world, nor have the soles of their feet yet found a resting-place. A nation scattered and spoiled, they are a bye-word, a proverb, and a hissing—nor land, nor temple, nor oracle, nor prince, have they, nor shall have, till turning to the hope of his best and oldest fathers, the Jew bows his proud head to the Nazarene, and kisses the feet that were nailed to a cross.

Looking at these words, therefore, in this light—taking them in a Gospel, not a Jewish sense—let us give our attention to some of the blessings which they announce—the benefits which, to use the words of our Catechism, "flow from justification, adoption, and sanctification." Let the believer look—

I. To the abundance of the blessings of grace.

A new-born infant is the most helpless of all creatures. In its nakedness, weakness, dumbness, how dependent on a mother's love! yet not more so than God's people are on his care and kindness. Theirs are therefore circumstances in which his promises are exceedingly precious. The condition of believers very much resembles that of a man of boundless affluence, whose wealth lies, not so much in money, as in money's worth—in bills and bonds, that, when due, shall be duly honored. With these promises the poorest Christian is really a richer man than any other men, with all their possessions; nor would he part with one of them for the world's wealth.

This rude and naked savage—the dupe of avaricious men—barters a coronet of gold for some worthless trinkets, and buys the wonders of a mirror, the tinkling of a bell, or a string of colored beads, with a handful of pearls, the fit ornaments of a crown. The child of God knows better than to sell what is of surpassing value, for any thing intrinsically worthless. With this promise, "thy bread shall be given thee, and thy water shall be sure," he holds himself richer, more sure of meat to eat, and raiment to put on, than he would be with the wealth of banks. And why? Is this reasonable? No doubt of it. No logician ever reasoned more soundly. These may fail; God's promise can not. The very stars shall drop like figs from shaken heavens, and these heavens themselves shall pass away, but not one jot or tittle of what his God has spoken shall fail, till all be fulfilled.

With such security as we have in the character of God, and such fullness as is promised in the text, it needs, therefore, only a prophet's faith to echo a prophet's speech, and—when gaunt famine walks our streets, and there are "clean teeth," and children cry for bread, and their mothers have none to give them —to repeat the boldest words that ever fell from mortal lips -"Although the fig-tree should not blossom, and there be no fruit on the vine; though the labor of the olive should fail, and the fields yield no meat; though the flocks should be cut off from the fold, and there be no herd in the stall, yet I will rejoice in the Lord, and joy in the God of my salvation." I can fancy a skeptic exclaiming—Extravagance! fanaticism—mad fanaticism! No such thing. In his promises God's people have meat to eat that others know not of, and these have proved like the breasts of a daughter to the aged captive who had been condemned to die of pining hunger. In that cell, where the gray old man each day took her infant's place, her love and ingenuity have found means to save a father's life, which his enemies never dreamt of; and the child of God, around whom fears of want are gathering, may rest assured, that he who inspired that daughter with the wit and will for such an emergency, will find ways and means to make his promise good. "The word of the

Lord is a tried word "—fail us who, and what may, that can not.

There are, indeed, times when the believer is ready to faint. Faith staggers beneath the burden, and hope all but expires. My sins are so many, my guilt so great, my burden so heavy! thus and thus they speak; now, with Jacob, complaining, "All these things are against me" and now, on finding Satan so often conquering them when they should have conquered him, crying with David, "I shall one day fall by the hand of this Saul." Well, let your burdens, sins, cares, be such as you describe. Let me ask you a question. Is it not as easy for yonder great sea to carry the bulkiest ship that ever rode her waves, as the sea-weed or foam she flings upon the shore? Is it not as easy for that glorious sun to bathe a mountain, as to bathe a mole-hill in gold? Is it not as easy for this mighty earth to carry on its back an Alp as a grain of sand—to nourish a cedar of Lebanon, as the hyssop on the wall? Just so, believer, it is as easy for God to supply thy greatest as thy smallest wants; even as it was as much within his power to form a system as an atom—to create a blazing sun, as kindle a fire-fly's lamp.

To one, indeed, whose standing point is on the ground, objects seem very various in their size. The cliffs tower above the level shore; piercing the horizontal cloud of smoke, the spires rise above the humbler tenements of the town; and from her throne of snow in high mid-summer, winter looks down on the valleys that lie smiling at the mountain's feet. Eyed from the low, dead level of shore or plain, objects do appear in strong contrast, high or low, great or small, big or little. But I rise on eagle's wings; I sit on the circle of the earth; higher still, I stand beside the angel whom John saw in the sun; still higher, I follow Paul up to the third heavens; and, seen from such elevations—if seen at all—dwarf and giant, the mountain and the mole-hill, are on one level. All these sublunary differences vanish, sink into insignificance—into nothing.

Now, here lies a believer's comfort, and here shines a sinner's hope. So vanish all distinctions between great and little wants in the eye of God; so disappears all difference between great and little sins, or great and little sinners, to the blood of Christ; and, when our cares are cast on him who invites the burden, so sinks every difference between light and heavy burdens, to the back of Jesus. It is as easy for Jesus Christ to save a Magdalene, a Manasseh, a hoary thief, as an infant, that (happy creature!) just leaves its mother's womb to make of this earth a stepping-stone to heaven. Whatever be your circumstances, trials, cares, and griefs, this promise fits them—"As thy day, so shall thy strength be." Be he dwarf or giant, no man can say of an assurance so well founded, "The bed is shorter than a man can stretch himself upon it; the covering is narrower than a man can wrap himself in it." Are you cast down because, while others have shallows, you have depths—dark depths—depths of sorrow, and suffering, to pass through? Be it so: it is as easy for God to march his people through the wide, deep sea as across the bed of Jordan. Are your corruptions strong? Be it so: Samson found it as easy to snap a new spun cable as withes fresh gathered on the river's bank; and believe me, it is as easy for God to break thy tyrant's strongest as his lightest chain. A chain of iron and a thread of flax are all one to God. The blood of thy Saviour cleanseth from all sin; and nothing being impossible, nay not even difficult to Omnipotence, be assured, that in your battle, and watch, and work, you shall find this promise true—"My grace is sufficient for thee."

II. Consider the happiness which God's people enter on at death.

Egypt pursued the Hebrews to the very shores of the sea. There, however, the people saw the last of them; of those tyrants who had made their burden so heavy and life so bitter, that their cry came up before the Lord. On this shore the oppressor and the oppressed are to part. In these weltering waves, from which they shrink back with dread—as some good men from death—their enemies and their griefs are to find a common grave. In these the wicked shall cease from troubling; beyond them the weary shall be at rest. Night has come; a sun they shall never see more has set on Pharaoh and his host. Under the light that illumined the camp of God, and flung a fiery luster across the deep, Moses stood up to address the people. Their redemption was nigh. It was now just that darkest hour which ushers in the dawn. With his foot on the shore, his rod in his hand, the fiery pillar lighting up his face, Moses pointed to the gloom where the Egyptians lay, and said, "The Egyptians whom ye have seen to-day, ye shall see them again no more for ever."

God's people are like his ancient Israel. They have enemies who will harrass them in life, and follow them to the very shores of time; but whoever, or whatever these may be—sin, sorrow, poverty, temptations, trials, fears, doubts, Satan himself—Oh! a death-

16*

bed shall be the death of them all. In leaving life
we leave these behind. Death is their destruction,
not ours. And how should it reconcile us to that
dark passage from which nature shrinks, that when
we stand in its gloomy mouth to take our last look of
this world, may feel assured that we shall take the
last look, not of friends in Christ—for we shall meet
them again in heaven—but only of these our enemies.
We "shall see them again no more for ever." Satan
may not only pursue God's people to their very death-
bed, but harrass them upon it. He knows that his
time is short. It is his last chance. Another day or
hour, and they are out of his grasp; and so—sum-
moning all the powers of hell—he drives down like
the Egyptians into the sea—into the very depths of
death—and aggravates by his horrible suggestions
the struggles of a dying hour. The saint has, in that
time of darkness, two enemies upon him—death, and
him that has the power of death, that is the devil.
Be it so; God shall take off their chariot-wheels;
they shall not reach the other shore, nor set foot in
heaven; there, there entereth nothing to hurt or to
defile.

The dead enter into rest. "Blessed are the dead
which die in the Lord, they rest." "He that is dead
is free from sin." And, as I have looked on the calm
and deep repose of the quiet sleeper, when the tossing
arms lie still, and the restless head reposes on its pil-
low, and the features which have now lost all express-
ion of pain, or passion, present an aspect of solemn,
sublime, beautiful, perfect rest, I have sometimes
thought that this was an emblem which the soul had
left us of its own still more profound, perfect, heavenly
rest

This is what the redeemed escape *from*, but, Oh! what they escape *to*—the joys they enter on when they go to be with Christ, who can tell? We know that "to die" *is*—not shall be at some future time, and after some intermediate state—but "to die *is* gain," gain immediate. One step—and, what a step!—the soul is in glory. Ere the wail has sunk in the chamber of death, the song of the upper sanctuary has begun. There is no delay; no waiting for an escort to travel that invisible, untrodden way. Angels unseen are moving in that chamber, looking on with tearless eyes where all else are weeping; and, the last breath out—the last quiver passed from the lip—and away, away, they are off with the spirit for glory. On angel's wings the beggar is borne to Abraham's bosom; and the shout of saints and angels, that greeted the Conqueror, is still ringing amid the arches of heaven, when the door opens, and the thief walks in. "This day thou shalt be with me in Paradise." He leaves his cross, and direct, as I have seen a lark drop singing into her nest, he goes up singing to his crown.

And what and where is heaven? I can not tell. Even to the eye of faith, heaven looks much like a star to the eye of flesh. Set there on the brow of night, it shines most bright—most beautiful; but it is separated from us by so great a distance as to be raised almost as high above our investigations as above the storms and clouds of earth. A shining object, we see it gleaming in the fields of space, but we see nothing more, even when our eyes are assisted by the most powerful telescope. By what beings it is inhabited; what forms they have; what tongue they speak; what the character the landscape wears in these upper worlds we do not know; and perhaps never shall, till we have cast loose a body which moors us to the earth, and, with a soul unchained, free perhaps as thought—we are left to roam the universe, and pass, on the wings of a wish, from world to world of our Father's kingdom. Never, at least, till then, shall we know either where heaven is, or what heaven is. The best description of it is to say that it is indescribable. Paul, on his return, attempted no other. There he "heard and saw things unutterable." Nor does the matter cost us the least anxiety. If God spared not his own Son, heaven shall want nothing to make us supremely happy. It is enough for me to know that heaven, the home of the blessed—the palace of the Great King—has joys which eye never saw, ear never heard, and which it hath not entered into the heart of man to conceive.

III. The complete blessedness of the saints at the resurrection in the restoration of all that sin forfeited.

There were periods in creation—progressive steps. Step by step the work advanced to its consummation. In creation, just as in conversion, the process began with light—letting light in upon the darkness. God said, "Let there be light, and there was light, and the evening and the morning were the first day." And then a wide-spread firmament of blue separates the waters above the earth from the waters beneath, and, the work completed, the evening and the morning are the second day. The third day begins a new epoch. The mountains raise their heads above the waters, like an infant, the earth comes naked from the womb, and when God has wrapped the new born world in a beautiful robe of flowers, green fields. and waving forests, the evening and the morning are the third day. The heavens next are garnished; and when their boundless fields are sown with countless stars, the evening and the morning are the fourth day. Thus the Creator goes on with his work. Each succeeding period brings it nearer to perfection, till, on the evening of the sixth day, as the sun was sinking behind the western hills, his slanting beams shone on our holy, happy parents—their home a garden, their estate a world, the creatures all their servants, in their hearts no taint of sin, in their eyes no tear of sorrow, and on brows too soon to be bathed in sweat, and blushing with shame, flashing crowns of innocence. Then, from the throne of his most excellent majesty, God looked on this world as it rolled away in its happy orbit, and, pronouncing all that he had made to be very good, the evening and the morning were the sixth day.

Like creation, the Gospel has had its periods of progress. It gradually advanced in its development from the first promise given by God, when he, the judge, and the culprits man and the devil stood face to face upon the ruins of Eden. First, we have a simple altar, with the smoke of sacrifice curling up to heaven from earth's unbroken forests;—none there but our two solitary parents, weeping, as well they might, when they gazed on the miserable wreck which they had made of their own and their children's fortunes; and yet, while they wept, lifting up their heads in hope of a coming redemption. The scene shifts, and next we have a desert, with a mighty host scattered over its sands, and in their midst a tented sanctuary with a cloud of incense floating, like a prayer, away to heaven. The scene shifts again, and Jerusalem sits upon her hills, and where hundreds of white-robed priests are serving, and thousands of worshipers are kneeling, a magnificent temple of marble, cedar, and gold towers high over all—the ornament and palladium of the land. The scene shifts once more. It is mid-day, and yet dark; the earth is trembling, graves are yawning to let out their dead, and, through the gloom of an unnatural eclipse, we behold the cross of Calvary with its bleeding victim. Son of God! He is dying, "the just for the unjust." He cries, "It is finished," and, Saviour of the world, he dies. The work, so long ago begun, is brought to a triumphant close. In the very act of death he swallows up death in victory. And thus you see how, from one garden to another, from the flowery bowers of Eden to the olives of Gethsemane, from the first promise to the final performance, redemption advances by successive steps. Jesus bows his head; and then, again, from the throne of his most excellent majesty, God looks on all the work, and over the bloody cross and his own dead Son, pronounces this judgment, "Behold, it is very good." And, ushering in an eternal Sabbath, the evening and the morning were the sixth day of redemption.

There yet remains an aspect of redemption in which it is not complete. The prince of this world is still out, and in the battle-field fighting—fighting like the devil he is for his kingdom. The body yet lies a captive in the tomb, and the grave must yield its ancient charge. Insatiate and insatiable devourer! thou robber of our pleasant homes! with thy black mouth ever opening, and thy cry, give, give, give, ever in our ear, thou thyself must give—thou must give up thy dead. The dust of saints is dear to Christ. He comes to claim it. All that death and Satan hold they must relinquish; all that Christ has purchased he shall possess. The soul wants her partner; and although the exile may return no more, nor see his native land, the redeemed shall return to claim their bodies from the earth—aye, and claim the very earth they lie in. "The saints shall inherit the earth."

A grand destiny awaits this world of sins and sorrows. This earth, purified by judgment fires, shall be the home of the blessed. The curse of briars and thorns shall pass away with sin. "Instead of the thorn shall come up the fir tree, and instead of the briar shall come up the myrtle tree." Of the thorns of that curse Jesus' crown was woven, and he bore it off upon his head. Under laws accommodated to the new economy, the wide world shall become one Eden, where, exempt from physical as from moral evils, none shall shiver amid arctic frosts, nor wither under tropic heat; these fields of snow and arid sands shall blossom all with roses. From the convulsions of expiring —or rather the birth-pangs of parturient nature—a new-born world shall come, a home worthy of immortals, a palace befitting its King. The blood that on Calvary dyed earth's soil shall bless it, and this theater of Satan's triumph, and of a Saviour's shame, shall be the seat of Jesus' kingdom, and the witness of his glory.

Then the saints shall inherit the earth. Some, like Abraham in the promised land, are poor wanderers here—the proprietors of nothing but a grave. Some own not even so much as that. The saints, like the descendants of a noble but decayed house, are strangers on the soil which was once the property of their fathers. But the time of their redemption draweth nigh. Man shall get his own again, and hold it by a charter writ ten in the blood of Christ. This world was gifted to him. It was his patrimonial estate. It was the land given to our fathers. And it seems most meet, that with the rank and title, the lands should come back to the old family; and, as forming the completest triumph over Sin and Satan, that our redemption should be altogether like that of Israel, when Moses turned round on Pharaoh, saying, "Not a hoof shall be left behind." Even so, come, Lord Jesus, come quickly.

The Security of the Believer.

I the Lord have spoken it, and I will do it.—EZEKIEL xxxvi, 36.

WHEN in a sultry summer day the sky gets over-cast, and angry clouds gather thick upon its brow, and bush and brake are silent, and the very cattle, like human beings, draw close together, standing dumb in their untasted pastures, and while there is no ripple on the lake, nor leaf stirring on the tree, all nature seems struck with awe, and stands in trembling expectation; then, when the explosion comes, and a blinding stream of fire leaps from the cloud, and as if heaven's riven vault were tumbling down upon our head, the thunders crash, peal, roar along the sky, he has neither poetry, nor piety, nor sense, who does not reverently bow his head and assent to the words of David, "The voice of the Lord is full of majesty."

When the God of glory thundereth in nature, his voice is full of majesty; when, in still louder thunders, the God of providence speaks by calamities that shake the nation, or shake to its foundations the happiness of our home, his voice is also full of majesty; and when the ear of faith listens to these august and lofty words, "I have spoken, and I will do it," the voice of the Lord again is "full of majesty." This language is stamped with divinity. And to God we may, with the highest propriety, address the words which the flatterers of royalty blasphemously offered to an orator, whose proud assumption of divinity the worms soon refuted. The lie of their adulation to Herod changes to truth on our lips, when—speaking of him who says, "I the Lord have spoken, and I will do it"— we exclaim, "This is the voice of a God, and not of a man."

The words of my text fit not mortal lips. Of that truth, Jephthah's calamity and Herod's crime afford memorable illustrations. In the full tide of patriotism, in the fierce excitement of the fight, with a warrior's proud ambition to win the field, Jephthah made his vow, and resolved to keep it—to do what he spake. Ah! little did he dream, that the first to leave his house, the victim for sacrifice, should be the daughter of his heart—his only child. And as little did Herod foresee, upon what a bloody path of remorse and crime the rash pledge extorted by the fiendish hatred of a paramour would lead him.

Often, we have not the power to do what we say, and to perform what we promise. "If the Lord will," should qualify all the future. And although the power were ours, some vows, some resolutions, are more honored in the breach than in the observance. The language of my text, therefore, belongs only to him whose glance penetrates eternity; to whose omniscience nothing is impervious, to whose power nothing is impossible. Weak, short-sighted, ignorant, erring mortals, such words in our mouths were impudent and impotent presumption; and we have no more right to assume the imperial tone of Divinity, than we have ability to launch his thunderbolts, or wisdom to guide his counsels.

These great words of power are also words of mercy. Connect them with the exceeding precious promises, the exceeding lofty offers of the Gospel, with such a

passage as this—"Believe on the Lord Jesus Christ,
and thou shalt be saved;" or this, "Come unto me
all ye that labor, and are heavy-laden, and I will give
you rest;" or this, "My grace shall be sufficient for
thee, and my strength made perfect in your weak-
ness;" or this, "With my dead body shall they arise."
"Awake and sing, all ye that dwell in the dust.   For
thy dew is as the dew of herbs, and the earth shall
cast out the dead"—and these words are as full of
mercy as of majesty.   God in them speaks with ab-
solute confidence.   And how is his confidence calcu-
lated to create and sustain in our hearts the firmest
assurance that he can and that he will do all he says?
He speaks "as one having authority."   There is no
obscurity about his language, or hesitation in its tone.
He speaks as one whose word is law, whose will is
power, whose smile is life, whose frown is death.   He
speaks as one who has entire confidence in his own
resources, and whose word is as efficient now as on
the day when he issued the creative fiat, and said,
"Let there be light, and there was light."

Were you ever at sea in a storm, when the ship
reeled to and fro like a drunken man, and struggling,
as for life in the arms of death, now rose on the top
of the billow, now plunged into the trough of the sea?
Partially infected with others' terror, did you ever
leave shrieking women and pale men below, to seek
the deck, and look your danger bravely in the face?
In such circumstances, I know nothing so re-assuring
as—when we have staggered across the slippery plank-
ing, and are holding by rail or bulwark—to see amid
these weltering foam-wreaths, that fierce commotion,
the hurricane roar of the wind among the shrouds,
and the loud dash of the billows beneath—calm con-

fidence seated on the brow of that weather-beaten man who, with iron strength, leans upon the wheel, and steers our ship through the roaring billows. Such- -only much higher—is the confidence which we draw from the confidence of God, as expressed in the words —" I have spoken, and I will do it."

In illustration of this, take the night of the storm in Galilee. The disciples gather round our Lord, and wake him, crying, Master, Master, "Carest thou not that we perish?" Look up, and see these mountain waves! Hark to the roaring of the storm! the boat fills—we sink. Save, Oh save, we perish! Had they known him fully, would they not have drawn courage from his very slumbers? With a boat-cloak protecting his wasted and weary form from the flying spray, they would have let him sleep on; and bold faith, arresting the arm of fear, had said, "Hush! wake him not; let him take his rest; he would not, could not, sleep, were disciples in danger."

When a mother, on a watch by a cradle where life has been feebly flickering, falls asleep, we are sure that the crisis is over—the worst is passed. Before sleep sealed these kind and anxious eyes, they had seen the tide, that had ebbed, returning. Let the storm wreck a hundred boats, and carry disaster, widowhood, or-phanage among the fishing hamlets upon Galilee's shores, to my eye the disciples had full assurance of safety in the fact that Jesus slept, and slept as soundly in that storm-tossed boat as when Mary rocked the cradle, or sung him over on her gentle bosom. In that sleeping form "there was the hiding of his power," and the confidence of high and worthy faith. But my text is one that meets the weakest faith; for who can doubt that God will make good all his promises, who marks the firm, unqualified, determined, supreme, sovereign tone of the words, " I the Lord have spoken, and I will do it." Man is often confident when he should be diffident; and yet, if the confidence of man inspires us with hope, and speaks peace to the apprehensions of a troubled heart, how much more should the confidence of God? With these words in our eye, we can look on the starry dome of heaven and this solid earth, and believe that sooner shall that arch fall, and bury a crushed world in its ruins, than that one good word spoken of his people shall fail till all be fulfilled.

I. The text announces a most important truth.

So long as there was pulse and breath in Lazarus, his sisters often left their brother's couch, and went to door and window to see if there was yet any sign of Jesus. Days ago a messenger had been dispatched with the tidings, "He whom thou lovest is sick;" and they felt like the mother of Sisera, when, wearying for her son's return, she looked for him in the glare of day, and listened for him in the gloom of night, crying, Why is his chariot so long in coming? why tarry the wheels of his chariots? Death at length quenches hope. The funeral is over; and, when four days have elapsed, a lingering Lord is seen descending the heights of Olivet in his approach to Bethany. One enters the house of mourning and whispers, "The Lord is come." Martha rises, advances to meet him and pour forth her regret for his absence, and her confidence in his power in this bitter cry, "Lord, if thou hadst been here, my brother had not died."

When we look at our text, we feel, in reference to the sad event of Eden, much as Martha did when she

turned her weeping eyes on Jesus. Would *his* pres
ence have preserved the life of Lazarus? No less
certainly had these words been present in their power
to Eve, they would have preserved her innocence, and
saved the world. Not Lazarus only, but no man had
died; there had been neither sin, nor sorrow, nor griefs,
nor graves, in this suffering world, had Eve, when she
stood by the fatal tree, but remembered, believed, felt
this sentence, "I have spoken, and I will do it."
Then, on the serpent saying, "Thou shalt not surely
die," with a voice as prompt and peremptory as her
Son's, she had replied, "Get thee behind me, Satan,
thou savorest not of the things that be of God." The
honor reserved for her seed had been her own. She
had placed her naked foot upon the serpent, and, stamp-
ing down a heel unbruised, had crushed his head.
Oh, the world had been saved, had she, taking up her
position on the high ground of my text, answered the
tempter thus, "The Lord hath said, In the day thou
eatest thereof, thou shalt surely die. He hath spoken,
and He will do it." Entrenched more strongly within
these lines than ever army that, behind batteries—
bristling with cannon—beat back the fierce sortie, she
had stood alone; within the impregnable barriers of
God's word, she had defied the powers of hell; and,
omnipotent in God, she had received the battle on her
single shield. Eden had still been ours, and our family
had still been blessed and holy, with God for a father
and Paradise for a home.

Some years ago, when autumn floods wrought great
devastation in our country, a strong man was swept
away into the swollen river. It bore him—as he and
others thought—by good fortune, to a tree, which
stood bravely up amid the sea of waters. He caught

it and climbed it. Seated on a bough he stretched
out his arms for help to the distant banks. Attempts
were made to rescue him before nightfall, but all in
vain. The day wore on, and the night at length came
down; and now a frantic wife, and weeping little ones,
and some kind neighbors, were left nothing to do, but
to listen amid the pauses of the tempest for his long,
shrill whistle. Ever and anon that came across the
flood to cheer them up; for he sounded it to let them
know that he was still alive, and that the tree was
yet breasting the roaring stream. About midnight
this signal ceased. They strained their ears, and
heard nought but the hoarse roar of the angry river,
mingled with the shrieking of the storm. Morning
at length arrived; the man was gone—tree gone—and
where it stood they saw but the whirling waves of the
red roaring flood. At this moment, one—considered
little else than a fool—stepped forward to say, "I could
have saved him." Any other but that heart-broken
group would have laughed him to scorn; and yet he
showed them how, by attaching a rope to a float, and
sending that away from the very bank where the lost
man had been carried off, he could have saved him,
since the current that bore the man to the tree would
have been certain to carry to him this means of com-
munication with the shore. The plan was perfect;
no doubt of it. But it came too late; and they had
to leave the scene with their grief exasperated and
embittered by the thought, that had they possessed
but the wisdom of this fool, their desolate home had
received a joyous family, to give God thanks for the
"dead that was alive again, and the lost that was
found."

I have told you, that had my text been present to

the mind, and felt in its power by the heart of Eve, we had not been lost. But when the deed has been done, and it is now too late, my object is not to show how man might have been saved. There is little kindness in telling me of a medicine that would have cured my dead. To tell me that had this or that been done, the grave had not held their loved dust this day, is not to close but open my wound—to drop not balm, but burning acid upon a raw and bleeding sore. Glory to the grace of God, I tell not that my text, if believed in, would have saved man, but, if believed in, shall still save him.

It would have kept us out of the grave. It can raise us out of it. It is like Jesus Christ. Had he been present, Lazarus had not died, but he who could have saved Lazarus from the tomb, when it has closed upon his friend, calls him out of it. The power that would have proved the sick man's remedy, stands at the mouth of that yawning sepulcher the dead man's resurrection. Let my text lay hold of the redemption of Christ, and it has all, and more than all the power it ever had—the cross, the crown, peace, pardon, grace in life, hope in death, heaven throughout all eternity— these are all wrapped up in a deep, solemn, heartfelt, divine conviction of this truth. " I the Lord have spoken, and I will do it."

Take, on the one hand, these precious invitations— " Ho, every one that thirsteth, come ye to the waters; come ye, buy and eat, yea, come, buy wine and milk without money and without price;" and this, " Look unto me, and be ye saved, all the ends of the earth;" and this, " The blood of Jesus Christ cleanseth us from all sin ;" and this, " I will take out of you the hard and stony heart;" and this, " Behold, O my people, I will

open your graves, and I will cause you to come up
out of your graves, and ye shall live;" and take, on
the other hand, these:—"They that sow to the flesh,
shall of the flesh reap corruption;" and this, "The
soul that sinneth, it shall die;" and this, "The wicked
shall be cast into hell." Now, would God by his Spirit
help us to lodge in men's hearts an earnest, cordial
belief of these truths as they appear in the light of the
text, man would not—man could not be lost. At once
warned and won by it, the Gospel would be glad news.
Men with all their hearts would embrace offered mercy.
Churches would become sanctuaries, and the place of
worship would be a gate to heaven. And ministers—
disheartened and despondent—would not have to return
so often to their Master, saying, "Lord, they are per-
ishing; yet they will not come to thee that they may
have life. I have brought back thine offer. They
will not take it. No man hath believed my report,
and to none has the arm of the Lord been revealed."

II. The comforts this truth imparts to a true Christian.
*Through his confidence in this truth, the believer com-
mits all his earthly cares to God.*

I do not say that we are not to embrace any oppor-
tunity of improving our circumstances, and acquiring
lawful objects of pursuit. Far from it. The Gospel
inculcates diligence, even in our worldly calling. "Go
to the ant, thou sluggard, consider her ways, and be
wise." Nor shall our lawful calling, whatever it be,
interfere with the best interests of our souls. Religion
is none the worse, but all the better for work; and a
man's work is all the better for his religion. The
morning prayer does for a good man's heart what the
morning meal does for his body. It braces him up

for the day and its duties. He has least need of a master's watchful eye, who feels that the eye of God is ever upon him. You may safely trust most to those who make conscience of the meanest work; who, in kindling a fire or sweeping a floor, have an eye uplift. ed to the glory of God; who ennoble life's humblest employment by aiming at a noble end; and who address themselves to their business in the high and holy belief, that when duty—however humble it may be— is well done, God is glorified; just as he is glorified as well by a lowly daisy, as by the garden's gaudiest and proudest flowers.

But while this truth gives no encouragement to indolence—to a languid and idle waiting upon providence—and no encouragement to cast our work itself on God, it teaches his people to cast the cares of the work upon him. Are not these among the words that he hath spoken, and will do, "The steps of a good man are ordered by the Lord." "Cast thy burden on the Lord, he shall sustain thee." "The lot is cast into the lap; but the whole disposing thereof is of the Lord?" Child of God! put in, then, a fearless hand into this lottery, and draw. With faith in God's superintending providence and his unfailing word. Child of God! shield thy heart from cares that are the torture of others, and from temptations that are often their ruin? Between a man, torn with anxieties, tossed with fears, fretting with cares, and the good man, who calmly trusts in the Lord, Oh! there is as great a difference as between a brawling, roaring, mountain brook, that with mad haste leaps from crag to crag, and is ground into boiling foam, and the placid river, which, with beauty on its banks and heaven in its bosom, spreads blessings wherever it flows, and pursues the noiseless tenor of its way back to the great ocean, from which its waters came. "It is better to trust in the Lord than to put confidence in man. It is better to trust in the Lord than to put confidence in princes." "They that trust in the Lord shall be as Mount Zion, which cannot be removed."

Through his confidence in the truth of my text, the believer is sustained amid the trials of life.

God casts his people into trial for the very same reason that the refiner commits his silver to the furnace. He tries them to purify them. He does not afflict willingly. Be assured that he has no more pleasure in their sufferings than a kind surgeon in his patient's groans, or a parent in his children's tears.

Trials are ill to bear. To be reduced from affluence to poverty—to become dependent on cold charity—to lie on a bed of languor—to pass nights of sleepless pain—to be exposed to evil tongues—to be hissed on the stage where we were once applauded—to sit amid the ruins of fortune—to lay loved ones in a lonesome grave—such things are not "joyous, but grievous." Winter, no doubt, is not the pleasant season that summer brings, with her songs and flowers, and long, bright, sunny days. Bitter medicines, no doubt, are not savory meat. Yet he who believes that all things shall work together for good, will be ready to thank God for physic as well as for food ; and for the winter frost that kills the weeds, and breaks up the soil, as for the dewy nights and sunny days that ripen the fields of corn. May God give us such a faith! With nature weak and grace imperfect, when there is no lifting of the cloud, and trials are severe and long-protracted! ah! though it may be easy for an on-looker to preach patience, it is not easy for a sufferer to practice it. In such circumstances, how prone we are to take the case out of God's hands, and, getting discontented with his discipline, how ready we are to cry, "How long, O Lord, how long?" "If it be possible, let this cup pass from me;" or, take away this, and give me any one else to drink. Yet let me have a firm faith in God's truth and love, let me be confident that he will do what he has said, and perform all that he has promised, and I shall discover mercy's bow bent on fortune's blackest cloud, and, under most trying providences, shall enjoy in my heart, and exhibit to others in my temper, the blessed difference between a sufferer that mourns, and a spirit that murmurs.

Through his confidence in the truth of my text, the believer cheerfully hopes, and patiently waits for heaven.

Home! to be home is the wish of the seaman on stormy seas and lonely watch. Home is the wish of the soldier, and tender visions mingle with the troubled dreams of trench and tented field. Where the palm-tree waves its graceful plumes, and birds of jeweled luster flash and flicker among gorgeous flowers, the exile sits staring upon vacancy; a far away home lies on his heart; and borne on the wings of fancy over intervening seas and lands, he has swept away home, and hears the lark singing above his father's fields, and sees his fair-haired boy brother, with light foot and childhood's glee, chasing the butterfly by his native stream. And in his best hours, home, his own sinless home—a home with his Father above that starry sky—will be the wish of every Christian man. He looks around him—the world is full of suffering; he is distressed by its sorrows, and vexed with its sins. He looks within him—he finds much in his own corruptions to grieve for. In the language of a heart repelled, grieved, vexed, he often turns his eye upwards, saying, "I would not live here alway." No. Not for all the gold of the world's mines—not for all the pearls of her seas—not for all the pleasures of her flashing, frothy cup—not for all the crowns of her kingdoms—would I live here alway. Like a bird about to migrate to those sunny lands where no winter sheds her snows, or strips the grove, or binds the dancing streams, he will often in spirit be pruning his wing for the hour of his flight to glory.

The holier the child of God becomes, the more he pants after the perfect image and blissful presence of Jesus; and dark although the passage, and deep although the river may be, the more holy he is, the more ready will he be to say, "It is better to depart, and be with Jesus." "Tell me," said a saintly minister of the Church of England, whose star but lately set on this world, to rise and shine in better skies—"tell me," he said to his physician, "the true state of my case; conceal nothing;" adding, as his eye kindled, and his face beamed at the very thought, "if you have to tell me that my dissolution is near, you could not tell me better or happier news."

Paul said, "I am in a strait betwixt two, having a desire to depart and to be with Christ, which is far better: nevertheless, to abide in the flesh is more needful for you." He judged it best for himself to go, out for others he judged it best to stay. And there are few nobler sights than to see that man, with his foot on the door-step of heaven, return to throw himself into the very thick of battle, and spend and be spent in his Master's work. The crown of martyrdom often within his reach, he drew back a hand that was eager to grasp it. He took as much care of life as the coward guilt that is afraid to die. He was not impatient of the hardships, wounds, and watchings of the warfare, so long as he could serve the cause of Jesus. It was sin, not suffering that he felt intolerable; and which wrung from him the bitter cry, "O, wretched man that I am! who shall deliver me from this body of death?" His a Saviour's spirit, he chose rather that Christ should be glorified through his labors on earth, than that he himself should be glorified with Christ in heaven. And so long as he had a tongue to speak for Jesus, and an arm to hold high above the battle's tumult the banner of the faith, he was willing to work on—not impatient for death and his discharge. His was a higher and more heroic wish than to get to heaven. He wished to make a heaven of earth; and, persuaded that nothing could separate him from the love of God, or, finally, from heaven, believing that all which God had said of him he would do for him, and knowing that, though the vision tarried, it would come, he possessed his soul in patience and peace—waiting for the Lord.

It is a cowardly thing for a soldier to seek his discharge, so long as his country's banner flies in the battle-field. The Christian should be a hero, not a coward; and with such faith as all may get, and many have enjoyed, God's people, while they look to heaven, will with patience wait for it. On his way home, the saint will prove himself a good Samaritan; ready to stop even on a heavenward journey, that he may raise the fallen, bind up the wounds of humanity, and do all the work that meets him upon the road. Nor shall this go unrewarded. "The sleep of a laboring man is sweet." And, Oh! heaven shall be sweetest to him who has wrought through the longest

day, and toiled the hardest at his work. Now and
then he will be lifting up a weary head to see how
the hours wear by—if there be yet any sign of his
Master coming. But upborne under the heat and
burden of the day by the confidence that "he who
shall come will come, and will not tarry," he works
patiently, and he suffers patiently. The most impor-
tunate and urgent prayer he ventures on, that of one,
who, trembling lest patience should fail and religion
suffer dishonor, cried, when her pain deepened into
agony, and the agony became excruciating—"Come,
Oh come, Lord Jesus! come quickly."

II. Both nature and providence illustrate the truth
of my text.

Nature assures us, that what God hath said, he will do.

It can never be wrong to do what Jesus did. That
must be sound reasoning, in the use of which he sets
us an example. I see him bring a flower to the pulpit,
and choose a lily for his text. He bids the people
listen to that sweet preacher—the little bird—that,
seated on the bending spray, with providence for its
song and sermon, neither sows nor reaps; without
harvests, suffers no wants; and without a barn, feels
no fears. Thus he taught his hearers to cast their cares
on God, and thus have I the highest authority for
summoning Nature here to bear witness to the char-
acter of God. We ask her then to say, whether her
God, who is our God, is true to his word? whether
he ever says, and fails to do? By the voices of
the sun, the stars, the hills, the valleys, the streams,
the cataracts, the rolling thunders, and the roaring
sea, she returns a majestic answer—it is an echo of
the text. Spring comes with infant nature waking in

her arms; Summer comes bedecked with a robe of flowers; Autumn comes with her swarthy brow crowned with vines, and on her back the sheaves of corn; old Winter comes with his shivering limbs, and frozen locks, and hoary head; and these four wit-nesses—each laying one hand on the broad table of nature, and, lifting the other to heaven—swear by him that liveth for ever and ever, that all which God hath said, God shall do.

No man looks for sunrise in the west. No soldier stands beneath the falling shell, expecting to see it arrested in its descent, and hanging like a star in empty space. We build our houses in confidence that the edifice will gravitate to the center; nor ever doubt, when we set our mill-wheel in the running stream, that as sure as man is on his way to the grave, the waters shall ever take their way to the sea. We consult the Nautical Almanac, and, finding that it shall be high water to-morrow at such an hour, we make our arrangements for being on board then, cer-tain that we shall find our ship afloat, and the seamen shaking out their sails to go away on the bosom of the floating tide. If fire burned the one day, and water the next; if wood became at one time as heavy as iron, and iron at another as buoyant as wood; if here the rivers hasted to the embraces of the sea, and there, as in fear, retreated from them, what a scene of confusion this world would become! In truth, its whole business rests on faith—on our belief, that God will carry into unfailing effect every law which his finger has written in the books of nature and of prov-idence. This is the pillow on which a sleeping world rests its weary head; this is the pivot on which its business turns. Now let us remember, that there are not two Gods; a consistent Divinity who presides over nature, and a capricious Divinity who presides in the kingdom of grace. "Hear, O Israel, the Lord thy God is one Lord." In regard, therefore, to all the precious promises and solemn warnings of the Bible, Nature lifts up her voice, and cries—"O Earth, Earth, Earth, hear the word of the Lord."

Providence assures us that what God hath said, he will do.

Some time ago the heavens were pouring down torrents of rain, the streams had risen into rivers, the rivers were swollen into seas, and, our fields changed into lakes, boats were plying were ploughs were wont to go. It looked like the beginning of a second deluge; and to some who had fled from their beds for safety to cottage roofs, the howling of the wind, the incessant pouring of the rain, the waters steadily rising on the walls, may have recalled the memory of that day when the ark began to float, and men hung round it knocking on a door which God had shut in judgment against a wicked world. Yet, I will venture to say, that the dread of a second deluge aggravated no man's sufferings, nor changed a sinner's curses into a penitent's prayers. Why not? Ah! men say the sea has never left her bounds. Apart altogether from the records of revelation, geology tells us that she has, and that round the rock where the eagle now has her nest, monsters of the deep have swam, and that the highest peaks of earth's highest mountains were once the islands of an ancient sea. Yes! but then, it is said, there is the bow in the cloud, and the promise in the Bible, "Neither shall all flesh be cut off any more by the waters of a flood; neither

shall there any more be a flood to destroy the earth.
This is the token of my covenant that I will make
between me and you, and every living creature that
is with you for perpetual generations. I do set my
bow in the cloud, and it shall be for a token of a cov-
enant between me and the earth." That indeed *is* a
security against a second flood. Now, shall God keep
his word to this doomed, sinful, polluted world—
shall he keep the covenant of the bow, and not keep
the covenant of the cross? The providences of four
thousand years assure us that he who is true to his
covenant with Noah, shall not be less true to the
blood-sealed covenant made with his beloved Son.

The voice of every storm that, like an angry child,
weeps and cries itself asleep—the voice of every shower
that has been followed by sunshine—the hoarse voice
of ocean breaking in impotent rage against its ancient
bounds—the voice of the seasons as they have marched
to the music of the spheres in unbroken succession
over the earth—the scream of the satyr in Babylon's
empty halls—the song of the fisherman, who spreads
his net on the rocks, and shoots it through the waters
where Tyre once sat in the pride of an ocean queen—
the fierce shout of the Bedouin as he careers in free-
dom over his desert sands—the wail and weeping of
the wandering Jew over the ruins of Zion—in all these
I hear the echo of this voice of God, "I the Lord
have spoken, and I will do it." These words are
written on every Hebrew forehead. The Jew bar-
tering his beads with naked savages—bearding the
Turk in the capital of Mohammedan power—braving in
his furs the rigor of Russian winters—over-reaching in
China the inhabitants of the Celestial Empire—in
Golconda buying diamonds—in our metropolis of the

commercial world standing highest among her merchant princes—the Hebrew every where, and yet every where without a country; with a religion, but without a temple; with wealth, but without honor; with ancient pedigree, but without ancestral possessions; with no land to fight for, nor altars to defend, nor patrimonial fields to cultivate; with children, and yet no child sitting under the trees that his grandsire planted; but all floating about over the world like scattered fragments of a wreck upon the bosom of the ocean—he is a living evidence, that, what the Lord hath spoken, the Lord will do.

True to his threatenings, Almighty God will be true to all his promises; and to both we can apply the words of Balaam—" Rise up, Balak, and hear; hearken unto me, thou son of Zippor: God is not a man that he should lie, nor the son of man that he should repent. Hath he said, and shall he not do it? hath he spoken, and shall he not make it good?"

THE END.